THE BROKEN PROMISE
OF A PROMISED LAND

By

William Hanna

The Broken Promise of a Promised Land
Copyright © William Hanna 2021
www.williamhannaauthor.com

Cover designer: Mariana Coello
Interior Formatting: Jackie Friesen

ISBNs:
Paperback: 978-1-77374-086-7
eBook: 978-1-77374-087-4

CONTENTS

Introduction

They deem him their worst enemy, who tells them the truth.
Plato, The Republic, c. 380 BC

If some Jewish people wish to believe they were chosen by a non-existent god who helped with an Israelite Exodus from Egypt that never occurred and allegedly promised them the land of Canaan, then such religious beliefs, even if unfounded, still qualify as an acceptable human right. That right, however, does not come with a carte blanche authorisation for the use of fictional biblical narratives — as justification for the barbaric ethnic cleansing of Palestinian people including a heinous and deliberate targeting of children — so that a Zionist Apartheid Jewish State can claim exclusive rights to a "Promised Land" disingenuously described as "a land without a people for a people without a land."

Israel's perversely persistent persecution of the indigenous Palestinian population and denial of its culture, history, existence, and human rights — for more than seventy years — has been largely misrepresented if not totally ignored by unprincipled mainstream media prostitutes; catastrophically tolerated by a world drenched in xenophobic thoughts, attitudes, and actions; unconscionably financed

1

by an inherently racist, degenerate, and declining US where democracy is suffocating and the "American Dream" has become a horrifying nightmare; and facilitated by the double moral standards of a spineless EU which like the US is also subservient to the pernicious and predatory lobbying of powerful and cash-rich pro-Israel groups relentless in pursuit of Zionist objectives which are presented as conscientious concern — with the bogus claim of preventing another Holocaust — for the wellbeing and safety of all Jews.

Preventing another genocide of the Jewish people, however, can hardly be either achieved, or morally justified, by having Jewish people exterminate another ethnic group in a deliberately calculated, viciously cruel, and sadistic manner. Zionist objectives are therefore actually destroying the moral principles — including justice, healing the world, charity and kindness to others, and the importance of the sanctity of human life that includes the concept of "saving a life" (Pikuach Nefesh), which is an obligation for all Jews — of the religion it claims to be protecting while with ruthless relish perpetrating the abominable crime of genocide against the Palestinian people.

> *The term does not necessarily signify mass killings . . . more often [genocide] refers to a coordinated plan aimed at destruction of the essential foundations of the life of national groups so that these groups wither and die like plants that have suffered a blight. The end may be accomplished by the forced disintegration of political and social institutions, of*

the culture of the people, of their language, their national feelings and their religion. It may be accomplished by wiping out all basis of personal security, liberty, health and dignity. When these means fail the machine gun can always be utilised as a last resort. Genocide is directed against a national group as an entity and the attack on individuals is only secondary to the annihilation of the national group to which they belong.

Raphael Lemkin (1900-1959), Polish-Jewish jurist, who in his book Axis Rule in Occupied Europe, coined the word "genocide" and subsequently served with the team of Americans working to prepare the Nuremberg trials.

Yes, It's Israeli Apartheid. Even Without Annexation . . . In other words, apartheid is a regime that, using all the tools at its disposal — law, policy, practice — creates the superiority of one group and imposes inferiority on another, usually manifested in institutional discrimination regarding rights and resources. Contrary to popular belief, in international law, a racial group is defined in accordance with sociopolitical classifications, not biological-genetic ones, thus the definition encompasses national or ethnic origin. It's not enough to impose inferiority on such a group; a condition for committing the crime is that the superiority is not temporary but meant to be permanent.

Hence, international law criminalises "inhumane acts" committed against the inferior group with the aim of preserving the superior group's control over it. You'd have to turn out the lights, plug your ears and close the shutters to evade the conclusion that the Israeli regime in the West Bank is an apartheid regime and that annexation would only deepen and expand it

Michael Sfard, expert Israeli attorney on international humanitarian law and international human rights law, in Haaretz, July 9, 2020

. . . So, apartheid is today accepted as an international crime defined as the commission of inhumane acts by one racial group against another racial group for the purpose of maintaining domination over that group and systematically oppressing it. The ICC is today considering the commission of this crime by Israel, resulting from its establishment of an Israeli settler regime in occupied Palestine and its policies of forcible removals of Palestinians from their land, home demolitions, torture, arbitrary imprisonment, denial of free movement and more. There is very little doubt among international law jurists that Israel's actions in occupied Palestine meet the requirements for the crime of apartheid . . .

Professor John Dugard, eminent South African human rights lawyer, October, 2020

Apartheid is a crime against humanity. Israel has deprived millions of Palestinians of their liberty and property. It has perpetrated a system of gross racial

discrimination and inequality. It has systematically incarcerated and tortured thousands of Palestinians, contrary to international law. It has, in particular, waged a war against a civilian population, in particular children.
Nelson Mandela (1918-2013)

1

Origins of the Universe, Planet Earth, and Life

Understanding the historical significance of a "god cho-sen people" also requires some knowledge about the calam-itous effect that all religions, with their concocted sacred texts and creatively imagined gods, have had on people and the planet they inhabit. One of those imaginary gods was al-leged to have promised Abraham — the common patriarch of Christianity, Islam, Judaism, and others — the land known as Canaan which was then situated in the southern Levant and currently includes Gaza, Israel, the West Bank, Jordan, and the southern portions of Syria and Lebanon. The ulti-mate validation for any imaginary god is to be credited with having created the universe and all that is in it.

In the beginning, God created the heavens and the earth.
Genesis 1:1-31

With most people from an early age being led to believe that in the beginning a god created the universe, the planets, and life itself, the question remains as to when and by which of the countless gods worshipped by humankind actually achieved that momentous task. As to the question of when, there is no definitive answer. Jewish years for instance are numbered according to the rabbinic understanding of when the Creation of the world took place. Though many calculations were attempted by different rabbis, it was the one by Rabbi Jose ben Halafta (second century CE) — declaring Monday 7 October, 3761 BCE to be the day Creation began — that gained the most favour at the time. Alternatively, Young Earth Creationism (YEC) holds as a basic tenet that the Earth and its lifeforms were created by a god over a relatively short period sometime between 6,000 and 10,000 years ago.

The truth of our faith becomes a matter of ridicule among the infidels if any Catholic, not gifted with the necessary scientific learning, presents as dogma what scientific scrutiny shows to be false.
Thomas Aquinas (1225-1274), Dominican priest, philosopher, and theologian

YEC followers claim that their conclusion has its earliest roots in ancient Judaism, citing, for example, the commentary on Genesis by Ibn Ezra (c. 1089–1164) who was one of the most distinguished Jewish biblical commentators and philosophers of the Middle Ages. Many modern Jewish theologians, however, have rejected such literal interpretations of the written text with various other Jewish commentators —

who oppose some aspects of science — generally accepting scientific evidence that the Earth is much older.

Scientific consensus — supported by a 2006 statement from 68 national and international academies — asserts that evidence-based fact derived from observations and experiments in multiple scientific disciplines show that the universe existed almost 14 billion years ago in an extremely hot and dense state. It was about that time, according to the Big Bang theory about how to how it all came about, that the universe then began to cool and expand towards its present dispersed state with the earth being formed 4.5 billion years ago and life first appearing no less than 2.5 billion years ago. That self-induced expansion is still ongoing to this day without any supernatural assistance from some supreme-being. That ongoing expansion makes it difficult to precisely know the actual size of the universe, but its furthest visible regions are estimated to be approximately 46 billion light years away. That's a diameter of 540 sextillion — 54 followed by 22 zeros — miles.

In a study published in the *Nature Journal*, astronomers were able to measure the galaxy's distance from Earth by analysing its colour. With the universe expanding and everything moving away from the Earth, light waves are stretched, making objects appear redder than they actually are. Such apparent colour changes are rated by astronomers on a scale that is called redshift. So with a redshift of 7.51, this galaxy — named z8_GND_5296 — is the most distant galaxy ever found. Though the system has a mass of only about one to two percent of the Milky Way and is rich in heavier elements, it has the surprising feature of turning gas and dust into new stars at a remarkable rate of hundreds of times faster than our own galaxy can.

In 1974, anthropologist Professor Donald Johanson and his student made an important fossil discovery in a maze of ravines at Hadar in Northern Ethiopia. While searching the scorched terrain for animal bones in the sand, ash, and silt they spotted a tiny fragment of arm bone. Johanson immediately recognised it as belonging to a hominid. Further up the slope they discovered more bone fragments of ribs, vertebrae, thighbones, and a partial jawbone. Eventually forty-seven bones were unearthed — about forty-percent of a hominid (human-like creature) which had existed some 3.2 million years ago. Its small size and pelvic shape suggested it was female and they named it "Lucy" after "Lucy in the Sky with Diamonds," the Beatles song which happened to be playing during their post-discovery celebration.

Though many of Lucy's characteristics were similar to those of a chimpanzee, the structure of her knee and pelvis showed that she routinely walked upright on two legs like humans. Known as "bi-pedalism," this form of locomotion is the single most important difference between humans and apes. As walking on two legs was one of the earliest defining characteristics of humans, Lucy was placed firmly within the human family. Johanson named Lucy's species Australopithecus afarensis, which means "southern ape of afar," after the Ethiopian region where Hadar is located. This species — existing 3.5 million years ago — foraged for fruit, nuts, and seeds within the savannah and woodland, and may also have obtained animal protein from termites and birds' eggs.

In 2001, palaeontologists in northeastern Brazil discovered fossils of what was believed to be an ancestor of Tyrannosaurus rex (T. rex), two words which mean tyrant lizard and king. The fossils — including two skulls and various bones — were from the high Triassic period from 235 to 240 million years ago and consequently predate and contradict the timescales for religious versions of the creation.

In September 2011 it was announced that a two million year-old fossil discovered in a South African cave may be the missing link between humans and our ape ancestors. The fossil, called Australopithecus sediba, had a human-like brain and hands, but its legs were more ape-like, suggesting that it walked upright but more like a chimpanzee than a modern human. Until now scientists have traced human ancestry to fossils discovered in East Africa of the species Homo habilis or Homo rudolfensis, but the newly discovered specimen is several hundred thousand years older. Professor Lee Berger, from the University of the Witwatersrand in Johannesburg, stated "the many very advanced features found in the brain and body, and the earlier date, make it possibly the best candidate for ancestor of our genus, the genus Homo."

More recently the science journal *Nature* revealed that

scientists believed that a new fossil discovery from China is the world's oldest known example of the bone structure that is recognisable as a face. The remarkably well-preserved fish (an example of the species Entelognathus primordialis) was discovered in Southeast China in a layer of sediment dating back to the Silurian period — marks the time when the first plants and animals colonised dry land — making the specimen roughly 419 million years old. The find is exceptional because it is the earliest known example of the basic facial bone structure that is currently recognised: the ancient predator has a jaw, a mouth, two eyes and a nose. All previous discoveries from this geological time period have been of jawless fish — of the type that is still in existence today as lamprey and hagfish.

What may be even more remarkable than seeing the world's oldest known face is the notion that this fossil might even be a direct ancestor of human life. The fossil is unique in that it displays characteristics of two types of ancient fish: placoderms, the heavily armoured fish that were thought to have gone extinct millions of years ago, and bony fish, a taxonomic group that gave rise to all modern vertebrate fish, and subsequently amphibians, birds, mammals, and finally humans.

Another recent report by the journal *Nature* said that water drilled from rock under Timmins, Ontario, is among the oldest yet found on Earth by scientists. Despite being far from any light source, particular types of micro-organism could survive in the water which had the right chemistry and was rich in dissolved gases like hydrogen and methane. Professor Chris Ballentine from Manchester University explained "there are similar waters in South Africa with almost identical chemistry that are tens of millions of years old, and they contain microbes that have adapted to that environment . . . These are microbes that can survive on the energy from the natural water-rock interactions . . . A positive identification had fascinating implications for our understanding of how life evolved on the early Earth and where it could exist underground today on other planets, such as Mars." Researchers recovered the water from mineworkers who had drilled new exploratory holes into deeply buried sulphide ores containing zinc and copper.

If despite such evidence and the advantage of current scientific knowledge there are people who still find it difficult to either comprehend or accept such scientific facts, then it must have been even more so for the earliest of our ancestors whose evolution as human beings — Homo sapiens — began in Africa where archaeological evidence of our ancestral Y chromosome and mtDNA (mitochondrial DNA) has been discovered.

It must be disconcerting for supremacists and god chosen peoples to learn that geneticists have identified groups of chromosomes called haplogroups — "genetic fingerprints" which define populations — that trace their ancestral origins to the "subhuman" races of Africa. The ethnocentric concepts of a god "chosen people," a master race, or Nazi breeding programme (Lebensborn) to produce perfect "purity" is nothing more than racist nonsense.

As the accrued mutations of mtDNA occur at a known rate, they can be used to calculate the timing of human existence. By combining all the available evidence of this mtDNA and Y chromosome with archaeology, climatology and fossil analysis, scientists have managed to tabulate the directions and timing of human migration. Though further archaeological discoveries could change estimates regarding the peopling of the world, it is currently believed to have begun sometime between 160,000 and 135,000 BCE when groups of hunter-gatherers from East Africa migrated northeast to the Horn of Africa, southwest to the Congo Basin, west to the Ivory Coast, and south to the Cape of Good Hope.

Around 125,000 BCE migration continued along the Nile through a green Sahara and the Levant. Those that reached the Levant died out by 90,000 BCE when a global freeze turned the area — including North Africa — into desert. The area was subsequently repopulated by Neanderthal man and about 5,000 years later groups crossed the mouth of the Red Sea and along the coast of the Arabian Peninsula towards India. All non-African peoples are the descendants of these migrants.

From 85,000 to 75,000 BCE migration pushed further along the Indian Ocean coastline to South China by way of Indonesia and Borneo which were then still part of the

Asian landmass from which they were later to detach. Then in about 73,000 BCE one of the earth's largest known eruptions occurred on Sumatra's Mount Toba and covered India and Pakistan with a five-metre deep blanket of volcanic ash that caused a six-year nuclear winter, a thousand-year ice age and a considerable drop in population.

Following that cataclysmic event repopulation occurred after about nine thousand years followed by migrations from Borneo to New Guinea, and Timor to Australia. Aboriginal DNA from a lock of hair has been dated to 70,000 BCE. A more recent study of DNA from Aboriginal Australians has shown that a further migration from India occurred about four thousand years ago at around which time dingoes also made their first appearance.

An ensuing warming in climate leading up to 50,000 BCE then allowed northward migrations back to the Levant, past the Bosphorus and into Europe. By the time of 45,000 BCE the Mini Ice Age had occurred and the early stages of the Palaeolithic culture moved from Turkey into Europe. Research suggests that the Modern humans who entered Europe at that time, outnumbered by as much as ten to one the Neanderthals who had lived there for at least 200,000 years. Human migration along the River Danube also introduced newly developed stone tools and overwhelming human settlement eventually drove the Neanderthals to extinction.

During this period migrations continued from Indochina across Tibet; from Pakistan into Central Asia; and westwards from the East Asian coast traversing the central steppes towards the north-east. Between then and 25,000 BCE Central Asians then migrated westwards into Eastern Europe, north-wards to the Arctic Circle, and accompanied East Asians to north-east Eurasia. This was also a time that witnessed the birth of impressive works of art such as those discovered in the Chauvet-Pont-d'Arc cave in southern France which contains the earliest known cave paintings.

Leading up to 22,000 BCE, due to low sea levels, the Bering Strait was in effect a land bridge across which ancestors of Native Americans travelled between Siberia and Alaska. But during the last Ice Age leading up to 19,000 BCE, populations in Northern Europe, Asia, and North America were drastically reduced with only a small number of groups surviving in isolated areas.

The findings of the biggest survey of Native American DNA published in the journal *Nature* by an international team of researchers concluded that though the New World was settled in three major waves, the majority of today's indigenous Americans descended from a single group of migrants that crossed from Asia to Alaska 15,000 or more years ago. Previous genetic data have suggested that America was colonised by a single migrant wave, but it is now apparent that there are at least three deep lineages in Native American populations. This latest research has settled the debate as to whether or not Native Americans stemmed from a single migration by casting light on patterns of human dispersal within the Americas.

Following the Last Glacial Maximum around 18,000

BCE, development in genes, diversity, culture and language continued with migration into South America. This period also saw the start of Australian rock art such as the elegant and impressive Bradshaw Paintings (or Guion Guion) in the Northwest region. The continued improvement in global climatic conditions opened American coastal routes and enabled human habitation as confirmed by the Monte Verde Excavation in southern Chile where finds have been radio-carbon dated from 11,800 to 13,600 years BCE.

The repopulation of North America began 12,500 BCE and a thousand years later groups migrated from the Beringian refuge to become the Aleut, Eskimo, and Na Dene speaking peoples. The ensuing and final demise of the ice age between 10,000 and 8,000 years BCE witnessed the emergence of agriculture with a Sahara grassland and a recolonised British Isles and Scandinavia.

Contrary to the existence of such evidence, a 2007 Newsweek poll discovered that 78 percent of people in the United States — a superpower whose astronauts have walked on the moon — doubt the traditional scientific view of "secular evolution" which is the long-term interaction between the galaxy and its environment such as gas accretion (the growth of objects that gravitationally attract gaseous matter in an accretion disk) and galaxy harassment (frequent high speed galaxy encounters that produce starbursts).

A 2012 Gallup poll discovered that forty-six percent of Americans believed in the creationist view that God created humans in their present form 10,000 years ago. Furthermore, Americans with postgraduate education were most likely of all educational groups to say that humans evolved without god's guidance; and least likely to say that God created humans in their present form 10,000 years ago. So it is the less educated who are more likely to have the creationist viewpoint. But then one does not have to be a genius to realise that ignorance, fear and poverty provide the fertile soil wherein groundless religious beliefs can best take root.

Human history becomes more and more a race between education and catastrophe.
H.G. Wells, The Outline of History, 1922

It must be bewildering for any reasonable person with average intelligence to comprehend how despite the vast advances that have been achieved with the help of science and technology in virtually every field of human endeavour, there is still a suicidal tendency for people to blindly embrace the tenets of crude religious myths even to the extent of inflicting unspeakable atrocities not only on the lives of others, but also on the lives of their own families. For some inexplicable reason mankind has from the beginning of time failed to establish a universal ethic based on unfettered perceptions of reality rather than the disastrous consequences of adherence to diverse forms of religious mumbo-jumbo.

Any system of education which with authority presents age-old religious myths as being factual, is only serving to shackle the minds of present-day youngsters with the same mumbo jumbo that warped the thinking of their forefathers.

Belief without evidence in what is told by one who speaks without knowledge, of things without parallel.

Ambrose Bierce (1842-1913), a definition of faith in his satirical lexicon The Devil's Dictionary

2

In the Beginning There Was Man

When one person is delusional, it's called insanity. When many people are delusional, they call it religion.

Atheism saying

Irrespective of any claims of some god having promised Canaan to the Jewish people (Genesis 15:18-21), the irrefutable fact remains that biblical Israel and today's "Jewish State" are two distinct concepts with the former being a myth, and the latter a consequence of the 1917 British government sanction — deceptively dubbed The Balfour Declaration but actually authored by Leopold Amery, a Zionist Briton of Jewish background — for what resulted in the ethnic cleansing of indigenous Palestinians so as to establish a "national home for the Jewish people."

While it was in the Hebrew Bible — written during various periods between about 1,200 and 165 BCE — that Jewish scribes created the god who was attributed with having chosen the Jewish people, the actual serious god creation industry began much earlier sometime around 10,000 BCE in ancient Egypt where the only habitable place in the eastern Sahara Desert at that time was the Nile Valley which began to be settled by tribes of possible Semitic origin from nearby African regions and western parts of Asia. Because of the valley's long, narrow geological features and the ever-present threat of possible attacks from other tribes, the settlers were forced to live in small, isolated groups adjoining the river which apart from providing the means to sustain life, also served as a natural barrier on one side in the event of attacks from hostile tribes.

The profound ignorance and primitive nature of those people inevitably led to superstition being rampant with reliance on amulets, charms, talismans, and rituals for everything from healing the sick to raising the dead; for knowledge of the past and prediction of the future; and even for curses that allegedly harmed enemies. Such ignorance also spawned a reverential fear and respect for the unexplained mysteries of nature including the heavenly elements and the surrounding wildlife with the result that religious worship became awe-inspired by the wonders of nature including animals, birds, and reptiles whose deification and purported existence was accepted by the mostly illiterate and superstitious masses.

In the time leading up to the Predynastic Period (5,500 BCE) such fictional gods only presided over villages or districts so that their stature and veneration was determined by the size and importance of their domains. Furthermore the line between secular and religious authority in such communities was so indistinguishable, that it was the priests with their self-proclaimed possession of wisdom and access to the gods, who with wilful coercion and enforced religious control were best positioned to fully exploit the prevailing ignorance so as to govern without any serious challenge.

The priests also developed both esoteric and exoteric religious doctrines, with the latter being the idolatrous faith fed to the ignorant and easily manipulated masses. The esoteric doctrine proclaiming the unity of God was reserved for the select few who like the priests themselves had undergone the mystery rites where initiates acknowledged their dedication to the Goddess Isis without being required to worship her exclusively.

In due course, however, changing social conditions forced the priests to defend their own privileged positions of power which they did by arming a select minority of the population so as to perpetuate existing repression and exploitation of the majority. Though the ploy was initially successful, it eventually backfired when restless ambition within the ranks of the military resulted in rebellion wherein the force of arms ended monopoly of religious authority and led to the establishment of a monarchy.

But despite the reality of an absolute monarchical government, religious influence remained unassailable with the priests — who in effect ruled alongside the monarchs — being allowed to retain their colleges, palaces, and temples as well as agricultural and commercial interests. Furthermore, having already established themselves as the bureaucrats of their societies, they continued to regulate every aspect of daily life by acting as advisors, magistrates, physicians, and teachers. They became a select and privileged minority who — by paying no taxes and soliciting donations — accumulated wealth, influence, and power that was eclipsed only by the monarchs. They were consequently well positioned to regulate compatibility between religious doctrines and ever changing sociocultural and political conditions.

One of the initial stages for ensuring socially compatible theology was the humanisation of the gods so that some of them were provided with human bodies to go with their animal, bird, and serpent heads. The aspects of nature, animal, and man that related to such worship, however, began to gradually fuse so that in due course animal gods with human characteristics began to appear. Thoth, god of wisdom and truth, was given a human body but retained the head of an ibis; Anubis, who assisted Osiris as judge of the dead, was given a human body with the head of a Jackal; and Hathor, the goddess of childbirth and love, was given a human head and body but retained an element of her animal manifestation with a pair of cow's horns.

Then as the masses gradually became more sophisticated and required gods with which they could identify, the gods were accordingly transformed and obligingly portrayed as having complete human forms. Having fictional gods — like the one who with glorified omnipotence chose the Jews — made it so much easier for rationalising the irrational and explaining the inexplicable. It was therefore such fictional omnipotence that was credited with creating the universe, rather than the cataclysmic event known as the Big Bang which occurred about 13.8 billion years ago

Apart from their physical transformations, the gods were also subject to the reality that religion was very much a part of politics so that whenever a political union occurred between two or more communities, a fusion of their gods was also necessary. That fusion was achieved by grouping them into families such as that of the Osirian triad consisting of Osiris, Isis and Horus who had initially presided separately over three different tribal communities. Such groupings inevitably led to varying degrees of syncretisation whereby the main gods acquired multiple names and each other's characteristics.

The situation was further complicated by the introduction of West Asian cosmic theology which maintained that in the beginning there existed only the darkness of boundless primeval water that had remained unproductive for a considerable period of time before its spirit felt the urge to create the seed from which sprang Ra, the sun god, within whose shining form was embodied the almighty power of the divine spirit.

Before spreading the cosmic faith to other parts of the

valley from their main cult centre in sun-city which the Greeks later referred to as Heliopolis, the priests had to first somehow include within the system of cosmic theology, the widespread worship of existing popular gods such as Osiris, Isis, Horus, and others without actually subordinating the importance of their own positions. This was achieved by re-writing the religious texts so as to form the Heliopolitan Ennead whereby Ra had apparently created the gods Shu and Tefnut; who in turn begat Seb and Nut; who in turn produced Osiris, Isis, Seth, and Nephthys. Consequently as a result of the gods and religious doctrines being customised to accommodate the political requirements of the ruling elite, the history of ancient Egyptian gods has no continuity and is full of interpolations that reflect the influence of changing political and social conditions over a period of many millenniums.

One such influence was that of the monarchy whose successive members became increasingly dissatisfied with only being monarchs who like everyone else, were also simply subject to birth, life, and death. It was therefore with the connivance of the priesthoods that a deification process — with its ramifications of immortality — was set into motion with subtle associations between the Pharaohs and the gods being gradually introduced. For instance the second Pharaoh of the Second Dynasty (c. 2890-2686 BCE) incorporated Ra's name with his own so as to become known as Raneb. The Pharaohs of the Fifth Dynasty (c. 2494-2345 BCE) went even further by claiming to have been directly descended from Ra as a result of a miraculous conception by a high priest's wife who was no doubt impregnated by a strong shaft of sunlight.

The "miraculous conception" story — a convenient way of explaining how ordinary human beings could also be gods — has since been used by the priesthoods of other religions including Christianity. As always such blatant fabrications were lent authenticity by their inclusion in texts such as that of the depiction of Pharaonic afterlife in the Pyramid Texts discovered in the burial chamber of the Fifth Dynasty's last Pharaoh, Unas (c. 2375-2345 BCE). The hieroglyphics have Unas ascending a stairway of sunlight so as to join in immortality with his father, Ra, from whose unquestioned supremacy flowed the Pharaonic Right to govern the land of Egypt.

Such immortality was initially a privilege reserved for the Pharaohs who after death could enjoy, embalmment, and reunification with their ancestors. A Pharaoh, however, could in his capacity as a god extend that privilege to high priests and favoured officials by allowing them to build their tombs within the confines of the royal necropolis, and to use secret formulae to facilitate their journey to the afterlife.

In their determined quest to retain their privileged positions, the ruling elite soon realised that the concept of immortality was a potentially powerful weapon with which to control an ever-growing and increasingly disaffected population. So as the advantages of retaining the privilege of afterlife for themselves began to be outweighed by the benefits of making the afterlife an entitlement for everyone, the necessary theological adjustments were begun so that by the onset of the Middle Kingdom (c. 1550-1650 BCE) the concept of the soul's immortality became universal.

By the time of the New Kingdom (c. 1550-1069 BCE) the priesthood had produced *The Book of the Dead* which was designed to help people prepare themselves for death and the consequences of the Final Judgment. Apart from preparations before death, it was also necessary — so as to ensure continued existence in the afterlife — that the body after death be kept intact as an "everlasting" depository that would provide a permanent place of refuge for the soul which would cease to exist in the event of the body being somehow destroyed. Consequently a period of seventy days was required for preparation and embalmment of the corpse during which time the soul wandered the underworld in search of Osiris, who, with the assistance of forty-two other gods known as the judges of the dead, would determine the soul's fate in the afterlife.

On finally entering the hall of judgment, the soul was required to render a full account of past actions, and in the event of an unfavourable judgment, was sentenced to a life of thirst and hunger in the darkness of Amenti, an area of the underworld that was reserved for the damned. So the concept of accountability and possible damnation in the afterlife for one's actions on earth was thus established, and its potential as a means of controlling the actions of the common people has since been fully exploited by all major religions. The Greek historian, Polibius (c. 200-118 BCE), author of books on the history of the Roman Republic and renowned for his ideas on the separation of powers in government which were later to be used as guidelines for drafting the United States Constitution — a Constitution recently savaged by a corrupt and deranged President Trump — had this to say on the subject:

The most important difference for the better, which the Roman Commonwealth appears to me to display, in their religious beliefs, for I conceive that what in other nations is looked upon as a reproach, I mean a scrupulous fear for the gods, is the very thing that keeps the Roman Commonwealth together. To such an extraordinary height is this carried among them in private and public business, that nothing could exceed it. Many people think this unaccountable, but in my opinion their object is to use it as a check upon the common people. Where it possible to form a state wholly of philosophers, such a custom would be unnecessary. But seeing that every multitude is fickle and full of lawless desires, unreasoning anger and violent passion, the only resource is to keep them in check by the mysterious terrors and scenic effects of this sort. Wherefore to my mind the ancients were not acting without purpose or at random when they brought in among the vulgar these opinions about the gods and the punishments of Hades.

While members of the ruling elite were prepared to share the concept of afterlife with the common people, they were not at all prepared to allow random access to the celebration of the mysteries for which there were two levels. The seven Crata Repoa, or Higher Degrees, were restricted to Pharaohs, high priests, and some top officials. The three Lower Degrees were reserved for a selective membership. Each degree had passwords and signs of recognition and initiation ceremonies were usually conducted in the subterranean chambers of pyramids which by virtue of their shape symbolised the ascending flame that was a sacred tribute to the sun.

Initiation into the first of the Lower Degrees required the Candidate to undergo instruction and lengthy rituals with secret signs and symbols before being formally pronounced an initiate of the mysteries of Isis whose character like that of other important ancient Egyptian deities, had evolved over many millenniums. Her portrayal as a faithful wife and loving mother who had conceived miraculously does not, however, appear to have become very pronounced until the Nineteenth Dynasty (c. 1295-1186 BCE) as is evident from numerous figurines of that period that have her seated on a throne clasping Horus to her left breast.

There is no doubt, however, that the position she occupied as the "Mother of God" was unique to her as no other goddess was shown suckling a child. All the attributes, qualities and powers of all the other goddesses were without exception combined in the person of Isis, and ancient Egyptian scriptures assert "in the beginning there was Isis, Oldest of the Old, she was the Goddess from whom all becoming arose." One of the Psalms in the Bible (89:14) which states "righteousness and justice are the foundation of thy throne; steadfast love and truth go before you," was plagiarised from an Egyptian hymn to Isis.

Isis worship was widespread and apart from becoming one of the principle goddesses of Rome, her cult was also to be found in many islands of the Mediterranean including Chios, Crete, Lesbos, Rhodes and Samos. Representations of her on many antiquities found in places such as Argos, Epirus, Corinth, Megara and Thessaly also bear witness to her popularity in numerous Greek cities where even the elite members of society felt the need to become initiates.

Though the mysteries of Isis continued to be performed by priestesses in the numerous temples built in her honour right up to the fourth century, her cult was eventually suppressed by Christianity's ruthless elimination of other religious movements. Isis as a goddess, however, was not eliminated but absorbed, and the identification of the Virgin Mary with her was part of a calculated syncretism that led to the creation of the Madonna cult.

The similarities between them are numerous and include Mary's wanderings in Egypt which follow a comparable sequence of events to those experienced by Isis as described in the Metternich Stela Texts (c. 380-342 BCE), a magico-medical style that is part of the Egyptian Collection of the Metropolitan Museum of Art in New York City. By bringing forth a human life which she then protected, fed and nourished, Isis became the personification of that great feminine capacity to conceive and give birth to new life. Drawings and sculptures depicting Isis suckling her child became the model for the Christian Madonna and Child, and many of the qualities that were originally attributed to Isis were then given to the Mother of Christ. In order to supplant popular pagan deities the Christian Church Fathers had to ensure that their own man-made Christian idols had characteristics similar to those of the popular pagan deities whom they were determined to replace. In his Egyptian Religion: *Egyptian Ideas of the Future Life* (1900), E. A. Wallis Budge (1857-1934) had this to say:

> *In Osiris the Christian Egyptians found the prototype of Christ, and in the pictures and statues of Isis suckling her son Horus, they perceived the prototype of the Virgin Mary and her child. Never did Christianity find elsewhere in the world a people whose minds were so thoroughly well prepared to receive its doctrines as the Egyptians.*

> *The Christian Trinity ousted the old triads of gods. Osiris and Horus were represented by our Lord Jesus Christ, Isis by the Virgin Mary, Set the god of evil by Diabolus [Satan] . . . and the various Companies of the gods by Archangels, and so on.*

Information regarding initiation into the Second Degree is scarce but it is known that in the Third Degree the Candidate was required to take part in a lengthy re-enactment of the murder of Osiris by playing the role of the victim. This was followed by the revelation of secret doctrines including the ineffable name AL-OM-JAK, the sacred name of the deity symbolising solar fire as the combined principle on which all existence was dependent. The word OM, or its trilateral form AUM, signified the Deity's capacity to create, to preserve, and to destroy; and was represented by an equilateral triangle. Great powers were attributed to this ineffable name which was to be contemplated in silence so as to avoid the dire consequences that would result from its vocalisation. This was a custom subsequently picked up by Judaism so that modern Jewish culture judges it forbidden to pronounce the name most often used in the Hebrew Bible and transcribed as YHWH (expanded into English as "Yahweh."

Osiris was a god whose coming was announced by Three Wise Men — the three stars of Mintaka, Anilam, and Alnitak in the belt of Orion which pointed towards his star, Sirius (the significator of his birth) which "rose in the east" at the time of the seasonal flooding of the Nile. The Osirian tradition is traceable to the Orient where in Tibet the rising of the same star in the east — named Rishi-Agastya, after an ancient holy king — marks the annual event of "setting free the waters of the springs." This same star was called Ephraim (or star of Jacob) by the ancient Hebrews. In Arabian, Persian, and Syrian astrology it was the Messaeil — the Messiah.

Osiris was without doubt the paradigm for Messiahs who as the god of gods came to be regarded as the son of Ra next to whom he sat as an equal in heaven. Egyptians regarded him as the only deity capable of bestowing upon them the gift of eternal life, and the events leading to his death were re-enacted in a passion play. His flesh was that of the Saviour and Truth, which when eaten in the form of communion wheatmeal cakes, made them just like him. The ancient Egyptians viewed the horrible consequences of death with its decaying aftermath with fear and trepidation and so believed that only Osiris could save them. Wallis Budge noted that the Egyptians believed according to the following:

> *The resurrection of the body in a changed and glorified form, which would live to all eternity in the company of the spirits and souls of the righteous in a kingdom ruled by a being who was of divine origin, but who had lived upon the earth, and had suffered a cruel death at the hands of his enemies, and had risen from the dead, and had become a God and king of the world which was beyond the grave . . . Although they believed in all these things and proclaimed their belief with almost passionate earnestness, they seemed never to have freed themselves from a hankering for amulets and talismans, and magical names, and words of power, and seem to have trusted in these to save their souls and bodies, both living and dead, with something of the same confidence which they placed in the death and resurrection of Osiris. A matter of surprise is that they seem to see nothing incongruous in such a mixture of magic and religion.*

This same mixture of magic and religion still exists worldwide to this day with even Christians displaying the same ancient Egyptian hankering for such objects including crucifixes, Saint Christopher medals, holy pendants, superstition-based incantations, holy name invocations, holy water blessings, saintly relics, and even the rosaries which Christianity copied from the ancient Egyptians.

The fact that early Christianity was more readily accepted in Egypt than in other places comes as no surprise when one considers that it was from the characteristics of Osiris that the Christ figure had evolved; and that from texts relating to the life of Osiris that many Biblical passages were plagiarised. It is for example evident that Psalm 23 was based on an Egyptian text that called on Osiris the Good Shepherd to lead the dead to the "green pastures" and "still waters" of the nefer-nefer land so as to restore the soul to the body and provide protection in the valley of the shadow of death (the Tuat). Even the Lord's Prayer was certainly influenced by a hymn to Osiris that began "O Amen, O Amen, who art in heaven" and which also ended with an "Amen."

The words by Jesus "Except a corn of wheat fall into the ground and die, it abideth alone; but if it die, it bringeth forth much fruit" (John 12:24) were from an Osirian tenet that a dying man is like a corn of wheat "which falls into the earth in order to draw from its bosom a new life." The Osirian text telling of the numerous Arits (Mansions) in the blessed land of Father Osiris is also apparently uttered by Jesus "In my Father's house are many mansions" (John 14:2). Just as Osirian worshippers were promised that they would rule the spirit-souls (angels) in heaven, so too were the Saint Paul's followers promised by him that they would rule even the angels (1 Corinthians 6:3). Even the healing by Jesus of a nobleman's daughter was long preceded by an Osirian priest who cured a princess. Numerous such examples exist as a testament to the popularity of a god who in spite of being a figment of primitive human imagination, became the obligatory prototype for any other man-made god who wished to replace him.

The portrayal of an eminent man or deity who as a member of a trinity, first perishes as the victim of an evil deed, and then resurrects into a greater glory, is by now an all too familiar theme and figures not only in religious legends, but also as part of initiation ceremonies in secular secret societies. Of the various legends relating to Osiris, it is perhaps the one by the Greek historian, Plutarch (c. 46-120), *Peri Isodos Kai Osiridos*, which best echoes the consensus of available accounts.

It is alleged that Osiris was a wise and just king who after civilising his own people through instruction in religious worship, the rule of law, and land cultivation, then proceeded, by means of reason rather than force of arms, to do likewise for the rest of humanity. While Osiris was carrying out this noble mission overseas, Isis, who was both his wife and sister, watched over the affairs of state so carefully, that the political ambitions of their envious brother, Seth, were completely frustrated.

By the time of Osiris' return, however, Seth had already devised a plan which was put into effect at a banquet when some of Seth's co-conspirators brought in an exquisitely ornamented chest which unbeknown to Osiris, had been made to accommodate his precise measurements. The chest was then playfully offered as a gift to the person whom it would best fit, and after some of those present had gone along with the charade, Osiris unwittingly stretched himself out in the chest which was then immediately slammed and nailed shut, covered with molten lead, and thrown into the waters of the Nile wherein it floated out to sea before drifting ashore at Byblos — present-day Lebanon — to become lodged in a Tamarisk bush.

On learning of the chest's location, Isis simply parted the waters for her journey to Byblos — thereby providing the story line for Bindumati (Kali as the mother of bindu or Spark of Life) whose miraculous crossing of the River Ganges was also used for the Moses myth — and eventually retrieved the chest which she then laid to rest in an isolated part of Egypt. The annual flooding of the Nile was said to have been caused by a teardrop from the eye of Isis as she lamented the deceased Osiris. The ensuing annual Nile Festival took place on the "Night of the Teardrop," and was subsequently taken up by Muslims in the June festival of Lelat al-Nuktah (Night of the Drop). Sometime later Seth accidentally found the chest while out hunting and in a fit of rage had the corpse cut into fourteen pieces that were then scattered throughout the land.

Isis once again set about finding her husband's remains and managed to locate every part except the phallus which had apparently been thrown into the Nile to be devoured by the fish. She therefore created and consecrated an imitation which by her decree was commemorated annually by the ceremonial procession of an Ark containing the seeds of various plants, a winnowing fan, and a representation of Osiris' pudendum. This gave rise to the worship of the phallus which was comparable in concept to that of the worship of the lingam in India.

After gathering Osiris's remains, Isis murmured powerful incantations that brought life to his body, and by raising up "the prostate form of him whose heart was still," she was able to take of his essence and thereby become full with child. In spite of his miraculous resurrection, however, Osiris was unable to resume his earthly life and instead went on to rule as Lord of the underworld and judge of the dead. Seth in the meantime took possession of the kingdom and imprisoned Isis who, with the assistance of the Seven Scorpion Goddesses managed to escape to the Papyrus Swamps in the Nile Delta. According to one version which sounds familiar, Isis applied to a rich woman for a night's lodging but was turned away and was eventually obliged to give birth to her son, Horus, on a cot made from papyrus plants after obtaining help from a poor family. She then raised Horus secretly and prepared him for the day when he would avenge his father's murder by defeating Seth in battle to become the new Pharaoh.

The myth of Horus' birth, however, was not confined to ancient Egyptian religion and is also to be found in the narratives of many other god-kings and eminent heroes. King Sargon of Akkad (the Akkadian Empire was a region in ancient Mesopotamia) was the virgin-born son of a temple maiden who set him afloat on the river in a basket of rushes. Sargon was rescued by the divine midwife, Akki the Water Drawer — now transformed into Aquarius — and then had to overcome the traditional obstacle of a sacred king: the menace of early destruction from an incumbent ruler, time spent in wilderness exile, evil spirit temptations, and finally ascension to the throne as spouse of the Goddess Ishtar.

This theme of a fatherless eminence born of "waters" (Maria) became universal and was repeated in many myths including that of Jason, Joshua son of Nun, Oedipus, Perseus, and Trakhan of Gilgit (a Central Asian dynasty). Such narratives were mostly based on the Goddess Cunti (Kali-the-cosmic-yoni) myth which had her give birth to the sun god and place him in a basket of rushes that was set afloat on the Ganges River. It was this selfsame sun god who was fathered by Apollo and reborn in Athens to the virgin Cruesa who left him in the obligatory woven basket.

So the concept of the "virgin birth" became an essential element for the creation of divine beings because the ancient religious scribes obviously felt that no self-respecting divine being would deign to have sexual intercourse with a mere mortal, let alone one who was a woman. And so long before Mary's "Immaculate Conception" of Jesus, a whole lot of other presumably "untouched" women where used as receptacles for the foetal development of divine beings.

Whenever broaching the subject of the mysteries in his writings, the Greek historian Herodotus (c. 485-425 BCE), always did so with caution and explained his reluctance by recounting the misfortunes of another who had been so foolish as to utter secrets that had been learnt through initiation. In *The Golden Ass*, which is in effect a description of the mysteries under the guise of a fable, Apuleius, the Berber Latin prose writer, is not much more forthcoming. When the narrative's protagonist, Lucius, regains his human shape and is initiated into the mysteries of Isis, he divulges very little:

> *Perhaps, inquisitive reader, you will very anxiously ask me what was said and done? I would tell you if it could be lawfully told. I approached to the confines of death, and having trod on the threshold of Proserpine, at midnight I saw the sun shining with a splendid light.*

Knowledge of the Higher Degrees or Crata Repoa is also based on a compilation of initiation facts sourced from the allusions of many separate ancient writers. Entrance to the Crata Repoa was by invitation only — usually from the Pharaoh himself — and required the Candidate to be continually tried during many years of work and study before eventually being accepted as a Propheta in the Seventh Degree where he was addressed as "Saphenath Pancah," or the man who knows the secrets. His acceptance entitled him to take part in elections for high office and read all the sacred books in the Ammonite language after which Amman, the capitol of present-day Jordan was named. Apart from a square cap for his tonsured head and a full-length, white-stripped tunic called an Etangi, he was also given a cross whose shape and special significance was related to the waters of the Nile.

The cross was a small replica of an upright pole with horizontal bars that was fixed into the riverbed of the Nile for judging the level of inundation. As a result of life in ancient Egypt being dependent on the flooding of the Nile, this form of measure for inundation came to be viewed as the symbol of life, health and prosperity.

Consequently the Tau cross — because it is shaped like the Greek letter T and also associated with Saint Anthony of Egypt — topped by a circle, was the "Cross of Life" representing the union of the male and female sexual symbols. It was regarded by the ancient Egyptians as an essential life-charm on whose possession depended the life of every human and divine being. Ancient Egyptian depictions have goddesses, gods and Pharaohs clutching such crosses in their right hands long before anyone ever heard of, or saw the Christian version which did not appear in Christian art until the fifth century. Needless to say, the Christian version dropped the female symbol of the circle and retained only that of the male. Such bias against Women has been a feature of Christianity to this day.

Variations of this cross —also known as an ankh, or ansate cross — were later adopted as an emblem by other religious and secular organisations including the Knights Templar. The Triple Tau, for example, is now regarded by Royal Arch Masons as the emblem of emblems with "a depth that reaches to the creation of the world and all that is therein."

One must state it plainly. Religion comes from the period of human prehistory where nobody — not even the mighty Democritus who concluded that all matter was made from atoms — had the smallest idea what was going on. It comes from the bawling and fearful infancy of our species, and is a babyish attempt to meet our inescapable demand for knowledge (as well as for comfort, reassurance and other infantile needs). Today the least educated of my children knows much more about the natural order than any of the founders of religion, and one would like to think — though the connection is not a fully demonstrable one — that this is why they seem so uninterested in sending fellow humans to hell.
Christopher Hitchens (1949-2011), author, orator, essayist, journalist, and columnist, God Is Not Great: How Religion Poisons Everything

3

Glorified Gods Galore

Man cannot make a worm, yet he will make gods by the dozen.
Michel de Montaigne (1533-1592), influential French Renaissance writer

The Brahmins

The use of religion with its proliferation of gods to coerce and control the masses was by no means restricted to the ruling elites of ancient Egypt. Sometime during the second millennium BCE a large group of light-skinned Aryans from Persia (now Iran) migrated through Afghanistan and into India which was mostly inhabited by dark-skinned Dravidians. The migrating Aryans introduced a Dark Age to an otherwise thriving civilisation where their priests devised a devilish caste system that relegated the indigenous population to a lower status while preserving their own elitist position with claims of divine ordinance.

Discriminatory caste system doctrines promoted the notion that all those born into the lower ranks were being punished for their sins in a previous life which they may not recall. Their duty therefore was to accept punishment without objection while toiling and obeying the demands of their superiors so as to gain an elevated position in the next life. It was in effect slavery fraudulently enforced with a quasi-religious promise of future benefits in an "afterlife."

The migrating Aryans were nomadic agriculturalists consisting of three main social classes of priests, warriors and husbandmen who after initially settling around the northern branches of the Indus River, then fought their way southwards to create more settlements in the central and southern parts of the country. Assimilation soon followed and the Aryan language gradually became part of the extensive folklore which in being passed from generation to generation, helped to develop Sanskrit, the language used in the most ancient and sacred religious writings collectively known as the Vedas.

Early Vedic religion involved the deification and worship of natural elements with each element often being represented by more than one god so that the sun was for example variously venerated as Vishnu, "the mighty one"; Bhaga, "the bestower of boons"; Savitar, "the enlivener"; Pushan, "he who causeth to flourish"; and Surya, "the glowing one." The gods in their abundance, however, were not worshipped by the priests who like their ancient Egyptian counterparts did not subscribe to the idolatry of the duped masses whom they considered incapable of either comprehending or observing the pure religion of the spirit which in its spoken and written form was the jealously guarded possession of a small circle of initiated men. It is evident in the following passage from the Mahanirvana that those chosen for initiation were taught to disregard such idolatrous inventions:

Numerous figures, corresponding with the nature of divers powers and quality, were invented for the benefit of those who are wanting in sufficient understanding . . . We have no notion of how the Eternal Being is to be described: He is above all that mind can apprehend, above nature . . . That only one that was never defined by language, and gave to language all its meaning, he is the Supreme Being and no partial thing that man worships . . . This Being extends over all things. He is mere spirit without corporal form; without extension of any size, unimpressionable, and without any organs; he is pure, perfect, omniscient, omnipresent, the ruler of the intellect and the soul of the whole world.

Despite assimilation, the caste system persisted and the priests evolved into the Brahmins from whose supposedly deep appreciation of the values that mattered most to humanity, emanated the power that governed every aspect of community life. The Kshatriyas, or warriors, provided the political and military leadership that maintained social order and enhanced the material welfare of the community. The necessary base for social cohesion was down to the artisans, farmers and merchants who were known as the Vaishyas. It was from the Vaishyas that a fourth group of unskilled labourers, or Sudras, came into being to carry out the menial tasks which in turn produced a people of such low status, that they were called Harijans or "untouchables," and as such they were not allowed to associate or even worship with their fellow human beings because the nature of their "impure" work was anathema to the purity of Brahmanism.

Such discrimination appears even in the Bible where it is written that outcasts could not be touched, but were permitted to exist as "hewers of wood and drawers of water" (Joshua 9:21). While Yahweh's Jewish scribes insinuated that traditions of the caste system had been passed down from their ancestors, they were in truth borrowed from the already established Asian caste system.

Brahmanism, the orthodox religion of India, developed in three main stages starting with the Age of the Vedas, dealing with meditation, philosophy, and spiritual knowledge. Next came Brahmanism and the doctrines of the Upanishads — texts with esoteric embodiment that were probably written between 400 and 200 BCE — which held that god was the transcendent reality of which man, nature and the material universe were manifestations. Finally came the Age of the Buddhist and Jainist Heresies which prompted a Brahmin Counter-Reformation in the form of relentless and sanguinary persecution that led to the rise of Hindu sects.

Acceptance into the priesthood required initiation into the mysteries with the Candidate enduring a long and arduous process including constant ablutions, fasting, prayer, and study under the tutelage and spiritual guidance of a Brahmin. After being elevated to the position of Brahmin which was attainable only to a man who belonged to the first three thrice-born classes, and of the four original divisions of the Hindu body, the Candidate attained a position that allegedly possessed supernatural powers capable of controlling and even changing the course of cosmic events by means of rituals and sacrifices; a position of esteem and unchallenged authority; and a position with contempt for "those who are wanting in sufficient understanding," for those who were Untouchables, and for those who were women.

It was the Brahmins who around 200 BCE composed the self-serving rules which they legitimised with attribution to Manu who was the Hindu version of Adam, or First Man. The Code of Manu, or Manusmĩiti, is the collection of laws based on custom, precedent and the teaching of the Vedas. It is alleged — as was the case with Moses — that Manu learnt these laws from the creator himself which he in turn passed on to the sages who were by definition profoundly wise men. Despite the written assertions by such wise men it would not be unreasonable to wonder what kind of benevolent and just god would have inspired the iniquitous laws of which the following are but a few examples:

"In childhood a female must be subject to her father; in youth, to her husband; when her lord (husband) is dead, to her sons; a woman must never be independent. She must not seek to separate herself

*from her father, husband or sons. By leaving them
she would make both her and her husband's families
contemptible."*

Manu Verses 148, 149

*Him to whom her father may give, or her brother
with the father's permission, she shall obey as long
as she lives. Though destitute of virtue, or seeking
pleasure elsewhere, or devoid of good qualities, a
husband must be constantly worshipped as a god by
a faithful wife.*

Manu Verses 151, 154

Though Mahatma (Great Soul) Gandhi to some extent
championed women's rights and travelled throughout India
condemning the degradation of the Untouchables, little has
changed to this day with the caste system and religious intol-
erance still prevailing. Irrespective of the religion that an Indian belongs to — Buddhist, Christian, Hindu, Jainist, Muslim, Sikh, or otherwise — he or she will regard their caste as
being the primary factor in their identities as Indians rather
than their religion.

Even in Western societies such as Britain, the tradition of
forced marriages persists within South Asian communities
where young girls can often be falsely lured to India, kidnapped, held against their will, beaten, and in some cases
even killed by their relatives. Those who rebel against such
an abhorrent tradition are regarded as having brought shame
on the family and are invariably punished with "honour" attacks that can include dousing with acid, abduction, mutila-

tions, beatings, and in some cases, even murder. It would be hard to find another animal species capable of punishing its offspring with the same degree of barbarity. But maybe that is because other animal species do not worship the false gods of hate-promoting religions.

Despite its abundance of gods and religious fervour, India is rated as one of the most hazardous countries in the world for women and young girls with high rates of human trafficking, prostitution and rape. The cultural preference for male rather than female offsprings has also encouraged foeticide and infanticide with an estimated 50 million females having gone missing over the past century. While India may be the world's largest "democracy" and is hailed as a rapidly "developing" country, it must also be recognised that actual democracy and social development are unattainable so long as a flagrant disregard for the human rights of women and the lower castes continues to prevail. Before India can rightly claim to be a developing democracy, it must first address the need for educating the masses and abandon the abysmal doctrines of fictional gods who are used as an excuse for horrendous human rights violations.

Zoroastrianism

Zoroastrianism, arguably the world's oldest monotheistic faith, was established sometime between 1,500-1,000 BCE by the Persian prophet Zoroaster — Zarathrustra in ancient Persian — who has been described as the father of ethics, the first rationalist, first monotheist, and first to articulate the notions of heaven and hell, judgment after death, and free will. Such Zoroastrian notions probably influenced other religious and philosophical systems including Second Temple Judaism, Gnosticism, Greek philosophy, Christianity, Islam, the Baháʾí Faith, and Buddhism.

Zoroaster's message initially met with strident resistance before he managed to convert king Vishtaspa — who though not epigraphically attested, was like Zoroaster traditionally assumed to have been a historical figure — eventually influenced his people's acceptance of the new religion. Thereafter, while in deep meditative prayer, Zoroaster received messages from Ahura Mazda which he then repeated to his disciples. The messages, which were answers to questions, were memorised by the prophet and his followers as a living scripture to be passed down from generation to generation in the ancient Avestan language. Zoroastrianism was embraced by the Achaemenid Empire (c. 550-330 BCE) and the Parthian Empire (247 BCE-224 CE) which maintained the oral tradition. Under the Parthians, a written record of the conversations between Zoroaster and Ahura Mazda was initiated.

Zoroastrian tradition maintained that the beginning of creation was achieved by the emanation of light by the Eternal, from whence issued the King of Light, Ahura Mazda, who by means of speech created the pure world, of which he was the preserver and judge. He was the Supreme Being, or Eternal Life, otherwise known as "Time without Limits" because no origin was assigned to him. He was enshrined in his glory with attributes and properties that were incomprehensible to human understanding, and to him belonged silent adoration. His first creations were threefold and began with the creation in his own image and likeness of six genii called amshaspands, who surrounded his throne and were his messengers to lesser spirits and men; and to whom they represented purity and perfection.

The second creation was that of the twenty-eight yazatas, who as models of virtue and interpreters of men's prayers, watched over the happiness, innocence and preservation of the world. The third creation was that of the far more numerous farohars, who represented the perceptions of Ahura Mazda before he proceeded with the creation of material things. They were in principle the spirits, or "guardian angels" of men, and the concept of their alleged existence was later to be adopted by the Greeks and the Romans.

Apart from Ahura Mazda, there was also Ahriman, who as the second-born (twin) emanation from primitive light by the Eternal, was also initially pure, but being very ambitious and haughty, he soon gave way to intense jealousy that was deserving of punishment. The Supreme Being consequently condemned him to the region of darkness for twelve thousand years, a period considered sufficient for ending the strife between good and evil. Ahriman in the meantime created numerous genii, daevas, who plagued the world with disease, guilt and misery. They represented cruelty, covetousness, impurity and violence. They were the demons of cold, hunger, leanness, ignorance, poverty and calumny. They provided Western Europe with the basic myth of Lucifer's downfall with its dualistic division of the universe between the forces of good and evil. The prediction by Persian prophets that Ahriman and his daevas would be defeated in the Apocalypse, the final destruction of the world, was also adopted by Judaeo-Christian prophets as noted in the Book of Revelation.

Ahura Mazda reigned for three thousand years before deciding to create the material world — in the same six stages that were later to appear in the book of Genesis — and then produced the initial being from whose seed the first human pair were formed, Meshia and Meshiane; but first the woman and then the man were seduced by Ahriman who corrupted their natures by feeding them certain fruits.

Ahriman also altered the natures of other forms of life by aligning insects, serpents, wolves and all other kinds of vermin against the good creatures. At the end of twelve thousand years, however, when the world was no longer afflicted by the spirits of darkness, there would appear three prophets whose power and wisdom would restore the world to its original pristine beauty. Ahriman, the demons and all men — no mention of women — would be purified in a sea of liquid metal, and the law of Ahura Mazda would prevail everywhere.

The Magi

The extent to which priesthoods were prepared to go

with theological fabrications that were designed to gain power, wealth, and control over the masses was also evident in ancient Persia where priests known as the Magi manipulated the masses and imposed their own primitive customs and superstitions. Initially the Magi were not priests in the strictest sense of the word, but shamans of a distinct tribal caste from Media which lay south of the Caspian Sea. The Medes like the Elamites from the nearby Kingdom of Elam, were aboriginal and in no way connected to either the Aryans or Semites who at that time shared most of Western Asia between them. As Shamans they did not subscribe to any established or organised form of religion and instead preached that the world was inhabited by both good and evil spirits which only they could control. Their rituals included both fire and animal sacrifices that were invariably accompanied by drunken shouting and dancing after liberal consumption of an intoxicating drink made from the fermented juice of the haoma plant.

Apart from being avid practitioners of consanguineous (related to or descended from the same ancestors) marriage which they rated highly for its accumulative benefits, the Median shamans also claimed expertise in the occult, practiced divination, foretold the future, interpreted dreams, transmitted and received omens, read signs in the flight of birds and the movement of the stars, and preached that they were the only seers capable of recognising the coming of the Messiah's star which would correctly identify the Divine Child on the occasion of his birth. Anyone currently naive enough to think that humanity has progressed since those days should consider the shamanistic tactics of televangelism in the US where millions of supposedly intelligent Americans have been duped into donating billions of dollars to finance the outrageously lavish lifestyles of televangelists.

The term "magus," or priest, was not one which was immediately acquired, and was said to have later come from the word *Maja*, or mirror, wherein according to Indian legend, Brahma, the Hindu god, from all eternity beheld himself and all his powers and wonders. The Maja implied a formation of a shape, a figure, or a creature from the potency of primeval and unstructured living matter. A Magus therefore was a person who studied the functional aspects of eternal life. It was from the term "magus" that words such as "image" and "magic" came to us via the Latin and Greek languages.

The ancients attributed mystic powers to any liquid or solid reflective surface and there were strict prohibitions on disturbing water in which a person was gazing as such a disturbance would supposedly endanger the soul. Endangerment of the soul-reflection was the actual basis for the Narcissus myth and not the misinterpretation suggesting excessive self-love. Apart from the superstition that broken mirrors will result in bad luck for seven years, there were numerous Christian superstitions that connect mirrors with death because mirrors do not reflect the images of demons and other creatures without souls. When there is a death in the house some Christians still to this day cover or turn mirrors to the wall in the belief that mirrors can delay or detain the souls of the dead while on their journey.

When Cyrus the Great invaded Media in 550 BCE during the establishment of the Persian Empire, the wily shamans made an unsuccessful bid for political supremacy by posing for some considerable time as the champions of the people against the Aryan aggressors. Their incessant quest for power was not only maintained throughout the reigns of Cyrus and his son, Cambysses, but also carried over into the first years of rule under Darius (521-486 BCE) when the Magus Gaumata, masquerading as Smerdis, the brother of the deceased Canbysses, ceased power while Darius was overseas. Darius, however, regained control by having Gaumata and associates executed,

Having therefore failed to gain power by political means, the Magi immediately proceeded to insinuate themselves as priests within the ranks of Persian nature-worship by emphasising the more obviously common aspects of both religions such as the veneration of fire and the sun. They also appear to have had no qualms over the self-imposed suppression of their own aboriginal affinities even to the extent of adopting the Persian funerary custom of encasement in wax as opposed to their own tradition of exposing the dead to scavenging animals and carrion birds. The tradition, however, was later reintroduced once their usurped position of theological eminence had been established and no religious ceremony could be performed without their presence. The

Greek historian, Herodotus (c. 485-425 BCE), accurately records that by the time of his travels, the Magi had compensated for the failure of their political endeavours by becoming indispensable to the ritual of Persian religion. This they achieved by not only highjacking the more popular aspects of nature-worship, but also by tenaciously attaching themselves to the religion of the Persian prophet Zoroaster.

So by publicly feigning acceptance of Zoroastrian traditions, the former Median shamans managed to establish their own worthiness as proselytes to serve at the altar of native Persians: and in so doing, were able to gradually and covertly hijack Zoroastrianism by introducing many aspects of their own primitive beliefs. Consequently as the transformation from shamans to Magi took place, drunken orgies and blatant deceptions gave way to a more acceptable public image that even impressed Greek and Roman scholars who commented favourably on various characteristics of Magian behaviour such as demeanour, discipline, ethics, laws of purity, and powers of divination. Their reputation had become so widespread as a result of the Persian Diaspora in Asia Minor, Syria, Mesopotamia and Armenia, that even in the infancy narrative of Jesus (Matthew 2:1-2) it was felt — despite Christian hostility towards the Magi — that the child's alleged divinity had to be substantiated by including the presence of the three Magi who had been guided by a brilliant star. The frequent Christian depiction of these three wise men bearing gifts as a token of their homage subsequently became known as the "Adoration of the Magi."

Becoming a member of such a religious elite, however, was not easy and after lustrations by fire, water and honey, the Candidate had to endure in silent solitude numerous probations that culminated in a fast of fifty consecutive days. The mental rather than the physical strain of the trials often caused varying degrees of derangement whose effects on occasion proved permanent. After having survived the novitiate, the Candidate was armed with various talismans for protection during his journey through a series of adjoining chambers where intermittent flashes of light and thunderous noise were accompanied by attacks from other members disguised as wild animals. The Candidate was then soothed with pleasant scents and melodious music; had a snake placed on his breast as a token of regeneration; and witnessed a display of the wicked torments of Hades. On finally being congratulated and welcomed into the illuminated Holy of Holies which sparkled with precious metal ornaments, the Candidate had to undertake not to divulge the secret rites of Zoroaster to profane outsiders. An Arch-magus seated on a throne and surrounded by the dispensers of the mysteries, then revealed the sacred words of which the Tetractys, or name of God, was the principle. The Tetractys is analogous to the Tetragrammaton, or name of the Deity as revealed to Moses on Mount Sinai. Transliterated Y H W H and regarded by the Jews as being too sacred to pronounce, it is articulated as Yahweh or Jehovah.

These initiation stages came to be known as the ascent of the ladder of perfection and subsequently gave rise to the legend of Rustam, the Persian Hercules who mounted a Simurgh, a monstrous griffin in Persian Mythology, and undertook the conquest of Mazendaraun which was reputed to be the perfect earthly paradise. After fighting his way through many dangers along a road of seven stages, Rustam finally reached the White Giant who smote all who assailed him with blindness. Rustam, however, proved triumphant and with three drops of the giant's blood restored sight to all the captives. The blindness with which the captives had been smitten was symbolic of the Candidate's mental blindness before initiation.

Zoroastrianism under the authority of the Magi flourished in Persia for many centuries until 651 when Persian sovereignty was ceded to the Islamic invaders, and what was left of Zoroaster's teachings soon gave way to those of Mohammed. The severity of the ensuing persecutions forced many Zoroastrians to flee to remote regions with the majority settling in Northwest India where they are to this day known as Parsis, or Persians. It is believed that there are now approximately 200,000 worshipers worldwide with Zoroastrianism being practiced as a minority religion in parts of Iran and India.

For those Zoroastrians who courageously remained in Persia (Iran since 1935), persecution has been a way of life and they are referred to as gabhr, or infidel. Whether or not the former shamans of Media allowed themselves to be martyred for Zoroastrianism, is not known. But one must wonder if those wily shamans who survived the Aryan invasion and then embraced whatever religious beliefs were fashionable at the time, would have had much difficulty in making the necessary theological adjustments to become ardent and influential members of the Islamic community.

> *All national institutions of churches, whether Jewish, Christian or Turkish, appear to me no other than human inventions, set up to terrify and enslave mankind, and monopolise power and profit.*
> **Thomas Pain (1737-1809), English-born American political activist, philosopher, political theorist, and revolutionary**

4

The Israelites and Judaism

*It is highly probable that the bulk of the Jew's an-
cestors "never" lived in Palestine "at all," which
witnesses the power of historical assertion over fact.*
**H. G. Wells, (1866-1946), English writer in many
genres including history, satire, and social commentary, The Outline of History.**

To successfully launch and establish a new religion requires a mind-boggling historical narrative of epic propor-
tions to legitimise its doctrines while beguiling the religiously inclined and hopelessly deluded. Consequently mythic
concoctions are at the very core of sacred texts which become instrumental in generating a folklore — as was also
the case for Judaism — that helps to explain, establish, and
exemplify nascent religions. But every narrative, factual or
fictional, has to have a beginning and many scholars now
regard Jewish history as having begun with the Exodus of
Jews who were led by Moses from Egypt and that any events
previous to that mentioned in the Bible were just an accumu-

lation of syncretic mythologies based on numerous non-Jewish sources.

According to the Bible, the Exodus occurred in circa 1300 BCE when some 600,000 oppressed Israelite slaves led by Moses — with neither map nor directions from the god who chose them — wandered through the wilderness for forty years before settling in the promised land. Unfortunately there is no mention or record of this Exodus in ancient Egyptian history and had such a momentous event actually occurred — 600,000 people would in those days have represented at least a quarter of Egypt's population — then surely it would have warranted being diligently recorded or at least mentioned.

Very briefly, this extravagant biblical myth — as related in the books of Exodus, Leviticus, Numbers, and Deuteronomy — started with the Israelites going to live in Egypt during a famine; the pharaoh eventually became concerned over the number and power of Israelites and enslaved them; he also ordered the slaughter at birth of all male Hebrew children; one child, however, survived, was placed in a basket on the Nile, and was found and adopted by the Pharaoh's daughter who named him Moses; Moses killed an Egyptian who was beating a Hebrew slave, and was forced to flee; Moses goes to Mount Horeb where god appears in a Burning Bush, commands him to free the Hebrew slaves, and take them to the promised land in Canaan; the Pharaoh refuses Moses' request to free the Israelite slaves; God smites the Egyptians with plagues; the Pharaoh finally agrees to let the Israelites go; when the Israelites leave, the Pharaoh changes his mind and pursues them to the Red Sea; Moses parts the Red Sea with his staff, the Israelites cross on dry ground, and the sea closes down on the pursuing Egyptians, drowning them all; god then provided water, food, and rained manna on the Israelites to eat; the Israelites reached the Sinai desert, god revealed himself, and established the Ten Commandments and Mosaic Covenant which was named after Moses; the Israelites kept god's torah (law/instruction), and in return would be given the land of Canaan; a series of deaths, disputes, and disasters then occurred before Moses addressed the Israelites for one final time on the banks of the River Jordan; and finally god instructs Moses to climb Mount Nebo from where he saw the promised land, and died.

Even though the Exodus story is discounted by Egyptologists, archaeologists and even Jewish scholars, it has nonetheless served to instigate a historical casting of Jews as the perennial victims. It is, however, possible that some Jews may have been expelled from ancient Egypt following an outbreak of plague that was likely to have been leprosy as noted by Manetho — the Egyptian priest and historian who during the third century BCE wrote the *Aegyptiaca* (History of Egypt) — and noted that some alien tribes in northwest Egypt were lepers and unclean.

There are no Egyptian documents to substantiate claims of Jews being expelled from ancient Egypt — and even if some were — it is highly unlikely that the number expelled was anywhere near the number claimed by Jewish scribes. Numerous Egyptian documents do, however, mention the custom of nomadic shepherds entering Egypt to camp in the River Nile Delta during periods of drought and the scarcity of food, but such harmless incursions were more likely to have been periodic occurrences rather than a solitary, exceptional event.

Furthermore, researchers have continuously endeavoured to locate Mount Sinai and the desert encampments of the wandering tribes, but despite considerable efforts, not a single site has been located to match the biblical narrative. Because the main events in the history of the Israelites are not substantiated by either archaeological discoveries or non-biblical documentation, most historians are agreed that the stay in Egypt and the events of the subsequent exodus may have occurred to a negligible number of nomadic families whose story was embellished to accommodate the need for establishing a historical narrative for a Jewish ethnic identity.

Even the historically important narrative of how the land of Canaan was conquered by the Israelites is subject to doubt as a result of the difficulties encountered in trying to locate the archaeological evidence to support this biblical contention. Excavations by different expeditions at Jericho and Ai — cities whose conquest is conscientiously detailed in the Book of Joshua — have yielded nothing apart from the conclusion that during the agreed upon period for the conquest in the late part of the 13th century BCE, there were no cities in either location and certainly no walls that could have come "tumbling down." In response to this lack of evidence, a variety of feeble explanations have been offered including the suggestion that Jericho's walls had since been washed away by rain.

Almost half a century ago, biblical scholars put forward the idea that the conquest narratives should be viewed as nothing more than mythical legends because with the discovery of more and more sites it had become apparent that the locations in question had at different times simply petered out or been abandoned. It was therefore ultimately concluded that there was no factual evidence in existence to support the biblical narrative of a conquest by Israelite tribes in a military campaign led by Joshua.

While the biblical narrative exaggerates the extent — "great cities with walls sky-high" (Deuteronomy 9:1) — of Canaanite city fortifications conquered by the Israelites, the reality was quite different with excavated sites uncovering only remains of unfortified settlements consisting of a small number of structures that could hardly be regarded as being cities. Consequently it is evident that culture in urban Palestine during the late 13th century BCE had disintegrated over a period of hundreds of years rather than being the result of military conquest by the Israelites.

It is evident that the authors of the biblical descriptions

were either unfamiliar with, or deliberately ignored the geo-political reality in Palestine which was subject to Egyptian rule until the mid-12th century BCE. Egyptian adminis-trative centres were located in Gaza, Japho (Jaffa), and Beit She'an with evidence of numerous Egyptian locations on both sides of the Jordan River also being discovered. The biblical narrative fails to mention such prominent Egyp-tian presence and it is obvious that the scribes were either unaware of, or deliberately ignored an important historical reality so that archaeological discoveries have demonstrated the biblical scenario of "great" Canaanite cities, impregnable fortifications with "sky-high walls," and the heroism of a few Israelite conquerors assisted by god against the more numer-ous Canaanites, were all theological concoctions devoid of factual foundations.

Even the phased emergence of the Israelites as a people was subject to doubt and debate because there was no evi-dence of a spectacular military conquest of fortified cities, or evidence as to the actual identity of the Israelites. Archaeo-logical discoveries, however, did indicate that starting some time after 1200 BCE which is identified with the "settlement" phase, hundreds of small settlements were established in the central hill region where farmers worked the land or raised sheep. As it had already been established that these settlers had not come from Egypt, it was proposed — because graves had been discovered in the hills area without settlements — that they were pastoral shepherds who wandered throughout the region maintaining a barter economy with the valley inhabitants by exchanging meat for grains. With the gradual disintegration of both urban and agricultural systems, however, those nomadic sheep herders were forced to produce their own grains which resulted in the establishment of permanent small settlements.

"Israel" is mentioned in a single Egyptian document dating from 1208 BCE, the period of King Merneptah, which states "plundered is Canaan with every evil, Ascalon is taken, Gezer is seized, Yenoam has become as though it never was, Israel is desolated, its seed is not." By referring to the country by its Canaanite name and mentioning several of the kingdom's "cities," Merneptah had provided evidence that the term "Israel" was given to one of the population groups residing in Canaan's central hill region toward the end of the Late Bronze Age, where the Kingdom of Israel was later to be established.

Archaeology also played a role in bringing about a change in establishing the reality of Kings David and Solomon's "united monarchy" period which the Bible describes as being the height of the economic, military, and political power of the ancient Israelites with David's conquests followed by Solomon's rule having created an empire stretching from the Gaza to the Euphrates River: "For he ruled over all the kingdoms west of the Euphrates River, from Tiphsah to Gaza, and had peace on all sides" (1 Kings 4:24). Archaeological discoveries at numerous sites, however, prove that the imposing buildings and magnificent monuments attributed to that era were nothing more than functional but unremarkable structures.

Of the three cities mentioned among Solomon's amazing construction achievements, Gezer proved to be only a citadel covering a small area and surrounded by a less expensive casemate wall consisting of two thinner, parallel walls with an empty space between them; Hazor 's upper city was only partly fortified — about 7.5 acres from total of some 135 acres — which had been settled in the Bronze Age; and Megiddo covered a small area with what would have been huts rather than actual buildings and with no indication whatsoever of having had a fortified wall.

Further contradictions also arose as a result of excavations in Jerusalem — the united monarchy's alleged capital — where extensive excavations over the past 150 years have uncovered some remains of the cities from the Middle Bronze Age and the Iron Age II (the period of the Kingdom of Judea). Apart from some pottery shards, no remains of any buildings from the united monarchy period have been found. In view of the existence of preserved remains from earlier and later periods, it may be concluded that Jerusalem in the time of David and Solomon was hardly a "city" with at most a small citadel for the ruler, but certainly not the capital of an impressive empire as described in the Bible.

As they were obviously aware of the 8th century BCE's wall of Jerusalem and its culture of which remains had been discovered in different parts of the city, biblical authors were able to transfer that scenario back to the age of the united monarchy. It may be assumed that Jerusalem's more prominent status was acquired following the destruction of its rival, Samaria, which had been besieged for three years by the Assyrian Sargon II before finally falling in 722 BCE.

Apart from justified doubts about historical and political details of the biblical narrative, questions regarding the doctrines and worship of the Israelites were also raised including the date at which monotheism was adopted by the kingdoms of Israel and Judea. For example in Kuntilet Ajrud in the southwestern part of the Negev hill region, and Khirbet el-Kom in the Judea piedmont, Hebrew inscriptions were discovered that mention "YHWH and his Asherah," "YHWH Shomron and his Asherah," "YHWH Teman and his Asherah." The authors were obviously familiar with a pair of gods, YHWH and his consort Asherah, and had sent blessings in the couple's name. These inscriptions from the 8th century BCE suggest the possibility that monotheism, as a state religion, was in reality an innovation of the Kingdom of Judea's era following the destruction of the Kingdom of Israel.

Archaeological discoveries have also proved to be consistent with the critical school of biblical scholarship's conclusions that David and Solomon might have been tribal kingdom chieftains who ruled over small areas with the former in Hebron and the latter in Jerusalem so that from the outset they were not only separate, independent kingdoms, but also at times adversaries. Consequently the much vaunted united monarchy narrative is an imaginary historiographic concoction written at the earliest during the time of Judea's Kingdom whose actual name has remained a mystery. What was astonishing about all of this, was the fact that a nation-state of the Jewish people was citing such blatant biblical falsehoods as justification for its current illegal and always brutal appropriation of Palestinian land, property, and resources.

Consequently the consensus amongst modern scholars is that the Bible fails to give an accurate account regarding the origins of the Israelites, who instead were likely to have become an entity in the central highlands of Canaan in the late second millennium BCE from the indigenous Canaanite culture. Some scholars believe that the story of the Exodus may have some historical basis, but that any such basis has little resemblance to the story told in the Bible.

> *Following 70 years of intensive excavations in the Land of Israel, archaeologists have found out: The patriarchs' acts are legendary, the Israelites did not sojourn in Egypt or make an exodus, they did not conquer the land. Neither is there any mention of the empire of David and Solomon, nor of the source of belief in the God of Israel. These facts have been known for years, but Israel is a stubborn people and nobody wants to hear about it . . . This is what archaeologists have learned from their excavations in the Land of Israel: the Israelites were never in Egypt, did not wander in the desert, did not con-*

quer the land in a military campaign and did not pass it on to the 12 tribes of Israel. Perhaps even harder to swallow is the fact that the united monarchy of David and Solomon, which is described by the Bible as a regional power, was at most a small tribal kingdom. And it will come as an unpleasant shock to many that the God of Israel, Jehovah, had a female consort and that the early Israelite religion adopted monotheism only in the waning period of the monarchy and not at Mount Sinai. Most of those who are engaged in scientific work in the interlocking spheres of the Bible, archaeology and the history of the Jewish people — and who once went into the field looking for proof to corroborate the Bible story — now agree that the historic events relating to the stages of the Jewish people's emergence are radically different from what that story tells.

Ze'ev Herzog — professor of archaeology at The Department of Archaeology and Ancient Near Eastern Cultures at Tel Aviv University specialising in social archaeology, ancient architecture, and field archaeology — debunks the historic Exodus myth in Deconstructing the Walls of Jericho

To begin with, the name Moses was in fact Egyptian as in Thutmose or Ahmoses, and meant "unfathered son of a princess." The Moses myth was probably modelled on the Egyptian demigod Heracles of Canopus — Ancient Egyptian coastal town located on the River Nile Delta — who was drawn from an arc in the Nile bulrushes, grew up to perform many great deeds, and eventually died on a mountaintop.

Moses's fortuitous meeting with Sinai's god — the Chaldean moon-god Sin — suggests that the Jews attempted to settle in that god's Cainite-Midianite mining community on the Sinai Peninsula, or land of Sinim ("Land of the Moon") whose consort was Mother Inana, who annually turned the waters of Sumer (present-day Iraq) into blood. Moses, who climbed the holy mountain where Sin dwelt, divulged that Sin was the same as the God of Abraham who apparently was not known by that name (Exodus 6:3). Ancient documents show that the name Abraham was itself a synonym for Ab-Sin, or "Moon-Father."

Abraham's god (Father Brahm) introduced himself to Moses with the words "I Am That I Am," thereby echoing the Brahmanic Tat sat's "I Am That that Is." He also commanded "Put off thy shoes from off thy feet, for the place whereon thou standest is holy ground" (Exodus. 3:5). The removal of footwear was an ancient Hindu custom — also attributed to ancient Egyptian and Roman witches — which in India is still practiced in temples where worshippers go barefoot in the belief that emanations from the holy ground can enter the body via the feet.

The narrative of Moses allegedly being given the tablets of stone was borrowed from the Canaanite god Baal-Berith, "God of the Covenant" — later to be regarded as a devil by Christian demonology — and the tablets' Ten Commandments followed the commandments of the Buddhist Decalogue. In ancient times such commandments were generally given by a god on a mountain top as was the case with the Greek Titan Queen of heaven, Mother Rhea of Mount Dicte (in Crete), and Zoroaster who received his tablets on a mountaintop from Ahura Mazda.

People are still being misled into believing that Moses wrote the Pentateuch (first five books of the Old Testament) despite the fact that scholars have long known that they were written by priestly scribes in Jerusalem late in the post-exilic period — between the end of Jewish exile in Babylon in 538 BCE and 1 CE — with a view to creating a mythic history for their nation based on the customs, pronouncements and legends of others. Because the character of Moses was conceived with a non-Jewish name and a selection of different myths, he remains shrouded in mystery that casts doubt on his actual existence.

Another groundless Judaic tradition includes the common assumption that the hexagram, with its two intersecting equilateral triangles, has been the emblem of Judaism since the time of David or Solomon. Though variously known as the Magen David (Shield of David), Star of David, or Solomon's Seal, the hexagram had nothing to do with either of them and was not even mentioned by Judaic scribes until the twelfth century. Furthermore its official acceptance as the Judaic emblem did not occur until the seventeenth century after it had been part of the medieval Cabala's system of sex worship.

The symbol originally represented the union between

males and females in Tantric Hinduism; with the upward pointing triangle representing the former and the downward representing the latter. The borrowing of this Tantric Hindu symbol was only a very small part of a lengthy and concerted effort by religious scribes to create a Jewish nation whose mythic history incorporated the traditions, maxims and legends of other religions and nations. Unfortunately Judaism has never been content to be just a religion, it has also always wanted its adherents to regard themselves, and to be regarded by others as a distinct race whom God had chosen. Growing up and living with that belief in one's own Jewish "superiority" — as a result of an unfounded assertion of being chosen by god — inevitably creates a barrier, or apartness, between the "chosen," and the less fortunate "unchosen."

The Tabernacle

During their period of wandering through the wilderness for 40 years the 600,000 Exodus Israelites were accompanied by The Tabernacle — which became redundant following the erection of Solomon's Temple in Jerusalem in 950 BCE — the portable sanctuary built by Moses as a place of worship for his people before they arrived in the promised land. It was initially a simple tent within which, it was believed, god manifested his presence and communicated his will. The Tabernacle's elaborate description in Exodus is generally regarded as being anachronistic with many scholars believing the narrative to have been written during or after the Babylonian Exile (586–538 BCE) following the destruction of the Jerusalem Temple.

The interior consisted of "the holy place" and "the most holy place," or Holy of Holies. The former contained the table on which the bread of the Presence (shewbread) was placed, the altar of incense, and the menorah, a seven-branched candelabrum. The Holy of Holies was believed to be the actual dwelling place of the Israel's god who sat invisibly enthroned above a solid slab of gold that rested on the Ark of the Covenant — a gold-covered wooden box with a cherub at each end — containing the tablets of the Ten Commandments.

The Ark of the Covenant

The word *ark* is an outdated predecessor of the modern word *arc* and was derived from the Latin *arca*, meaning a box, chest, or coffer, so that items kept concealed in such containers were regarded as being *arcane* while something deeply mysterious was an *arcanum* as in alchemy and the Tarot (from the Italian *tarocchi*). A depository for document preservation was an *archive*, with objects of antiquity being *archaic*. Consequently the excavation and examination of archaic objects came to be known as *archaeology*.

There was, however, some Biblical confusion over the stone tablets with for example Exodus 40:20 — stating "he took the tablets of the covenant law and placed them in the ark, attached the poles to the ark and put the atonement cover over it" — contradicting a later retrospective in Deuteronomy. It was apparently at that point that the Israelites before carrying the Ark into Jordan were reminded by Moses of its great power, and of the earlier events on Mount Horeb. He recalled how the stone tablets, written upon with god's finger, were those which he had thrown on the ground and broken before their eyes. He then recounted how he had been ordered to hew two more tablets — on which was to be written that which had been written on the original tablets — and that it was those tablets that he had placed in the Ark.

The assertion that the original stone tablets on which God had written were in fact not the ones placed in the Ark, had understandably been the cause of some dismay because the Ark narrative was based on that very premise which Judaic scholars reluctantly acknowledge to be factually suspect. In order to reconcile this troublesome issue, a compromise was conceived in the Middle Ages by theologians who concluded that there must have been two Arks: the one that Bezaleel built (Exodus 31), and the replica containing the tablets broken by Moses. It was nonetheless stressed that it was Bezaleel's original Ark that eventually came to rest in Solomon's Temple. The fate of the replica with the Commandments has since been an issue which Jewish historians have religiously avoided broaching and it was left to an Ethiopian Christian fraternity to exploit the fable.

It was some 700 years after Moses had passed away that Deuteronomy was written in a way that suggested the words were coming straight from the mouth of Moses. This was also the case with Exodus and was part of creating folklore that would substantiate the Israelite invasion of Canaan narrative by alleging it had been the will of god with Moses supposedly stating "and when the Lord your God delivers them before you and you defeat them, then you shall utterly destroy them. You shall make no covenant with them and show no favour to them" (Deuteronomy 7:2); "but thou shalt utterly destroy them namely, the Hittites, and the Amorites, the Canaanites, and the Perizzites, the Hivites, and the Jebusites; as the Lord thy God hath commanded thee" (Deuteronomy 20:17); "the Lord your God himself will go over before you. He will destroy these nations before you, so that you shall dispossess them, and Joshua will go over at your head, as the Lord has spoken" (Deuteronomy 31:3). Today in the promised land, those concoctions of ancient Hebrew scribes, could be construed as justification for the ethnic cleansing of the Palestinian people while the world shamefully looks the other way.

The consensus of scholarly opinion is that such accounts were derived from four different written sources which were brought together over a period of time to produce the first five books of the Bible in a composite form. The sources were referred to as J, the Jahwist source (from the German transliteration of the Hebrew YHWH); E, the Elohist source; P, the priestly source; and D, the Deuteronomist source. Consequently the Pentateuch (referred to by Jews as the Torah) consists of material gathered from six centuries of folklore which had been combined to provide a conceivable narrative of both god's creation of the world and his relationship with people in general, and Jews in particular.

There was also an apparent contradiction regarding the

Ark's portable sanctuary, the Tabernacle of the Congregation, whose elaborate details as described in the Priestly ("P") Pentateuch do not resemble the far simpler description of a mere tent with one Elohist ("E") account stating that "now Moses used to take a tent and pitch it outside the camp some distance away, calling it the 'tent of meeting'. Anyone inquiring of the Lord would go to the tent of meeting outside the camp" (Exodus 33:7). This is in stark contrast to the Priest description which has a magnificent Tabernacle located in the middle of the camp with attendants and Levite Guardians. This version of the Tabernacle — which subsequently came to be viewed as the one replicated in Solomon's Temple — had its heavy plank walls draped with thick linen and goat skins and was complete with a Brazen alter, furnishings, hangings, rings, and other adornments. A hardly portable and altogether different sanctuary from the simplicity of the Elohim tent sanctuary.

It should also be noted that by the first-century Gospel period there was still no single combined Judaic text available and that only a collection of different individual texts existed as was demonstrated by the discovery of scrolls in the caves of Qumrân located some two kilometres inland from the north-west shore of the Dead Sea. Such scrolls were for use in synagogues rather than for availability to the general public. The first combined set of texts to be recognised as a Hebrew Bible did not exist until after the fall of Jerusalem to the Romans in 70 CE with the Old Testament being written in a Hebrew style consisting only of consonants.

This led to a Greek translation — referred to as the Septuagint (from the Latin *septuaginta*: seventy) because seventy-two scholars were responsible for the translation — to cater for the increase in Greek-speaking Hellenist Jews. During the 4th century CE, Saint Jerome produced a Latin translation referred to as the Vulgate that was subsequently used by Christianity. Unfortunately impartial scholarly research and evidence strongly suggest that the Septuagint Greek translation of the Hebrew narratives — actually undeserving of being referred to as a Bible — were a rather crude forgery whose pernicious deception has to this day continued brainwashing gullible multitudes and negatively affecting the fate of millions.

By about 900 CE, Jewish scholars known as the Masoretes — because they appended the *Masorah*, a collection of traditional notes to the text — produced from the old Hebrew text a new form known as the *Codex Petropolitanus*. So irrespective of whether it is the Masoretic text, the Latin Vulgate, the English version, or other language translation, the reality is that they are all of the Current Era, the period beginning with the traditional birth year of Jesus, and as such have suffered from translational and interpretational adjustments by scribes committed to presenting a narrative — even if it necessitated stretching the truth — that would serve as a common religious conviction for the unification of a people desperate to establish and preserve a unique identity. It is equally important to recognise that historic references to the Ark in the book of Exodus and onwards through most of the Old Testament were frequent and included accounts of its pivotal role in the Israelites' conquest of Canaan; its apparent power to kill without warning all those who disobeyed the rules for its handling; and the fury of its unleashed power to cause tumours on a pandemic scale.

Since then it has been variously conjectured by historians and scholars that the Ark may have been taken away and destroyed; intentionally concealed under the Temple Mount; removed from Jerusalem before the Babylonian invasion; taken to Ethiopia by the Ethiopian prince Menelik I the supposed son of King Solomon and the Queen of Sheba; relocated by Jewish priests during the reign of Manasseh; or simply miraculously removed by divine intervention. Though the last known allusion to the Ark being in the Temple dated from 701 BCE when the Assyrian king Sennacherib surrounded Hezekiah's forces in Jerusalem, its existence and destruction or removal from the Temple remains subject to much debate.

While the current location of the Ark remains unknown, there are nonetheless a number of theories including the one about the Well of Souls, or Holy of Holies, an allusion to the former inner sanctuary within the Temple in Jerusalem. Despite the lack of certainty regarding the actual existence of the Well of Souls, its location is said to be on Haram al-Sharif/Temple Mount below a natural cave under the rock upon which according to Jewish tradition Abraham prepared to sacrifice his son Isaac, and from where Islamic tradition maintains Muhammad ascended to heaven. While knocking on the floor of the cave elicited a mysterious hollow sound, renowned nineteenth century British explorers Charles Wilson and Sir Charles Warren believed that the resounding echo was due to some small fissure below the floor and they failed to either prove or disprove the existence of any such chamber.

Though there had never been any officially organised archaeological exploration of either the site or Haram al-Sharif/Temple Mount itself — which is theoretically under control of the Waqf Muslim religious trust — it was known to be riddled with a network of some forty-five cisterns, chambers, tunnels, and caves. Shimon Gibson, senior fellow at the W. F. Albright Institute of Archaeological Research in Jerusalem, who with colleague David Jacobson wrote a definitive review — *Below the Temple Mount in Jerusalem: A Sourcebook on the Cisterns, Subterranean Chambers and Conduits of the Haram Al-Sharif* — asserted "since the 19th century, no Westerner has been allowed access to the subterranean chambers on the Temple Mount . . . I would have liked to disguise myself as a local Waqf worker and infiltrate these sites, but I wouldn't want to run the risk of creating an international incident." Taking that risk was no longer a problem for those Israelis wanting to replace the Muslim monuments that have stood on Temple mount for over 1300 years, with a Jewish Temple.

According to biblical accounts, the Ark — constructed with gold-covered shittah-tree wood (acacia) known to the ancient Egyptians as the Tree of Life with importance in traditional medicine and in many cases containing psychoactive alkaloids (hallucinogens) — had been hidden in a chamber under Haram al-Sharif/Temple Mount. If that were the case, then it was unlikely for it to have survived the adverse and damp conditions. It was Shimon Gibson's opinion that "the Ark probably would have disintegrated. Unless, of course, it had holy properties. But I, as an archaeologist, cannot talk about the theoretical holy properties of a wooden box." Even if that were the case, then surely there would still be some presence of either the gold that covered the Ark, or of the gold pot that contained manna, the "bread of the wilderness" which god gave to the 600,000 children of Israel when they were wandering for forty years from Egypt to the promised land.

Ethiopian tradition has maintained that the Ark was preserved in the ancient holy city of Axum, where apparently it has been kept for centuries in the Church of Mary of Zion. The Emperor Iyasu — member of the Solomonic dynasty who reigned from 1682 to 1706 — was recorded as having seen and spoken to it in 1691. The Ark is said to be kept in the Chapel of the Tablet — built adjacent to the church during the reign of the last emperor, Haile Selassie — where it is entrusted to a single guardian, who burns incense and recites the Biblical Book of Psalms in front of it. No one —

kings and bishops included — is allowed to approach the Ark other than the a guardian who was not only a monk, but also a virgin serving the Ark until when he approaches his own death, he appoints a successor.

The classic account of Ethiopia's Ark comes from Kebra Nagast's medieval epic, *The Glory of Kings*, written in the Ge'ez Ethiopian language. It describes how Bilqis, the Queen of Sheba, on hearing of King Solomon's immense wisdom, traveled to Jerusalem so as to acquire more knowledge and wisdom on how to better govern her own people. Being much impressed by both her beauty and intelligence, Solomon began desiring to have a child by her: a desire not driven by lust, but apparently by an unselfish aspiration to fill the earth with sons who would serve Israel's God. It was claimed that Bilqis did have a son who as a grown man travelled to visit his father in Jerusalem. After anointing his son as king of Ethiopia, Solomon instructed the elders of Israel to send their own sons to Ethiopia to serve as counsellors. As they were unhappy at the prospect of never again seeing Jerusalem and its Temple, the young Israelites decided to take the Ark along with them. *The Glory of Kings* narrative asserts that it was the Ark itself that decided to leave Jerusalem because the Jews had ceased to practice the faith revealed to them by God.

This raises the questions of when the tradition of the Ark being in Ethiopia began. It was known from coins and inscriptions that the ancient kings of Axum were pagan until the 4th century at which time they converted to Christianity

— which was declared the state religion in 330 — with no record in existence of them either claiming descent from King Solomon or of being associated with the Ark of the Covenant. The earliest report of the Ark's presence in Ethiopia appears towards the end of the twelfth century when an Armenian in Cairo, Abu Salih, wrote in Arabic that the Ethiopians were in possession of the Ark of the Covenant which was carried by descendants of King David's family who had blond hair and red and white complexions. While some historians have justifiably claimed that Abu Salih was mistaken in asserting the Ark had been carried by Europeans rather than by Ethiopians, his account cannot be discounted because he may have relied on the authority of the Bible's *Song of Solomon* (Song of Songs) — which in modern Judaism is read on the Sabbath during the Passover in commemoration of the Exodus from Egypt — which states that Solomon had white and red cheeks and hair like fine gold.

> *My beloved is radiant and ruddy, outstanding among ten thousand.*
> *His head is purest gold; his hair is wavy and black as a raven.*
> **Song of Solomon 5:10-11**

Solomon's Temple

One of the numerous questionable claims in the Hebrew Bible is the assertion that Solomon beseeched god "Give Thy servant an understanding heart to judge Thy people and to know good and evil" (1 Kings 3:9). God apparently replied "Since you have asked for this and not for long life and wealth for yourself, nor have you asked for the death of your enemies but for discernment in administering justice, I will do what you have asked . . ." (1 Kings 3:11-12).

Despite being on speaking terms with the one and only true god who apparently endowed him with great wisdom for discernment, Solomon went on not only to dabble in idolatry, but also to accumulate seven hundred wives and three hundred concubines whose sexual demands alone must have somewhat curtailed the energy and time available for the administration of justice.

The Hebrew Bible also mentions the building of the First Temple by Solomon which was achieved with the help of King Hiram of Tyre (part of present day Lebanon) who provided the architect Hiram Abiff, skilled craftsmen, and quality materials for which Solomon was obliged to pay King Hiram an annual tribute of 100,000 bushels of wheat and 110,000 gallons of pure olive oil (1 Kings 5:11).

So far no archaeological evidence has been unearthed for Solomon's First Temple and the only reference to what might have been contemporary with its supposed existence comes from the Hebrew Bible. Even architectural descriptions of the First Temple are lacking in technical detail and appear to feature combined characteristics from other temples in Egypt, Mesopotamia and Phoenicia. So regardless of any reality or truth, the Bible relates how Solomon's wisdom, prolific writings, and building accomplishments gained him a widespread fame that intrigued Bilqis, the Queen of Sheba.

When the queen of Sheba heard about the fame of Solomon and his relationship to the LORD, she came to test Solomon with hard questions. Arriving at Jerusalem with a very great train — with camels carrying rare spices, large quantities of gold, and precious stones — she came to Solomon and talked with him about all that she had on her mind.

1 Kings 10:1-2

An alternative version of the visit by Bilqis, has her being welcomed with fanfare, festivities and a tour of the great buildings including the Temple which filled her with awe and admiration. On being captivated by her beauty, Solomon — despite having all those wives and concubines — proposed marriage which a flattered Bilqis accepted. Following several subsequent visits to the Temple, however, Bilqis insisted on meeting the architect of such magnificence, and when brought before her, she found the architect Hiram Abiff's appearance and manner totally beguiling. On regaining her composure she not only questioned Hiram at length, but also defended him against Solomon's evident ill will and rising jealousy. When she asked to see the men who had built the Temple, Solomon protested at the impossibility of assembling the entire workforce consisting of apprentices, fellow-crafts and masters. But Hiram, jumping up on a large rock so as to be better seen, described with his right hand the symbolical Tau, and immediately all the workmen hastened from the different works into the presence of their Master. Bilqis was so impressed by such a display of authority that she realised she was in love with the great architect and regretted her promise to Solomon. She eventually got out of her pledge to Solomon by removing the betrothal ring from his finger while he was under the influence of wine.

Solomon's reaction was to let his fellow-conspirators know that Hiram's removal would be welcome and so when the great architect next visited the temple he was attacked by the three villainous fellow-crafts. Before dying, however, Hiram managed to remove from around his neck the golden triangle on which the master's word was engraved and threw it into a deep well. Hiram's corpse was carried by the killers to a solitary hillside where it was placed in a grave over which a sprig of acacia was then planted.

After Hiram had been missing for seven days, the public's outcry forced Solomon to mobilise a search for Hiram whose body was eventually discovered by three masters who because of the missing golden triangle decided as a security precaution to change the master's sacred and secret word. The three suspects were pursued but rather than face justice they committed suicide and their heads were brought to Solomon. After being later found in the well, the golden triangle was taken to the remotest part of the temple and placed in a triangular alter within a vault concealed by a cubical stone bearing the inscription of the sacred law. The vault, whose location was known only to the twenty-seven elect, was then walled up.

The portrayal of an eminent man or deity who as part of a trinity, first perishes as a victim of envy or evil, and is then restored to a far greater glory, is the often mandatory and by now an all too familiar story line that is central to numerous fraternal and religious rituals to which a significant percentage of humanity still subscribes in one form or another. Hiram Abiff's legacy is that the myth of his malevolent demise is still being reenacted in the twenty-first century by intelligent men of substance whose influential social status, when corrupted, can adversely affect the lives of millions. The fraternal organisation that is the main exponent of the reenactment of Hiram Abiff's death — with no mention of Bilqis so as to eliminate the female principle — is the secret society of Freemasonry whose origins surreptitiously evolved from the trade associations of the past.

The Bible, however, conveniently omits to mention that the historical facts relating to King Solomon's lifetime (c. 990-931 BCE) were loosely based on a selection of legends from Egypt, Phoenicia, and southern Arabia where the land of Sheba had long enjoyed a genuine Golden Age as a result of being the main source of frankincense and important spices that were essential for religious and funerary functions as well as food preservation. It is therefore highly unlikely — even if Solomon had actually existed — that Bilqis, one of a long line of matriarchal Sheban queens that had ruled over the entire Sinai Peninsula, a land renowned for fabulous wealth, would have stooped to paying him homage. It is far more likely that this far-fetched link with Bilqis was merely a name-dropping exercise intended to enhance Solomon's legend.

In reality there was no Golden Age; the Israelites were by no means a great nation; and there were no great cities with magnificent structures. The "city" of Meggido for example covered an area of less than several dozen acres and the only "magnificent structures" were mud-plastered huts where the standard of living was certainly below that of other nations in the ancient Near-East. The character of Solomon, or Sun God of On, was the Israelite version of the Egyptian sun god, Ra of Heliopolis. Furthermore, most of what is known about Solomon was not written until some two thousand years later so that there are no factual records traceable to the time of his reign.

There is no evidence of a United Monarchy no evidence of a capital in Jerusalem or of any coherent, unified political force that dominated western Palestine, let alone an empire of the size the legends describe. We do not have evidence for the existence of kings named Saul, David or Solomon; nor do we have evidence for any temple at Jerusalem in this early period. What we do know of Israel and Judah of the tenth century does not allow us to interpret this lack of evidence as a gap in our knowledge and information about the past, a result merely of the accidental nature of archeology. There is neither room nor context, no artefact or archive that points

to such historical realities in Palestine's tenth century. One cannot speak historically of a state without a population. Nor can one speak of a capital without a town. Stories are not enough."
Thomas L. Thomson, The Bible in History: How Writers Create a Past, 1999

In his next book, *The Mythic Past: Biblical Archaeology And The Myth Of Israel*, Thompson further asserted — with the benefit of continued advances in Palestinian, biblical, and cutting-edge archaeology, textual studies including the history of agriculture and technology, settlement patterns, climatology, sociology, and economics — that talk of pre-exilic prophets and writings was without foundation; that a time for the patriarchs never existed; that Israel at the time was only a small highland patronate lying north of Jerusalem and south of the Jezreel Valley (also known as Valley of Megiddo) ; and that Israel's history was nothing more than literary fiction.

Any honest examination by archaeologists and scholars of available facts would conclude that the Israelites were unlikely to have been in Egypt, could hardly have wandered in the desert for forty years, had lacked the military means to conquer the Promised Land, and consequently could not have passed it on to the twelve tribes of Israel. None of this, however, was going to discourage those intent on the complete Judaisation of East Jerusalem for the building of a Third Temple as fulfilment of a cherished aspiration for a united

Jerusalem as the undivided and eternal capital of the Jewish people at the expense and obliteration of the indigenous Palestinians, their culture, and their history.

> *We have to condemn publicly the very idea that some people have the right to repress others. In keeping silent about evil, in burying it so deep within us that no sign of it appears on the surface, we are implanting it, and it will rise up a thousand fold in the future. When we neither punish nor reproach evildoers . . . we are ripping the foundations of justice from beneath new generations.*
> **Aleksandr Solzhenitsyn (1918-2008), the Russian novelist, historian, and outspoken critic of Communism and the Soviet Union**

5

Christianity's Pagan Origins

Long before the Islamic threat to Zoroastrianism, Ahura Mazda faced another challenge to his authority which came not from Ahriman, but from Mithra who should not to be confused with Mitra who in Hindu Scriptures represents the light of day. Mithra, the first of the twenty-eight yazatas, or spirits of light that were invoked with the sun, eventually came to be regarded as being the sun. As the beneficent genius and most powerful of the yazatas, Mithra was the intercessor between Ahura Mazda and man, and though he was technically below the six amshaspands, the cosmic aspects of his position were allowed to become so perverted by the Magi, that with the passing of time he acquired the attributes of divinity. Such usurpation of a deity's rank by an inferior was not uncommon in mythology as was the case with Serapis in Egypt, Jupiter in Greece and Suva and Vishnu in India. Deification of an inferior being simply occurred when the symbol itself became confused with that which it was intended to symbolise.

Though Zoroaster's "purer" version of the Persian faith

which held that Ahura Mazda was the Supreme Being eventually gained prominence and spread even to the West where it influenced Middle Platonism and Judaism — many of Zoroastrian doctrines were adopted by Judaism to formulate the laws of Yahweh including the anti-female sentiment that only those women who were "submissive to control, who had considered their husbands as lords" could enter heaven — Mithra nonetheless remained an influential force when the Magi reintroduced aspects of their pagan worship which were legitimised in supplements to the scriptures. This is illustrated by the following quote from the Mihr Yasht (Hymn to Mithra):

> *Ahura Mazda spake unto Spitama Zarathustra, saying: "Verily, when I created Mithra, the lord of wide pastures, O Spitama! I created him as worthy of sacrifice, as worthy of prayer as myself, Ahura Mazda."*

By being accorded equal status with Ahura Mazda, Mithra became a supreme being in his own right and the emergence of Mithraism as a separate cult soon followed. Mithra's predominantly male attributes, however, had to be somehow balanced with some feminine presence and he was consequently paired with Anahita, an important female yazata who along with Ahura Mazda formed the mandatory great triad. The kings of the latter part of the Achaemenid dynasty from about 485 BCE became ardent votaries of Mithra and Anahita and introduced the religion to their winter capitol in Babylon. This furthered the cause of Mithraism as an independent religion and brought it into contact with the Babylonian priesthood who identified Mithra with Shamash, the Babylonian sun god.

The main source of influence on Mithraism, however, came from the Babylonian region of Chaldea whose Semitic inhabitants observed the planets in the belief that heavenly bodies had sway over people's destinies and guided the passage of their souls through the spheres. By plotting the movement of the stars, the Chaldeans were able to note that after a given period of time, some of the stars returned to their original position. This, they reasoned, meant that the stars were eternal and that the creating power responsible for their capacity for perpetual motion was therefore, if such were conceivable, even more eternal. Such reasoning gave birth to one of the concepts of eternity that led to belief in eternal life. Evidence of Chaldean influence can be seen on Mithraic monuments that invariably depict as prominent symbols the sun, the moon, and the circle of the zodiac. During the Mithraic initiation ceremony into the Fourth Degree the neophyte was required to wear a mantle adorned with signs of the zodiac and was hailed as a "Lion of Mithra," an allusion to the zodiacal sign in which the sun attained its greatest power.

The worship of Mithra spread from Babylon to Armenia and on to Asia Minor — the Anatolian peninsula of present day Turkey — where it made contact with the indigenous worship of Cybele, the Phrygian goddess of nature worship and mother of all things. Just as Isis was associated with Osiris, and Venus with Adonis, so also was Cybele with Attis: and together they symbolised relations between Mother Earth and her fruitage. So despite the fundamental differences in both character and function between Attis and Mithra, the two soon became assimilated in art and folklore so that the way was paved for an alliance between Cybele — with whom Anahita was easily identifiable — and Mithra. The ensuing association with the Cybele cult gave Mithraism its first experience of the mysteries that were to become an important part of its subsequent evolution.

Alexander the Great's conquest of the Persian Empire in 328 BCE, however, does not appear to have greatly assisted the westward advance of Mithraism, and it was not until after the collapse of his empire that the faith reinvigorated when rulers of the loosely formed federation of independent Near Eastern states became fervent worshipers in the hope that his association with Ahura Mazda — the first possessor of the legendary hvareno, or talisman of the Royal House of Persia — would lend a token of legitimacy to their dynasties. With Mithra firmly established as the region's favourite deity, Mithraism itself began from about 300 BCE — a time when the mysteries were enjoying a renaissance — to gain the interest of potential recruits in the West by exploiting the belief that access to the fabled wisdom of the East was only possible through initiation into the mysteries.

According to one of the most commonly known legends, the Magi who were much later to attend the birth of Jesus, brought gifts and were also present along with shepherds in the cave when Mithra was born of a female Rock, the petra genetrix, which had been fertilised by the Heavenly Father's phallic lightening. As a Peter, the son of petra, he carried the keys to the Kingdom of heaven. This led to Christianity's legend of Saint Peter which portrayed him as holder of the symbolic keys as was also the case with Shiva's trident and the Osirian ankh (known as key of the Nile and heavenly key to the Nile in the Sky, or Milky Way). Such key-holding enabled the holder to either admit or deny admittance to the land of the dead. The actual roots of Saint Peter's legend are to be found in pagan Roman myths of the city-god Petra, or Pater Liber, assimilated to the Mithraic pater patrum (Father of Fathers) whose title was initially corrupted into papa before becoming "pope."

The myth of Saint Peter was the false foundation on which the authority of the Roman papacy was built with a passage from the Gospel of Matthew stating that Jesus made a pun by giving Simon son of Jonah the new name of Peter — "Rock," or Latin petra — saying that he would found his church on this rock (Matthew 16:18-19). This so-called Petrine passage, however, was a forgery deliberately inserted into the scripture in the third century as a political ploy to establish the primacy of Christianity over equally competitive religions from the East. It was all part of the power struggle where the main weapons were bribery, forgery, collusion, intricate falsehoods, and fraudulent passages slipped into the sacred scriptures.

After first proving his invincible strength by overcoming the sun, Mithra then had to capture the bull — the first animal created by Ahura Mazda — which he dragged back to his cave. The bull, however, managed to escape and thereby caused Ahura Mazda to order its recapture and sacrifice.

When Mithra plunged his knife into the bull, its body gave forth all the useful herbs; from its spinal marrow, there issued wheat; from its blood came the grape that produced the wine used in the mysteries; and from its seminal fluid, all the useful animals were born. The Bull's death was therefore the birth of life, and the heavenly drama of its sacrifice was subsequently reenacted on earth as the central act of Mithraic worship in tauroboliums wherein devotees would lay in a trench beneath a lattice frame on which a bull was being slain so as to bathe in its blood. The ritual was believed to activate the renewal of life to the soul and probably originated from the Cybele cult.

Mithra, the predecessor of Jesus, performed the now familiar array of miracles by restoring health to the sick; sight to the blind; mobility to the lame; and even life to the dead. The Mithraic festival of the Epiphany which celebrated the arrival of the sun-priests or Magi at the Saviour's birthplace, was not adopted by Christianity until the year 813.

Mithraic ceremonies were usually conducted in subterranean caverns or crypts that had been converted to resemble caves that were symbolic of Mithra's birthplace. As the majority of such Mithraea were understandably small, membership averaged between fifty and sixty but rarely exceeded a hundred people who consequently experienced the kind of brotherhood and feigned equality — similar to that found in Freemasonry — that could not otherwise be found in the unjust social conditions of the Roman Empire.

The practice of equality, however, was not accorded to women and like its replacement Christianity, it was an ascetic, anti-female religion whose priests were celibate men. Women in Mithraic families were not allowed into Mithraea and the female principle was removed from the creation myth by replacing the Mother of All Living in the primal garden of paradise (Pairidaeza) with a bull named the Sole-Created. So instead of Eve, the bull was partnered with the first man. This masculinisation of the birth-giving ability, however, still required the bull to be castrated, sacrificed, and having its blood delivered for mystical fructification to the moon which being the source of a women's mystical lunar "blood of life" was responsible for producing life on earth.

An examination of all Mithraic inscriptions will reveal nothing to suggest the existence of even a single female participant in the mysteries. The concept of women's inequality to men was, and has been a hallmark of fraternal and religious organisations throughout the ages. There has to be something fundamentally wrong with the psychological state of men who allegedly subscribe to the highest of ideals and yet cannot accept women as either their social equals, or when it is patently evident on the basis of ability alone — as their superiors.

Initially Mithraism had only two degrees of initiation, but the need to exaggerate the extent of the mysteries and to create an aura of exclusivity eventually led to there being seven because that number was considered sacred. Beyond the Seventh Degree there was a priesthood under the authority of a high priest in Rome whose title of Pater Patrum was later appropriated to become the Christian Papa or Pope. The priests were responsible for the daily conduct of worship towards the East in the morning, the South at noon, and the West at night. They also kept the sacred fire burning, offered prayers to the planet that governed the day, and officiated at initiation ceremonies.

According to comments of what is left of the writings of the Phoenician neoplatonist philosopher, Porphyry (c. 232-302) whose fifteen books Against the Christians failed to survive the sentence of burning that was pronounced against them in 448, the first three degrees were of a preparatory nature and included the customary lustrations, a symbolic offering of bread and water to Mithra, and the marking of a sign on the Candidates brow. After being crowned, the Candidate removed the crown to the declaration "Mithra is my crown" and then armed himself in defence as he "ran the gauntlet" of priests who in various animal guises assailed the Candidate with blows and shouting.

It is reported that during his initiation, the deranged Emperor Commodus (180-192) became overenthusiastic in his own defence and accidentally killed one of his assailants.

Beyond these few details, there is little else known of the preparatory degrees and virtually nothing at all regarding initiation into the mysteries. One commentator does speak of "eighty punishments" by fire, water, frost, hunger, thirst, and wanderings of increasing severity; and it may be assumed that it was only after the surmounting of such trials that the Mithraic mysteries, representing the progress from darkness to light, were revealed.

Mithraism was also promoted by the enlistment of Hellenistic art with the creation of sculptured reliefs — the most common depiction being that of Mithra slaying the bull — that became the hallmark of every Mithraeum and sanctuary as the cult moved westward from Asia Minor. The eventual extent of the cult's diffusion, however, was mostly due to the Roman armies. Even before their annexation and while still client-kingdoms of the Roman Empire during the first century BCE, some regions of Asia Minor such as Armenia, Cappadocia, and Pontus served as recruiting grounds for Rome's legions and foreign auxiliary corps. It was these oriental soldiers, who while on garrison duty in far off outposts, established the numerous Mithraic sanctuaries that stretched from Africa to Britain. During 1954 rebuilding work in London's Walbrook, a Mithaeum was discovered and is now rated as the most famous of all twentieth-century roman discoveries in the City of London and is open to visitors.

Despite its popularity within military ranks, Mithraism was not immediately successful in Rome and was obliged to resort to the customary device of acquiring legitimacy by registering its sanctuaries as burial associations. Apart from Mithraism, there was also the monotheistic sun-worshipping cult of Sol Invictus, or "Invincible Sun," whose doctrinal belief that its god possessed the attributes of all the other gods precluded the need for competition with its rivals. It was therefore to the relative success of this cult that Mithraism attached itself by various means including depictions that had Mithra sharing the banquet with Sol after the former had sacrificed the bull.

As both cults regarded Sunday as being sacred and attached the same importance to the status of the sun whose rebirth they celebrated annually on the December 25, it was only natural that a gradual merging took place and what had previously occurred in Persia — the supplanting of a superior deity by an inferior through the confusion of attributes — reoccured in Rome. Mithra then came to be variously known as "Invictus Mithra," "Deus Invictus Mithra," or by the full title of "Deus Sol Invictus Mithra."

Despite its apparent success, however, Mithraism had no official recognition and it was not until the Emperor Commodus became an initiate that progress towards that goal was begun and culminated with the Emperor Aurelian (270-275) finally providing state recognition. The adoption of such non-Roman form of worship by Roman Emperors at that time was probably influenced by the belief of oriental cults that the sun was the attendant and patron of the ruler. Consequently by promoting the concept of their own deification, Roman Emperors hoped that like the Egyptian Pharaohs, they too would be regarded as human manifestations of the sun god. Diocletian, who in 277 instigated the dedication of a temple to Mithra, was also a devotee and as Emperor from 284-305 was responsible for the last of the severe persecution of Christians prior to the more tolerant rule of Constantine the Great.

Christian historians and scholars have since tried to have us believe that the survival of Christianity owes much to the tolerance of Constantine (c. 272-337) who they claim became the first Christian Roman Emperor when prior to the Milvian Bridge Battle he saw a vision of the Christian God who promised victory if the Christian monogram was daubed on the soldiers' shields. This legend was invented by Eusebius — the Roman historian, exegete, and Christian polemicist — who also transformed Constantine's nefarious activities into acts of piety. Furthermore the "Christian monogram" which was already on Constantine's standard, was the labarum which displayed the "Chi-Rho" symbol with no Christian connections whatsoever and was in truth the emblem of Mithra, the deity most worshipped by the legions of Rome. A series of inscriptions from the island of Philae in Upper Egypt prove that the labarum evolved from the Egyptian ankh.

The tolerance resulting from what came to be known as the "Edict of Milan," which was more of an informal agreement between Constantine who ruled the western parts of the empire and Licinius who ruled the eastern, was not intended by Constantine as specific assistance for Christianity, but as part of his scheme to bring about unity in the Empire which he then proceeded to do by orchestrating a campaign to blacken Licinius's reputation, to eventually bring about his death, and finally to stigmatise his memory with infamy that resulted in the removal of his statues and the abolition of all his laws and judicial proceedings.

While Constantine also recognised that unity required the establishment of social, political and religious tolerance, his support for religious tolerance, however was not due to some altruistic concern for his subjects, but to his desire to avoid offending any of the gods who might seek retribution against him personally. Though he has been hailed for establishing Christianity as the official religion of Rome, such official recognition of Christianity did not occur until after his lifetime and was the work of his bishops. He was not so much a man who worshiped Christ, but one who revered himself.

While recognising the advantages offered by cults to government, Constantine was also aware that the vested interests of paganism had for too long exercised a divisive and dangerous influence through corruption of government officials in particular, and the people in general. Christianity on the other hand, as a relatively new religion, had not yet had enough time to become seriously involved with intrigue and corruption. He also recognised Christianity's educative and stabilising potential which more than any of its dogmas commended it to the interests of government.

As to his own religious credentials, Constantine did not share Christianity's view that pagan gods were devils and was himself an initiate of the Sol Invictus cult which regarded him as a high priest in deference to his imperial position. When he moved his capital to Byzantium in 330 to allegedly create the "first purely Christian" city, he renamed it Constantinople after himself and had many pagan relics taken there for preservation. His life was hardly one of piety, but one filled with an obsession for his own self-preservation. He murdered his eldest son, his second wife, his father-in-law, his brother-in-law, and numerous others. Despite having several wives and a legion of concubines, Christian apologists claimed that he was "wedded to chastity."

Constantine's conversion to Christianity appears to have been a deathbed insurance policy that came about when Christian bishops were successful in convincing him that their God would absolve him of his sins and install him in heaven. So with death approaching, Constantine decided "the salvation which I have earnestly desired of God these many years I do now expect. It is time therefore that we should be sealed and signed in the badge of immortality." He was then duly baptised and passed away with the deluded expectation of a heavenly resurrection. Despite that, his had been a "sun emperorship" under which Christianity enjoyed a degree of freedom and tolerance, but at no time during his reign (306-337) did Christianity come close to replacing the state religion of Sol Invictus whose symbol was prominent on many public features including banners and coins.

State recognition and political power were nonetheless urgent priorities which Christianity was prepared to acquire by any means even if it meant temporarily playing down the role of Jesus as the Messiah from the heaven above, and instead becoming associated with Constantine's more tangible accomplishments down here on earth. Jesus had after all been a Jewish Zealot agitator — a fact from which Christianity wished to distance itself — whose condemnation and crucifixion resulted from his outspoken criticism of social injustice which the Roman authorities regarded as subversive political activity. Consequently in 321 as part of the "shedding" of its Jewish heritage, Christianity switched its sacred day of observance from Saturday, the Jewish Sabbath, to Sunday, the state's sacred and "venerable day of the sun." Further changes included "borrowing" the aureole of light that crowned the sun god's head to create the Christian halo and Christ's birthday was changed from January 6 to December 25 in keeping with the sun's rebirth celebration. The Orthodox Church in Armenia still adheres to the January 6 date, while the Eastern Catholic and Orthodox churches observe a January 7 date.

Though Constantine is regarded as the effective architect of the Christian Church, his zeal for its teachings never quite matched that of his mother, the Empress Helena. It was she who deemed that extensive searches should be carried out until all the holy sites were identified and appropriately marked with some imposing shrine. Imperial subordinates eager to please the supposedly devout Helena wasted no time in not only identifying the site of the crucifixion below Jupiter's temple, but also in locating Christ's place of burial. Most impressive of all, if it is to be believed, was the discovery of the precise spot where Mary Magdalene had been standing when she received the glad tidings of Christ's resurrection. Whether by arrangement or coincidence, it was Helena herself who found the True Cross with its unmistakable "King of the Jews" plaque.

Churches were then established at the alleged site of Christ's birth in Bethlehem and on the Mount of Olives from where His Ascension is said to have taken place. Helena's achievements were certainly impressive considering that all of these discoveries were made subsequent to the city's destruction by the Romans and some three hundred years after occurrence of the events. Most remarkable of all, however, was the pinpointing of the exact spot where God spoke to Moses from the burning bush on top of Mount Herob in the Sinai Desert. The site is currently the location of St. Catherine's Monastery which was built by the Emperor Justinian (reigned 527-565) so as to enclose the Chapel of the Burning Bush which Helena had ordered to be built. The monastery's full, official name is The Sacred and Imperial Monastery of the God-Trodden Mount of Sinai, and its patronal feast is the Transfiguration. Associated with Saint Catherine of Alexandria — whose relics were said to have been miraculously transported there by angels — the monastery is now a favourite pilgrimage destination and sacred to Christianity, Islam and Judaism.

Comparisons between Christ and Mithra will show that both were born in a cave; both were part of a trinity; both were mediators between God and man; both committed a sacrifice for the benefit of mankind — though in different ways — wherein blood was the symbol of regeneration; and both celebrated with their respective twelve followers who in Mithra's case were represented by twelve signs of the zodiac. Christianity's seven sacraments were a follow-on from the seven degrees of Mithraic initiation; both religions promulgated concepts concerning man and the immortality of his soul; and both had mysteries from which the lower ranks were excluded. Confirmation as to the secrecy surrounding the Christian Eucharist comes from Tertullian (155-240) the Christian Carthaginian writer who stated that which is holy should not be cast to the "dogs," and that it was "a universal custom in religious initiation to keep the profane aloof and to beware of witnesses." Christianity also concurred with Mithraism over doctrines regarding heaven and hell; judgment after death; and the triumph of good over evil.

In trying to provide some explanation for the numerous similarities that existed between the pagan religions that had long preceded Christianity, Christian writers such as Tertullian, came up with the rather novel idea that Satan, having anticipated the coming of the true faith, proceeded to imitate it long before Christ was born. Such anticipation no doubt included ensuring that the Magi would be present at Mithra's birth. Tertullian went even further to suggest "the observances of Mithraism were cunning parodies devised by Satan to seduce the souls of men from the true faith by a false and insidious imitation of it." St. Augustine (354-395) who had himself been an adherent of Mithraism for some ten years, was later to offer the more realistic explanation of "what is now called the Christian religion existed amongst the ancients, and was not absent from the beginning of the human race until Christ came, from which time the true religion, which existed already, began to be called Christian." In other words it was just a different name for the same old concoction of fables heavily laced with blatant lies.

Christianity's quest to be recognised as the official state religion was in the meantime pursued with an impressive ruthlessness and Mithra's temple which was located on the ancient site of Vaticanum, or Vatican Hill, was seized in 376. The temple, over which St. Peter's Basilica was built, is still accessible to this day. Persistent efforts by Bishop Ambrose of Milan eventually succeeded in persuading the initially tolerant Roman Emperor Theodosius I (reigned from 379 to 395) to prohibit pagan sacrifices and to destroy pagan temples so that Christianity could by the default of the others become the state religion.

The relentless and often barbarous persecutions that ensued were not, however, totally successful and elements of oriental paganism persisted in various forms including that of Manichaeism which had been developed by Mani (216-274 or 277), a former Persian slave and an initiate of the Mithraic mysteries. Mani had cunningly utilised Christian names and rites to mask a mixture of Zoroastrian and Mithraic traditions laced with gnostic and Cabalistic ideas to produce a puritanical religion that viewed all things material as evil. He maintained that the Satan responsible for the creation of the material world with all its temptations was the Jewish Jehovah, and that it was in truth the Prince of Darkness who spoke to Moses, the Jews and their priests. Thus the Christians, the Jews and the Pagans are involved in the same error when they worship this God. Mani regarded Zoroaster, Buddha, and Jesus — but not Moses — as predecessors who like himself had been chosen as "messengers" to the people. He declared Jesus to be mortal and emphasised that any allusion to divinity had to be regarded as being merely symbolic.

Unfortunately for Mani, the "messenger" business in those days was not without its hazards and it was at the instigation of the Magi that in 276 King Bahram of Persia sentenced him to death by flaying and crucifixion. His martyrdom, however, only served to fuel the spread of his teachings and Manichaean schools promoted the ideas from which under different names and guises there evolved other similar sects such as the Cathars, the Paulicians, and the Bogomils of

Bulgaria who all in their own way challenged the Christian view that Christianity was the only legitimate religion for the worship of God.

The subsequent crusades which enabled the Holy Roman Empire to take punitive military measures against Europe's heathens and heretics and Christianise the West at the cost of between 8 to 10 million lives included the Albigensian Crusade (1209–1229) which was declared by Pope Innocent III with the promise that Cathar lands would be given to French noblemen willing to take up arms against the Catharan heretics in the Languedoc region of Southern France. In what is still to this day one of the darkest and bloodiest chapters in the history of Christian persecutions, an estimated one million Cathars were massacred.

With Constantine's reign being the first important turning point in the history of the Holy Roman Empire, the second occurred under Charlemagne, the Frankish emperor who reigned from 786 to 814. Being a Christian was for Charlemagne a matter of convenience because the Holy Roman Empire — unlike the pagan tribal religions — tolerated his wars of acquisition for a share of the spoils and eventually recognised his barbarous achievements by giving him the crown of the Empire. He was also accorded special status regarding the holy sacrament of matrimony in that he had four wives and numerous concubines which the church explained away as "marriages of the second rank."

During his reign, Charlemagne ruthlessly destroyed pagan clan shrines, enforced conversion to Christianity with the choice of either Christ or immediate execution, and imposed vassalage. One reprehensible aspect of vassalage was the feudal emergence of "The Lord's Right" — also known as jus primae noctis (the law of the first night) — which equated the ownership of land with the ownership of women. This droit du seigneur meant that every serf's bride on her wedding night had to be deflowered by the lord of the land and not by her bridegroom. The church upheld the droit du seigneur as a God-given right of the nobility and declared that consummation of marriage by a vassal bridegroom within three nights after the wedding was blasphemous and equivalent to "carnal Lust." The landowner's carnal lust was, however, judged to be just and proper. Even the Eastern Church had provisions for punishing any man who tried to consummate his marriage before his lord had raped her. Droit du seigneur lasted throughout the feudal period — between the ninth and fifteenth centuries — and until the nineteenth century in Russia.

During thirty-three years of continuous war that built the Holy Roman Empire, Charlemagne shed so much blood that historians have baulked at the task of trying to establish the extent of the slaughter. His conversion method by the sword was so successful that the church subsequently supported Christian rulers who indulged in similar military pursuits. The French heroic poem *The Song of Roland* (La Chanson de Roland) — based on the Battle of Roncesvalles in 778 — clearly states "the bishops bless the waters and convert the heathen. If any man protests, he is burned or put to the sword." On occasions it was the blessed water itself that served as executioner of unregenerate pagans with converts made under the rule of Saint Goar — who died in 575 and was honoured by Charlemagne — being held under "holy water" until they either accepted Christ or drowned. That was how the Holy Roman Empire was built.

Many Western historians have since unconvincingly tried to explain the causes responsible for triggering the collapse of that Holy Roman Empire and the onset of the Dark Age with its intellectual famines, economic hardships, and social regressions. Many such historians have, however, had neither the integrity nor the courage to firmly lay the blame at the door of Christianity. It was after all the Christians themselves who maintained that the diabolic symptoms of the approaching end to the world was "the spread of knowledge" which they attempted to halt by their opposition to education for laymen, their destruction of libraries and schools, and their indiscriminate burning of books. After years of persistent destruction and vandalism, Saint John Chrysostom (c. 347-407) was able to boast with holy pride "every trace of the old philosophy and literature of the ancient world has vanished from the face of the earth."

Pope Gregory the Great (540-604) condemned secular education as folly and wickedness and even proscribed the reading of the Bible by laymen. He had the library of the

Palatine Apollo burned "lest its secular literature distract the faithful from the contemplation of heaven." By the end of the fifth century — with the church maintaining that all opinions other than its own were heretical and diabolical — Christian rulers had forcibly terminated the study of geography, mathematics, philosophy and even medicine, because diseases were the work of the devil.

The result of insane Christian persecution and wanton destruction was that numerous scholars fled eastwards for refuge in Persia where the King of the Sassanian Empire — the last Persian empire before the rise of Islam — helped them establish a school for medicine and science that was to become the world's intellectual centre for several centuries. In 529, when Justinian I (c. 482-564) shut the Athenian schools, all Hellenistic knowledge was dispersed to Gupta India, Celtic Ireland, and Sassanian Persia. And because Christianity could only flourish — and like most religions still does — on ignorance, it became necessary for it to relentlessly promote ignorance with the result that Western Europe was deprived of the learning and knowledge that would have unleashed its potential for social advancement.

One of Christianity's numerous cardinal sins has been the historic physical and sexual abuse of children by priests, clergymen, and even nuns — an abuse also prevalent amongst rabbis and imams but hardly ever reported — whose paedophilic perversions were for decades covered up by church authorities before eventually being exposed. While most people are familiar with the sexual abuse scandals that have rocked the Roman Catholic Church over the past 20 years, very little has been said about sexual abuse occurring within churches of the numerous Protestant denominations including the Baptist, Methodist, Lutheran, and the Latter-day Saints. Evangelical churches across the US have routinely failed to protect victims of sexual abuse among their members. According to a recent study sponsored by LifeWay Christian Resources, ten percent of Protestant churchgoers under 35 have previously left a church because they felt sexual misconduct was not taken seriously.

Another prominent characteristic of Christianity is its sheer hypocrisy as exemplified by the religious right — an informal coalition of conservative evangelical Protestants and Roman Catholics additionally supported by politically conservative mainline Protestants, Jews, and members of the Church of Jesus Christ of Latter-day Saints — which advocates socially conservative positions on such issues such as homosexuality, birth control, and pregnancy termination.

This compassionate coalition vociferously — and at times even violently — opposes terminations with provocative proclamations about the "sanctity of human life"; "every child, born and unborn, is a sacred gift from God"; and even assertions equating terminations with the crimes of Adolf Hitler and Joseph Stalin. By way of contrast, a deafening and hypocritical silence prevails amongst members of this conscientious coalition in whose name the US government has since the end of the Second World War killed over 20 million people and is continuing to kill millions more.

These civilised and commendable Christians with their dedication to the "sanctity of human life," however, have also remained noticeably silent when the human life lost is not White Anglo-Saxon Protestant (WASP) as has been the case in Palestine, Myanmar, Yemen, and numerous other places around the world.

> *The civilised have created the wretched, quite coldly and deliberately, and do not intend to change the status quo; are responsible for their slaughter and enslavement; rain down bombs on defenceless children whenever and wherever they decide that their "vital interests" are menaced, and think nothing of torturing a man to death: these people are not to be taken seriously when they speak of the "sanctity" of human life, or the "conscience" of the civilised world.*
> **James Baldwin (1924-1987), American novelist, playwright, and activist**

6

Islamic Schisms and Sects

The histories of most religions, Islam included, have featured a series of endless dissensions and divisions with mayhem and murderous intent still prevailing to the present day. Islam's problems began after the Prophet Muhammad (c. 570-632) died without either naming a successor, or establishing a procedure by which one could be chosen. This led to a succession dispute between the "Emigrants" who had accompanied him from Mecca to Medina, and the local "Supporters" who by joining his movement had enhanced it both materially and spiritually. Though Ali, Muhammed's son-in-law, was an obvious candidate, community elders felt he lacked the necessary experience and decided instead that Muhammed's father-in-law would become the caliph thereby facilitating the institution of a caliphate whereby the caliph acted as both the religious and secular authority. This difference of opinion eventually led to Islam's most consequential schism resulting in serious repercussions for both the Sunni and Shia groups.

The Sunnis have six beliefs, or six articles of faith that

are to be found in the Hadith which some believe is a record of the words, actions, and the silent approval of the prophet Muhammad: belief in one Allah (Tawhid); belief in angels (malaikah); belief in holy books (kutub); belief in the prophets (nubuwwah); belief in the Day of Judgement and the afterlife (Akhirah); and belief in predestination (Al-Qadr).

Though Ali's supporters, who became known as shi'at Ali, or party of Ali, did not take any immediate overt action, they nonetheless covertly laid the foundation for Islam's main schism between Sunni — derived from *sunnah*, meaning "the trodden path" — and Shia Muslims who to this day resort to ungodly violence towards each other. The Shias lived by a strict social code that demanded absolute obedience to their imams, or priest-kings, who were the direct descendants of Muhammed through the union of his daughter Fatima and Ali. They believed that in the coming millennium one of the past imams would return to earth as the Mahdi, or "guided one," to establish the rule of justice.

In the meantime, in order to avoid persecution while working to undermine the orthodox doctrines of the Sunni majority, the Shias established a discipline of secrecy that required them to conceal their true religious beliefs and to outwardly conform to the state religion. In Shia Islam, this religious dissimulation — a form of deception that concealed the truth — was known as taqiyya and provided legal dispensation whereby believers could conceal their true religious beliefs when under threat, persecution, or compulsion. The concept of taqiyya was developed to protect the Shias who were invariably in the minority and under threat. The Shia view was that taqiyya was lawful in situations of overwhelming danger such as loss of life or property but where danger to the religion would not occur. The term "taqiyya" did not exist in Sunni jurisprudence because denying the faith under duress was only permitted in the most extreme circumstances.

As part of their deception, the Shias also dispatched specially trained missionaries, or da'is, throughout the Arab world to preach doctrines that belied most of the orthodox beliefs. They maintained that Muslim Law and Scriptures contained a hidden meaning known only to the imams, and that there were seven prophets: Adam, Noah, Abraham, Moses, Jesus, Muhammed and Ali. It was also held that the sevenfold chain of creation was as follows: the prophets were second only to God at the level of Universal Reason; Ali, the "Prophet's companion," at the level of Universal Soul; the seven imams, at the level of Primal Matter; the chief da'i, or Grand Master, at the level of Space; the da'i, at the level of Time; and finally at the lowest level, stood man. Though God himself was unknowable to man, a man could work his way upwards through the grades and thereby acquire a new revelation up to that of Universal Reason.

Early Shia leaders agreed on five key beliefs which are often referred to as the five roots of Shia Islam or the five roots of Usul ad-Din which are to be found in the Koran and Hadith: the belief that God is one (Tawhid); the belief that Allah is always right and just (Adl): the brlief that the prophets provide guidance from God and should be respected (Nubuwwah); the belief that leaders such as the imams are necessary to protect the religion and give people guidance on how to live correctly (Imamah); and the belief that Shia Muslims will be resurrected and judged by God (Mi'ad).

The celebrated sixth imam, Ja'far al-Sadiq (702-765 BCE), was the start of the first major division amongst the Shias. Those who backed the succession of Ja'far's son, Musa and his descendants, believed that the millennium would come with the return of the twelfth imam in that line, and were called the "Twelvers." The remainder who supported Musa's older brother, Ismail, believed that his son Muhammed, who had disappeared in 770, was the seventh and last imam, and that his return to earth as the Mahdi would mark the millennium. Ismail's supporters were known as the Ismailis or the "Seveners." With the passing of time the Ismailis also quarrelled amongst themselves and divided to create even more secretive sects such as the Batinites, Qarmatians, Druzes, Bretheren of Sincerity, Rosheniah, and the Nizari Ismailis who were the "Assassins."

Because the ruling administration of any given Islamic society could be toppled by the removal of just one man, assassination became the obvious solution for those with nefarious political ambitions. Such elimination of the competition, however, was not without precedence and there is evidence that the Prophet Muhammed — knowing full well that his faithful followers would carry out his wishes — used to rid himself of troublesome critics and rivals by simply implying that they were undeserving of life.

By far the most successful exponent of political assassination, however, was Hassan-i Sabbah (c. 1050s-1124), the Persian Nizari Ismaili missionary and founder of the Hashshashin or Assassins, who in his youth was reputed to have attended school with the subsequently famous astronomer and poet of the *Rubaiyat*, Omar Khayyam (1048-1131), and the Sunni statesman, Nizam al Mulk (1018-1092). Though the likelihood of that being factual is contradicted by chronology, its mention in the introduction to Fitzgerald's version of the *Rubaiyat* as well as other sources would suggest that they at least knew each other, especially as Nizam was later to become one of Hasan's first victims.

In 1090 Hassan ceased Alamut Castle which became his mountain fortress, was the site of intense activity until 1256, and functioned as the headquarters of the Nizari Ismaili State which included a series of strategic strongholds dispersed throughout Persia and Syria, with each stronghold being surrounded by hostile territory. Alamut, the most renowned of these strongholds — fabled for having heavenly gardens, a library, and laboratories where philosophers, scientists, and theologians were able to debate with intellectual freedom — was believed to be impregnable to any military attack.

When the Mongol Hulago Khan (c. 1217-1265), Genghis Khan's grandson and scourge of Islam, overran Alamut (meaning "eagle's nest") in 1256, Mongol historians made note of what was considered important before allowing the libraries to be destroyed. It is therefore known that Hasan was born of a Twelver Shia family in the Persian city of Qom. As a youth he sought the secrets of science and religion and for a while apparently experienced a period of doubt and depression prior to being recruited and converted to the Ismaili cause. Having then overcome a serious illness and being spiritually rejuvenated, Hasan travelled to Cairo to obtain the eighth Fatimid Caliph's permission to spread the Ismaili doctrine in Persia which was under the authority of the Seljuk Turks. Permission was given on the understanding that Hasan would support the Caliph's oldest son, Nizar, to become the ninth Fatamid caliph, and thus was born the Ismaili sect of the Nizaris who came to be known as the Assassins.

There are numerous tales relating to the travels and missionary subversion of the cunning Hasan prior to his acquiring Alamut from whence he only ventured out twice in more than thirty years. His "invisibility" as the "Old Man of the Mountain" enhanced rumours of his omnipotence and he continued to seize other mountain fortresses as regional centres of subversion. The summary execution of deviants, including two of his own sons, was a common feature of the ascetic severity of his regime which was elevated to include authority over the body as well as the soul.

Marco Polo (c. 1254-1324) — the Italian merchant traveller from the Republic of Venice who embarked on an epic twenty-four-year journey to Asia — described Aladdin quite differently from the mythic character who in Arabian Nights was master of a cave full of treasure. The cave in question was actually real and was located in the fortified valley of Alamut near Kazvin. Aladdin was the Old Man of the Mountain, the hereditary title of the Hashshishin starting with Hassan-b Sabbah whose name meant Son of the Goddess. The name Aladdin was subsequently adopted following the bloody conquest of Gujarat in 1297 by Ala-ud-din Khilji, the second ruler of the Turco-Afghan Khilji dynasty in India.

In order to accomplish his single-minded pursuit of religious power through violent political action, Hasan altered and increased the grades of Ismaili initiation from seven to nine and transformed the role of the lowly devotee from aspiring supporter to that of an active Assassin. Wily da'is with knowledge about the manipulation of the human character would "hook" potential recruits by first revealing the kind of information that would initially capture interest, and then imply that the divine mysteries could only be attained by those who swore allegiance to the imam. By using a combination of drugs and pleasurable experiences, Hasan was able to give the newly recruited "self-sacrificers" a taste of the "paradise" to which they would return as soon as they had accomplished whatever it was that he had required them to do.

The word *assassin* is a corruption of the Arabic word Hashshishin meaning "users of hashish," and it was alleged that the Assassins were heavily drugged before being dispatched to murder their victims. As each aspirant then progressed upwards through the grades of initiation, he was inspired to gradually discard the basic tenets of Islam so that by the ninth degree he was free of all authority and could subscribe to whatever system he deemed most suitable for his own needs. Such freedom of action, however, did not include exemption from the inviolable oaths and assurances that he would never lie to his fellow members, reveal their secrets, or lend a hand to an enemy against them.

Following the caliph's death and Nizar's failure to succeed in 1094, Hasan established himself as an independent prince by severing relations with the Egyptian Fatimids and unleashing his Assassins in a campaign of terror against the Persians. This led to the Turks and Sunnis retaliating by wiping out Ismaili communities in the Levant and Persia. While the Assassins remained powerful within their own areas of influence, they were by 1110 no longer regarded as a serious military threat and remained that way until Hasan's death in 1124.

Though Hasan's two immediate successors did little to alter his policies, the fourth Grand master, Hasan II who ruled between 1162 and 1164, claimed to be the Mahdi and thus ended the Shia discipline of secrecy. He seceded from Islam to found a more liberal religion which only served to alienate the more entrenched Nizaris who rejoiced at his death at the hands of his brother-in-law, and welcomed a return to the more orthodox version of the faith. Though still remaining independent, the Persian Assassins were never again to become the power they once were and in time the arrival of the Mongol Hulago resulted in the massacre of all Persian Assassins.

In the meantime the Syrian branch of the Assassins which was ably led by Rashid ad-Din Sinan (c. 1132-1192) and had some time previously become independent of the Persian Grand Master's authority, began carrying out assassinations on a "contract" basis for either money or the equally useful political and religious considerations. Sinan's numerous intrigues with and against Saladin (c. 1137-1193) — A Sunni Muslim of Kurdish ethnicity who became the first sultan of Egypt and Syria — and the Knights Templar are legend and there was a period during which in order to avoid being caught between the two factions, he made an annual tribute payment to the Templars of two thousand gold pieces. Sinan became a Syrian hero who maintained independence from the surrounding powers by terrorising them.

Saladin (Salāh al-Dīn Yūsuf ibn Ayyūb), who at the height of his power ruled over Mesopotamia, Syria, Yemen, Egypt and Hejaz (a western region in present-day Saudi Arabia), also led the Muslims against European Crusaders and recaptured Palestine from the Crusader Kingdom of Jerusalem. Consequently an apprehensive Sinan decided to have Saladin killed but his Assassins met with failure on several occasions. According to legend Saladin stopped persecuting the Ismailis because he awoke one morning to find by his pillow a poisoned dagger that had been placed there by the Assassins as a warning. The more likely explanation, however, is that Saladin and Sinan had pooled their resources, at least temporarily, against the Crusaders. Sinan appears to have helped Saladin's cause by dispatching two Assassins to kill Conrad of Montferrat, Prince of Tyre and King of Jerusalem in 1192.

> *. . . two youths lightly clad, who wore*
> *No cloaks, and each a dagger bore,*
> *Made straight for him, and with one bound,*
> *Smote him and bore him to the ground,*
> *And each one stabbed him with his blade,*
> *The wretches, who thus wise betrayed*
> *Him, were of the Assassin's men . . .*
> *Twelfth-century Chronicle of Ambroise,*

The Crusades were "holy wars" specifically waged to seize property from the heretic and heathen enemies of orthodox Christianity and were usually fought by vassals of Christian overlords and well-heeled clergy. As well as the to be expected spoils of war, the crusaders were also rewarded with indulgences such as remission of sins and a guaranteed admission to heaven irrespective of how heinous a crime they may have committed.

The Ismaili sect did manage to survive and there are now an estimated fifteen million adherents worldwide whose leader, claiming direct descent from the Prophet Muhammed, is the Aga Khan. The most colourful of the Aga Khans was Sultan Mahommed Shah, Aga Khan III (1877-1957) who enjoyed the "sport of kings" including the ownership of thoroughbred racing horses who achieved a total of sixteen wins in British Classic Races. Another of his distractions was a succession of women with three of his four marriages being to European Christians all of whom did not convert to Islam. In defence of his fondness for alcohol, Sultan Mohammed Shah is credited with having justified his tippling by asserting "I'm so holy that when I touch wine, it turns to water."

Following his death, he was succeeded by his grandson Shah Karim al-Hussayni Aga Khan IV, who apart from also being a racehorse owner and breeder, is an international business magnate whom Forbes magazine described as one of the world's fifteen richest royals with an estimated net worth of $13 billion. His Highness Aga Khan IV apparently inherited his father's penchant for European ladies with both his marriages to date being to former British model Sarah ('Sally') Frances Croker-Poole (1969-1995 with a £20 million divorce settlement and the sale of jewellery worth £17.5 million), and a German-born princess Gabriele zu Leiningen (1998-2011) with a £50 million divorce settlement following a long-standing adulterous affair between His Highness and air hostess Beatrice von der Schulenburg. Even his father Prince Aly Khan, who was passed over for succession as Aga Khan, was a renowned playboy and man-about-town in his youth whose many affairs included high-profile lovers and a second marriage to American actress Rita Hayworth from 1949 to 1953.

When commentators discuss the Sunni-Shia dispute as an issue in international affairs, they invariably allude to the divide between Sunnis and Twelvers as being the one with the most current political significance. Other Shia groups, including the Agha Khan's Ismaili followers, tend to have minor roles in the politics of most Muslim countries. The Alawis of Syria (who are an offshoot of the Twelvers) and the Zaydis of Yemen (who are not) are only of political consequence in countries where they are located.

But even the Ismaili sect had its dissenters so that by the eleventh century the Druze religion emerged without attempting to reform mainstream Islam, but instead to create an entirely new faith that combined various Christian, Iranian, and Jewish elements influenced by Greek philosophy and Gnosticism including a form of reincarnation whereby the Druze reincarnated as future descendants. They regard themselves theologically as "an Islamic reformatory sect," calling themselves Ahl al-Tawhid ("People of Monotheism") or al-Muwahhidūn ("Monotheists"). The origin of the name Druze is traced to Muhammad bin Ismail Nashtakin ad-Darazi, one of the first preachers of the religion.

Before going public, the movement was secretive with closed meetings being held in what was known as Sessions of Wisdom. During this stage a dispute occurred between ad-Darazi and Hamza ibn Ali ibn Ahmad — considered as the founder of the Druze and the primary author of the Druze manuscripts — mainly concerning ad-Darazi's Ghulāt ("exaggeration"), which referred to the belief that God was incarnated in human beings (especially Ali and his descendants, including al-Ⱨākim bi-Amr Allāh, who was the caliph at the time) and to ad-Darazi naming himself "The Sword of the Faith," which led Hamza to write an epistle refuting the need for the sword to spread the faith and several epistles refuting the beliefs of the Ghulāt, or exaggerations.

The Druze reside mostly in Lebanon (30-40%), Israel (6-7%), Syria (40-50%), and to a lesser extent in Jordan (1-2%) where they are officially recognised as separate religious communities with their own religious court systems. Expatriate communities of Druze also live in Australia, Canada, Europe, Latin America, the US, and West Africa. They speak Arabic and regard themselves as Arab in every country they inhabit apart from Israel where they are granted a privileged status in exchange for their loyalty to the state which includes fighting for the Israeli Defence Force alongside Jews. Their willingness to fight for Israel has understandably strained relations with the Palestinian people.

The Druze symbol consists of five colours with each pertaining to a symbol defining its principles: green for ꜥAql "the Universal Mind"; red for Nafs (cognate of the Hebrew word Nefesh) "the Universal Soul"; yellow for Kalima "the Truth/Word"; blue for Sabq "the Antagonist/Cause"; and white for Talī "the Protagonist/Effect." The number five, representing those principles, has a special significance in the Druze community, and is usually represented by a five-pointed star.

The Druze are split into two groups with members of the inner spiritual elite group called al-ʿUqqāl "the Knowledge-able Initiates" having undergone secret initiations that gives them access to the secret teachings of the Druze religious doctrine, the hikmah, Women — being regarded as spiritually superior to men — are considered especially suitable to become ʿUqqāl and as such can opt to wear al-mandīl, a transparent loose white veil, especially in the presence of religious figures. The al-mandīl is worn on the head to cover the hair and wrap around the mouth and sometimes over the nose. Female ʿuqqāl wear black shirts and long skirts covering their legs to their ankles. Male ʿuqqāl sport moustaches, shave their heads, and wear dark clothing with white turbans.

Members of the outer group, called al-Juhhāl "the Ignorant," who are not allowed access to the secret Druze holy literature, comprise some ninety percent of the Druze and form the political and military leadership while mostly distancing themselves from religious matters.

Of all the Islamic schisms, however, the Sunni-Shia division has remained as the most serious with awareness of the situation in the West becoming increasingly apparent following the 1978 Islamic revolution in Iran when the Shia clergy — dismissed as irrelevant "black crows" by the soon-to-be-toppled Shah — began to be regarded as having relevance by political analysts including those in the CIA and MI6 whose understanding of them is best described as being scant.

Such lack of understanding has led commentators on

international affairs to assert that the Sunni-Shia divide is the root cause of all difficulties being faced by the Middle East, while failing to mention Israel's mischief-making contribution to the region's turmoil. This view of Islam is not restricted to Neo-conservatives or right-wing capitalists who pontificate about the struggle for the soul of Islam to justify their own preconceptions of the religion being inherently violent. Even former President Barack Obama believed that "ancient sectarian differences" were behind today's instability in the Arab world and that the Middle East was undergoing a generational transformation rooted in conflicts dating back millennia.

One of the main reasons for Sunni-Shia sectarianism becoming toxic is Saudi Arabian tolerance of anti-Shia hate speech because the government — especially after accumulating vast oil revenues from 1973 onwards — has been exporting its fragile Wahhabi ideology. The Saudis see themselves as the promoters of Muslim solidarity and a conservative rallying point against Arab nationalism, socialism, and democracy. This, however, is a contradiction because the founding ideology of Wahhabism demonises the Shia as idolaters.

Another reason was the 1979 Iranian Islamic revolution with the Ayatollah Khomeini endeavouring to persuade all Muslims including Sunnis and Shias to follow in his footsteps. The spread of Iranian revolutionary ideas, however, was regarded as a threat by the Saudis and all other western-aligned, conservative states with Muslim populations. Consequently the Saudis and the Iranians have since been trying to persuade Sunni and Shia communities to join their side in the struggle for regional power. In Pakistan for example, during the 1977-88 military regime of General Zia ul-Haq, Saudi influence was responsible for a strict form of Sunni Islam becoming the governing ideology of the state whose exclusion of the Shia led to sectarianism in Pakistani politics.

The third reason was the decline of Baathism — A toxic mix of secular Arab nationalism and Eastern Bloc-style socialism — which from the 1960s dominated Syria and Iraq for decades while making the regimes of the al-Assad family in Syria and Saddam Hussein in Iraq completely unique in the Arab world. Baathism, was even more instrumental than US presidents George W. Bush and Barack Obama in instigating the violent Hobbesian nightmare — unrestrained, selfish, and uncivilised competition between participants — that engulfed the lands from the Mediterranean Sea to the Iranian plateau including a series of military coups and political intrigues.

Though Baathism pledged to remove religion from politics entirely, the manner in which Baathist regimes used their power ended up having the opposite effect. In their attempts to establish power bases, military dictators relied on patronage with men like Saddam Hussein in Iraq (a member of the Sunni minority) and Hafez al-Assad in Syria (a member of the Shia Alawi minority) promoting family members; childhood friends from their own town or village; people from their own tribe and province; and invariably co-sectarians. Consequently Saddam Hussain's Republican Guard were recruited from Sunni tribes near his home town, and a disproportionate number of Hafez al Assad's secret policemen were Alawites — who revere Ali ibn Abi Talib, believed to be the first imam of the Twelver school — from the mountains where he grew up.

While The foreign policy of the US and its Western allies is premised in large part upon prejudices against people of different ethnicity, race, and religion, it is the Muslims in particular who are demonised the most by the Western Mainstream media. Westerners of Aryan or Caucasian decent are invariably portrayed as being good and honourable while Muslims are painted as evil terrorists. Such demonisation of certain ethnic or religious groups strongly suggests deeply racist thinking with strong undertones of social-Darwinism — the concept of "survival of the fittest" where some people are more powerful in society because of being innately better — which is typical of traditional European thinking that serves as justification for eugenics, imperialism, racism, and social inequality.

With that in mind, it should also in fairness be noted that some negative perceptions of Islam need to be positively addressed including the belief that men are superior to, and the masters of women.

Family law in Islamic countries generally follows the prescriptions of the Koran which include veiling (the hijab), divorce laws, a very young legal age for marriage, custody of children, and polygamy; an absence of basic rights for women in matters of employment, travelling, and choice of residence; and honour killings which are all aspects of Islamic Sharia based on the Koran and Islam's doctrine. Women can also be stoned to death for engaging in voluntary sexual relations while being stripped of their basic human rights.

One particular totally barbaric and unacceptable tradition that persists and is still tolerated is Female Genital Mutilation (FGM) which is a violent violation of the human rights of girls and women involving either the partial or total removal of the external female genitalia, or the causing of some other injury to the female genital organs for non-medical reasons.

FGM poses immediate risks to the health of its victims with severe pain and bleeding, difficulty in passing urine, infections, and even death due to hemorrhagic or neurogenic shock. Other effects include long-term scars, post-traumatic stress disorder, chronic pain, HIV infection, cysts, abscesses, genital ulcers, difficulty and pain while having sex, and an increased risk of complications affecting menstrual cycles that could result in infertility. The disturbing extent of this barbarity was made apparent in a UNICEF report showing that despite FGM being internationally recognised as a human rights violation, at least 200 million girls and women alive today have undergone ritual mutilation in 31 countries across three continents, with more than half of the victims living in Egypt, Ethiopia and Indonesia.

Senior Muslim religious authorities agree that FGM is neither required nor prohibited by Islam. While the Koran does not mention either FGM or male circumcision, FGM is nonetheless praised in a few Hadith (sayings attributed to Muhammad) as noble but not required. This is a religion whose laws written by men, encouraged men to regard women as being deficient in intelligence and no better than pieces of property.

> *Men are in charge of women by [right of] what Allah has given one over the other and what they spend [for maintenance] from their wealth. So righteous women are devoutly obedient, guarding in [the husband's] absence what Allah would have them guard. But those [wives] from whom you fear arrogance - [first] advise them; [then if they persist], forsake them in bed; and [finally], strike them. But if they obey you [once more], seek no means against them. Indeed, Allah is ever Exalted and Grand.*
> **Koran 4:34**

7

Colonialism's Three Cs: Christianity, Commerce, and Civilisation

When in 1095 the Byzantine Emperor Alexius I Comnenus (1057-1118) sent envoys to the West requesting military assistance against the Seljuk Turks, it was a timely event for the Holy Roman Empire which had itself been harassed for the past two centuries by Norsemen who possessed numerous northern trading centres and dominated the sea routes. Furthermore, negotiations with North African and Middle Eastern powers had culminated in 834 with an Arabian delegation visiting Denmark to complete military and trade alliances that left the Holy Roman Empire trapped between two anti-Christian forces.

The Byzantine Emperor's request for assistance therefore provided Pope Urban II at the Council of Claremont in 1095 with an excuse to initiate a crusade — as a penitential pilgrimage and a war of conquest — against the infidels with the alleged intent of regaining the Holy Land for Christianity. So with the promise that volunteers would be placed above restrictions of law, receive forgiveness for all their sins, and enjoyment of eternal bliss in heaven without time in purgatory, a ragtag force — consisting mostly of social outcasts and soldiers of fortune — of between 150,000 to 300,000 was assembled.

As the force crossed southern Europe they pillaged, tortured, and murdered with one division slaughtering 10,000 Jews in the Rhineland before abandoning thoughts of the Holy Land and disbanding. Two other divisions perpetrated so many atrocities in Hungary that native soldiers were eventually roused to oppose and wipe them all out. Of the others, thousands died en-route from starvation, disease, or wounds resulting from violence. Those who survived then despoiled the Greeks before making their way to Constantinople where the more powerful of them financed their own existence by selling off the decrepit amongst them as slaves. Of the 7,000 who eventually crossed the Bosphorus, none survived the merciless onslaughts by Turkish forces.

Despite the utter failure of this initial crusade, more were to follow which with hindsight were better organised with seasoned soldiers and fewer penitential pilgrims. For the next 400 hundred years Christian knights in the Holy Land waged wars whose barbarity in the name of god, knew no bounds. One contemporaneous report stated that after laying siege to Jerusalem for one month, the Crusaders rode into the city with their horses "knee-deep in the blood of disbelievers." Jews were herded into their synagogues and burnt alive, and on the following day Christian knights slaughtered "a great multitude of people of every age, old men and women, maidens, children and mothers with infants, by way of a solemn sacrifice" to Jesus.

Following the siege of Acre which ended in 1191, King Richard I of England, Richard the Lionheart (1157-1199) broke his promise of truce by having his Muslim hostages slaughtered:

> *His conduct stands in strong contrast with the dignity and forbearance of Saladin, before whose eyes the outrage was committed, and who would not stoop to retaliate on his dastardy.*

Establishment of the ongoing crusades also enabled the Holy Roman Empire to take punitive military measures against Europe's heathens and heretics so that the sword became the traditional method of Christianising the West at the cost of between 8 to 10 million lives. The Catharan or Albigensian heretics in the Languedoc region of Southern France — who regarded the Roman Church as the Synagogue of Satan and called for a return to the Christian message of perfection, poverty, and preaching — became the recipients of particularly barbaric treatment after Pope Innocent III declared a crusade in 1209 against the Languedoc with the promise that Cathar lands would be given to French noblemen willing to take up arms.

The Albigensian Crusade remains to this day one of the darkest and bloodiest chapters in the history of Christian persecutions. When it was enquired of a papal legate as to how heretics were to be distinguished from the faithful, he replied, "Kill them all; God will know his own." The ensuing slaughter lasted for twenty years with an estimate of more than a million lives being lost. In trying to justify the scale of such wanton carnage, the best that Christian apologists could come up with was, "The Church, after all, was only defending herself." Justifying ethnic cleansing and genocide by claiming it was carried out in self-defence is the kind of mendacious mitigation that Israel has been using for over seventy years.

> *The barbarities and desperate outrages of the so-called Christian race, throughout every region of the world, and upon every people they have been able to subdue, are not to be paralleled by those of any other race, however fierce, however untaught, and however reckless of mercy and of shame in any age of the earth.*
> **William Howitt, Colonisation and Christianity: A Popular History of the Treatment of the Natives by the Europeans in All Their Colonies, 1838**

Despite the carnage in Europe, it was the crusades to the Holy Land that received the most attention especially after the formation of the Knights Templar who became a force to be reckoned with. The seed for the founding of the Order of the Poor Knights of Christ and the Temple of Solomon was sown in 1118 when Hugues de Payen, a nobleman from Champagne, and eight comrades presented themselves at the palace of Jerusalem's King Baudouin I whose elder brother,

Godfroi de Bouillon, had captured the Holy City nineteen years earlier. Their stated objective was to protect the pilgrim routes to Jerusalem and other holy places.

Having from the beginning pledged themselves to poverty, obedience, and chastity, the Templars began to attract an extraordinary band of cavalrymen including excommunicated knights who had nothing to lose. It could be said that the Templar Order became the forerunner of the French Foreign Legion in that it used discipline and war to purge the sins of those within its ranks. Templar ranks were increased by "rogues and impious men, robbers and committers of sacrilege, murderers, perjurers, and adulterers" whose unkept demeanour and maverick methods the influential French abbot, Bernard of Clairvaux, praised highly in a letter to Hugues de Payen. Armed with Clairvaux's letter, de Payen attended the Council of Troyes in 1128 where he was granted papal sanction and exemption from excommunication for the Templars.

As religion in the Middle Ages was the beneficiary of much generosity by its followers, the Templars were themselves bequeathed many estates in England, France, and Spain by returning crusaders or Christians who believed that their own route to heaven was being guarded by those keeping watch over the road to Jerusalem. The "Order of the Poor Knights of Christ" consequently ended up with a great deal of wealth which led to them becoming a moneylending institution that attracted both envy and ill will.

As bankers to the Levant their clients included Muslims who feared that the changing fortunes of war might in the future require them to ally themselves with the Christians. Even the courts of Europe made use of the Templar banking operation which could not only provide loans, but also arrange — because of its widespread network — international money transfers. Though at that time usury was forbidden to Christians, the Templars would repay an agreed sum less than the original amount that was either banked or transferred. Debtors repaid a greater amount than that borrowed. As a result the Temple in Paris became the hub of the world's money-market.

The Templars, like most other religious sects, also had their own regulations (The Rule of the Temple) and secret initiation ceremonies which distinguished them from other orders such as the Knights Hospitallers and the Teutonic Knights. The Order was open only to men who were obliged to observe strict vows of celibacy with the prohibition that they could neither marry nor remain married. Wives of men who became Templars were expected to join other religious orders as nuns. Templars were prohibited from kissing their mothers, wives, sisters, or any other women. They were also cautioned to beware the wiles of women who were not even to be looked upon. During the entirety of its historical preoccupation with protecting its celibate clergymen from the wicked wiles of women, the Catholic Church has unfortunately not only neglected to protect innocent young children from the diabolic lust of its paedophile priests, it has also more often than not taken steps to cover up such religious criminality. It should be reiterated that the physical and sexual abuse of children by "holy men" is not peculiar to Christianity and exists within many other religions including Judaism and Islam but is not as widely reported.

The first three Templar Grand Masters were men of faith, capable, and well-organised diplomatic leaders whose banners proclaimed *Non nobis, Domin, non nobis, sed nomini tuo da gloriam* (Not to ourselves, Lord, not to ourselves, but to Thy name give the glory). Their successor Bernard de Tremelai, however, during the siege of Ascalon in 1153, ordered his knights to beat back their Christian allies so that the Templars would get all the credit for taking the town.

The ensuing succession of Templar Grand Masters were at best mediocre with the seventh of them, Philip de Milly, becoming involved in the political intrigues and quarrels that disunited Jerusalem. His successor, Odo de Saint-Amand (1170-1179) proved to be even worse — in believing that Templar independence meant being bound by no treaty — and accordingly breaking the King of Jerusalem's treaty with Saladin by which no further Templar fortresses were to be built on the frontier. His arrogance was rewarded when the fortress he built fell to Saladin with the Templar garrison being massacred and Odo himself later dying in prison in 1180 after refusing to be ransomed with the declaration "A Templar can only offer as ransom his belt and his sword."

When Odo's nondescript aged successor died in 1184, he was succeeded by the young and ambitious Gerard de Ridfort who was destined to play a major role in Jerusalem's destruction. During the succession squabble following the death of boy-king Baldwin V (1186), Ridefort backed the unpopular Guy de Lusignan and had him crowned king instead of the regent, Raymond III of Tripoli who had Hospitaller support. The inevitable divisions amongst the crusaders were then ruthlessly exploited by Saladin whose peace treaty with the Crusaders had been broken by the treacherous Prince of Antioch, Reynald de Chatillon. Saladin's response was to join forces with Raymond in 1187 and during their march to Jerusalem they encountered Ridefort and 150 of his knights outside of Nazareth. The Templars had no chance against Saladin's force of 7,000 and were all massacred apart from Ridefort who managed to escape with three of his men.

On realising that the Crusader kingdom was on the verge of obliteration, Raymond severed his alliance with Saladin and joined the Christian forces led by Guy de Lusignan whose equipping of an army to fight Saladin was financed by the Templars. Ridefort then persuaded the indecisive Guy de Lusignan to go on the offensive against Saladin rather than adopt Raymond's preference for a campaign of delaying tactics. By taking the offensive, the Crusaders were obliged to leave behind their water supplies and then advance across a searingly hot and inhospitable desert to eventually come to a halt on the scorched double hill that formed the Horns of Hattin.

Saladin who had just captured the nearby town of Tiberias (now in present-day Israel), had the Crusaders surrounded and forced up the hill slopes. Being crazed with
thirst, the Crusaders made repeated unsuccessful attempts
to reach the freshwater lake of Tiberias (Sea of Galilee).
Though Raymond and his knights managed to break through
the Muslim encirclement, the remaining Crusaders were less
fortunate with the result that most of them were slaughtered.
The surviving Templars and Hospitallers, who had fought
valiantly in a desperate situation, were not spared by Saladin
who had them — apart from Ridefort — all beheaded. Ridefort, who as a free man was vocally courageous and physically aggressive, turned out to be a cowering yellow-belly in
captivity who ordered the garrisons of the remaining Templar fortresses to surrender to Saladin. The fall of Jerusalem
followed months later in October 1187.

Ridefort's brief rule as Templar Grand Master was a calamity from which the Templars never recovered. So despite
subsequently regaining some of their former wealth and
power even in the Levant, the Templars had forever lost their
renown for religious zealotry and instead — to best serve
their own interests — sheathed their swords along with compromises that accommodated Muslim rule and custom. The
fact that they — unlike other Christian orders — also spoke
Arabic and wore long beards in the Muslim fashion, provided ammunition for their detractors who had never forgotten
that the first Templar home had been situated in a mosque

built on the alleged site of Solomon's Temple in Jerusalem.

After a series of subsequent ineffective crusades and set-backs, the Templars hoped to regain some of their lost stature in the Seventh Crusade (1248-1254) led by King Louis IX of France who despite Templar advice to the contrary, advanced into Egypt and suffered defeat at the battle of Mansura in 1250. From that point on Templar fortunes declined rapidly while back in France King Louis IX's concern for what was left of the Crusader states — because as a result of the Templars being squeezed between the Egyptians and the Mongols, they had gradually lost most of their strongholds — prompted his launching of the Eighth Crusade (1270) which like the Ninth Crusade (1271-1272) was limited in scope and short on achievement. In 1291 Tripoli fell and was quickly followed by the fall of Acre which signalled the end of any further Crusades to regain the Holy Land from the Muslims.

The Three Cs

One adverse consequence of the Crusades was that Christianity — primarily Catholicism and Protestantism — became the instrument that European powers used to initially discover new trade routes and to subsequently colonise parts of the "Old World" and much of the "New." Colonialism's Three Cs of Christianity, Commerce, and Civilisation actually involved Christianising and civilising the indigenous "savages" while exploiting them as slaves and stealing their natural resources.

During the heyday of colonisation, cruel Portuguese exploitation in present-day African countries such as Guinea-Bissau, Angola, and Mozambique never came close to being as barbaric as Belgium's rape of the Congo where it was estimated that Belgium's King Leopold was responsible for the enslavement and massacre of well over half of the total population of some 30 million Congolese through starvation, disease and overwork. Because those victims were "inferior" black Africans, they were subsequently deemed undeserving of the "holocaust" memorials, museums, and annual remembrance days — accompanied by the hypocritical Western media fanfare — that they would have otherwise received had they been white, sanctified, and superior European Christians, or even more superior Jews deserving of the divine preference that led to them being "chosen" by god himself who apparently in his impartial and infinite wisdom promised them a Palestine cleansed of indigenous Palestinians.

The German historian Jürgen Osterhammel — in his 1997 book *Colonialism: A Theoretical Overview* — noted that by "rejecting cultural compromises with the colonised population, the colonisers are convinced of their own superiority and their ordained mandate to rule." The abhorrent perception of superiority by Europeans who regarded dark-skinned people as inferior, backward, and uncivilised, initially stemmed from the eighteenth century self-absolving need to justify slavery and subsequently served as the rationale for the colonial oppression of the sub-human species which Cecil Rhodes — British businessman, Freemason, diamond mining magnate, and politician who seized control of what are now Zimbabwe and South Africa — described as "the most despicable specimens of human beings."

Following the Slavery Abolition Act which took effect on August 1 in 1834 and ended slavery in most British colonies — by freeing more than 800,000 enslaved Africans in the Caribbean, South Africa, and a smaller number in Canada — the British government paid some £20 million (equivalent to about £300 million today) in compensation. It was not, however, to the victims of slavery or their descendants who were compensated, but the slave owners who included some of Britain's wealthiest businessmen. Such payments continued for 182 years and did not end until 2015 so that British tax-paying descendants of slaves have been conceivably contributing towards the compensation paid to those responsible for the enslavement of their forefathers.

The first intrepid European explorer was Bartolomeu Dias, a nobleman of the Portuguese royal household, who in 1488 sailed around the southernmost tip of Africa to discover the eastern sea route to the Indian Ocean. Dias was the first European during the Age of Discovery to anchor at what is present-day South Africa while setting up the route from Europe to Asia.

It was Christopher Columbus who in October 1492 — while endeavouring to discover a direct westward route from

Europe to Asia — instead landed on what was probably Watling Island in the Bahamas which he claimed for Spain. Later that month, he sighted Cuba which he thought was mainland China, and in December he landed on Hispaniola which he thought might be Japan.

Rather than being revered, Columbus deserves to be remembered with repugnance for presiding over unspeakable atrocities against native peoples including the kidnap and rape of native women; forcing Indians to either collect gold for him or die; beheading of Indian slaves; causing some 50,000 Indians to commit mass suicide rather than comply with Spanish rule; the fact that 56 years after Columbus's first voyage, only 500 out of 300,000 Indians remained on the island of Hispaniola; and the selling of nine to ten-year-old girls into sexual slavery by settlers about which he boasted.

Sexual abuse and brutal depravity by Columbus stemmed from the odious belief that native "others" were inherently of less "value" and consequently justifiably deserving of sexual debasement. In the course of his four separate journeys starting in 1942, Columbus landed on a number of islands in the Caribbean including those now known as the Bahamas where he sexually abused and enslaved girls as young as nine years of age, a fact of which he made note.

A hundred castellanoes [Spanish coins] are as easily obtained for a woman as for a farm, and it is very general and there are plenty of dealers who go about looking for girls; those from nine to ten are now in demand.

Claims about Columbus were exaggerated fables woven over time to create an impressive legendary character. To begin with the assertion that he disproved the "flat Earth" theory is without foundation because as early as the sixth century BCE, Pythagoras — and subsequently Aristotle and Euclid — wrote about the Earth being a sphere with there also being no doubt that educated Europeans during the time of Columbus were fully aware that the Earth was round.

The notion that Columbus discovered the Americas is equally fallacious because they were already inhabited by Native American descendants of the nomadic tribes who sometime around 22,000 BCE were able — due to low sea levels — to travel between Siberia and Alaska, to gradually settle in the Americas, and to become the Native Americans who eventually numbered in the tens of millions.

Furthermore, some 500 years earlier, a band of Vikings — seafaring Scandinavians who explored, raided, and traded in areas beyond Scandinavia from the eighth to eleventh centuries — set out in search of a new world. Led by Leif Ericsson, they crossed the Atlantic and encountered a rocky, barren land which researchers believe was probably Baffin Island, now part of present-day Canada. The Norsemen then sailed south to Labrador, before eventually establishing a base camp located on the northern tip of Newfoundland.

Archaeologists have since unearthed evidence of expeditions to America by the Vikings and in 1960, Norwegian explorer Helge Ingstad searched the coasts of Labrador and

Newfoundland and discovered signs of settlement on the northernmost tip of Newfoundland at L'Anse aux Meadows. An international team of archaeologists including Ingstad's wife, Anne, excavated artefacts of Viking origin dating from around 1,000 BCE, and the remains of the village are now part of a UNESCO World Heritage site.

Columbus's transatlantic voyages did, however, open the way for European colonisation and exploitation of land and resources in the Americas and trade was soon established between the continents. Such trade would in due course also pave the way for the inhumane slave trade. With the gradual increase of Europeans settlers arriving in North America, the frontier — the territory between the white man's so-called civilisation and the untamed wilderness — became an area that witnessed a clash of vastly different Native American and European cultures with the latter's sentiments being frequently expressed with explicit genocidal intent towards the indigenous Native Americans.

> *A war of extermination will continue to be waged between the two races until the Indian race becomes extinct.*
> **Peter H. Burnett, Governor of California (December 1849 to January 1851)**

Such sentiments became instrumental in the US government authorising over 1,500 attacks, raids, and wars against the Native Americans, the most ever carried out by any colonial power against an indigenous population. When the

146

Indian Wars finally ended in the late nineteenth century, no more than 238,000 indigenous people remained: a dramatic decline from the estimated tens of millions who inhabited North America when Columbus first reached the Americas in 1492.

> *They have neither the intelligence, the industry, the moral habits, nor the desire of improvement which are essential to any favourable change in their condition. Established in the midst of another and a superior race, and without appreciating the causes of their inferiority or seeking to control them, they must necessarily yield to the force of circumstances and ere long disappear.*
> **President Andrew Jackson, an infamous slave owner, in his fifth annual message on December 3, 1833**

The killing of some 100 million Native Americans was documented by author D. E. Stannard who in his *American Holocaust*, stated *"the destruction of the Indians of the Americas was, far and away, the most massive act of genocide in the history of the world."*

In the meantime, as all this "extermination" of the Indian race was ongoing, the first African slaves had already arrived in Jamestown, Virginia in 1619, in what was to be the start of a blatant exploitation of African people as slave labourers to help build the new nation into an economic powerhouse through the production of lucrative crops such as cotton and tobacco. But by the mid-nineteenth century, America's westward expansion and the abolition movement provoked a great debate over slavery that tore the nation apart in a bloody Civil War. Though the Union victory theoretically freed the nation's four million slaves, the legacy of slavery continued to influence the racist and unjust nature of white American society which more recently a deranged and barely literate Donald Trump fully exploited to become President. Novelist James Baldwin, had the following to say about white Americans in his essay *My Dungeon Shook*:

> *They have had to believe for so many years, and for innumerable reasons, that black men are inferior to white men. Many of them, indeed, know better, but, as you will discover, people find it very difficult to act on what they know. To act is to be committed, and to be committed is to be in danger. In this case, the danger, in the minds of most white Americans, is the loss of identity.*

Amongst some of those most responsible for brutally exercising white man "superiority" so as to preserve their precious "identity," was British General Jeffery Amherst whose numerous "achievements" included advocating the extermination of the race of Indigenous people during the Pontiac's War — also known as Pontiac's Rebellion by a loose confederation of dissatisfied Native American tribes primarily from the Great Lakes region — by means of biological warfare that involved giving them handkerchiefs and blankets infected with smallpox.

Amherst was renowned for being the architect of Britain's successful campaign to conquer the territory of New France during the Seven Years War. He commanded the British forces responsible for capturing the cities of Louisbourg, Quebec City, Montreal, and several major fortresses. As a result of being the first British Governor General in the territories that eventually became Canada, Amherst had numerous places and streets named for him in both Canada and the US.

Amherst was by no means alone in favouring Canada with the Christian concept of civilised white justice and his achievements for the new nation were surpassed by another who was given a knighthood for his infamy. Sir John A. Macdonald, Canada's first prime minister, deliberately starved thousands of Indigenous people to clear a path for the Canadian Pacific Railroad (CPR) which helped open up the prairies for European settlement. Macdonald's "National Dream" caused Canada's First Nations — Indigenous peoples — to lose their health, their independence, and in many cases even their lives.

Indigenous peoples were also afflicted by both nature and contagious diseases beginning with the European fur traders who infected them with smallpox, measles, and influenza to which they had no immunity. Then came the building of the CPR, and the near-extinction of the bison — on which they were dependent for food — leading to malnutrition. In desperation, they sought assistance from Ottawa, in the expectation that Macdonald would honour the treaties he had signed with them — in anticipation of thriving agrarian economy in the western plains — guaranteeing food and a livelihood in times of famine.

Needless to say Macdonald refused their request and ordered officials at the Department of Indian Affairs in Prince Albert to withhold food from them until they moved to federally designated reserves far from the path of the CPR. By complying with this condition, they became trapped within reservations and could leave only with the permission of the government's Indian agent. Without the necessary freedom of movement, Aboriginal men could not hunt for food, and without arable land could not resort to farming. When they complained, they had their already meagre food rations cut, and even if they were compliant, the food was invariably substandard with one contaminated shipment causing a mass outbreak of tuberculosis. And if you think that humanity has progressed for the better since those days, then you should take an unbiased look at what the Israelis are doing to the Palestinian people.

The starving of Canada's Indigenous peoples was not accidental, but a deliberate policy — to solve the "Indian problem" — with Macdonald having sent directives to federal officials ordering them to deny food to the First Nations. He even unashamedly bragged about his despicable inhumanity which kept the indigenous population "on the verge of actual starvation" so as to save the government money. Solving of the "Indian problem" involved scalping bounties being paid for each Mi'kmaw man, woman and child killed; providing smallpox blankets to Indigenous peoples to spread lethal diseases; deliberately infecting Indigenous children with infectious diseases in residential schools; resorting to acts of solitary confinement, electric chair punishment, rape, sodomy, torture, and assaults on Indigenous children in residential schools with some never being seen alive again; and the stealing of thousands of Indigenous children for adoption by "civilised" European Christian families.

In the meantime, apart from being starved, aboriginal women were also being indiscriminately raped and brutally murdered thereby creating a racist, depraved, and violent colonial past that has endured to this very day with a culture where no Indigenous woman or girl is safe. A report released in 2019 — Reclaiming Power and Place: The Final Report of the National Inquiry into Missing and Murdered Indigenous Women and Girls — confronted Canada's dark history of crimes against humanity.

Even today, sexual predators are still able to commit horrendous crimes against Indigenous girls and women with relative impunity because the country's civilised society chooses to look the other way. It is a civilised society where predators can physically assault little Indigenous girls, drive them to remote locations, and rape them before leaving them without their clothes to fend for themselves. A disproportionate number of Indigenous women and girls continue to be brutalised, raped, murdered, and go missing without their families getting the "satisfaction" of justice or closure.

The existence of that culture evolved from the methodical and strategic racist policy of sexually objectifying the bodies, minds, and spirits of Indigenous women as a means of deliberately brutalising and oppressing them. That colonial policy is still in existence globally where even today, imperialism still seeks subjugation of an occupied territory's population through the dislocation, isolation, rape, and murder of women and girls. Part of that inhumanity is evident in Canada where even though Indigenous people account for only four percent of the total population, 43 percent of women federally sentenced to prison, were Indigenous. Furthermore over 25 percent of all inmates in the Canada's federal prisons are indigenous.

> *In Canada, human rights are protected by federal, provincial and territorial laws. Canada's human rights laws stem from the Universal Declaration of Human Rights. In 1948, John Humphrey, a Canadian lawyer and scholar, played a significant role in writing the Declaration. When it was complete, the Declaration provided a list of 30 articles outlining everyone's universal human rights. The first two articles are about equality and freedom from discrimination, the foundation of the Canadian Human Rights Act.*
> **Canadian Human Rights Commission**

Also in 2019, the National Centre for Truth and Reconciliation, in partnership with Aboriginal People's Television

Network, unveiled a national memorial register with 2,800 names inscribed on a red scroll. The names belonged to some of the Indigenous children who died in Canada's residential Schools where for more than a century attempts were made to assimilate thousands of native children who were physically and sexually abused by priests and nuns. Despite an acknowledgement of, and an apology for such crimes by Canada's Prime Minister in 2008, his government continued to deny that it was a form of genocide. Even His Holiness the Pope remained silent instead of having at least the common, if not hypocritical Christian decency to apologise for the abuse inflicted on those Indigenous children by Catholic priests and nuns at as many as 80 forced-conversion gulags, euphemistically referred to as "residential schools."

Meanwhile, European global expansionism between the 1760s and 1870s differed from that of previous centuries due to industrialisation which required new markets for the machine-produced merchandise. Consequently the leading colonial powers, led by England, consolidated their hegemonic positions by either creating overseas empires, or conquering territories in the form of a continental colonialism where they could sell their goods.

A prime example of such exploitation occurred in India where most notoriously under British rule from 1765 to 1947, more than 60 million people died during a series of twelve major famines starting with the Great Bengal Famine (1769-70) and ending with the Bengal famine of 1943. Even today fifteen percent of the Indian population goes to sleep hungry every night with some 194 million Indians being undernourished.

Apart from the famines, recent research has revealed that the UK stole $45 trillion from India which is more than 17 times the total of the UK's current annual gross domestic product (GDP). During the precolonial period, Britain used to buy goods such as textiles and rice from Indian producers by paying for them mostly in the normal way with silver. Then in 1765, after the East India Company took control of the subcontinent and monopolised Indian trade and began collecting taxes about a third of which it used to fund the purchase of Indian goods for use in Britain. In other words, instead of paying for Indian goods out of their own pocket, British traders acquired them for free by "buying" from peasants and weavers using money that had just been collected from them.

While some of the "acquired " commodities were used for British consumption, the remainder were re-exported to other countries, thereby enabling Britain — which pocketed not only 100 percent of the original value of the "acquired" goods, but also the markup — to finance the import from Europe of materials including the iron, tar, and timber that were essential for industrialisation. It could be claimed with justification that Britain's Industrial Revolution was financed to a large extent by the systematic theft of goods from India.

After the British Raj took over in 1858, colonisers added

a special new twist to the tax-and-buy system. As the East India Company's monopoly broke down, Indian producers were allowed to export their goods directly to other countries. But Britain made sure that the payments for those goods nonetheless ended up in London. This was made possible because anyone wanting to buy goods from India would do so using special Council Bills, a unique paper currency issued only by the British Crown. And the only way to get those bills was to buy them from London with gold or silver. So traders would pay London in gold to get the bills, and then use the bills to pay Indian producers. When Indians cashed the bills in at the local colonial office, they were "paid" in rupees out of tax revenues that had been collected from them. So, once again, they were not in fact paid at all, but defrauded. Meanwhile, London ended up with all of the gold and silver that should have gone directly to the Indians in exchange for the goods they exported.

Further British "contributions" to the colonies included the transportation of convicts to the American colonies with such transportation ending when the American Revolution started. In 1770, James Cook charted and claimed possession of the East coast of Australia for Britain as part of its policy of pre-empting the French colonial empire from expanding into the region. Australia was subsequently chosen as a site for penal colonies, and in 1787, the First Fleet of eleven convict ships set sail and arrived at Botany Bay on January 20, 1788, to establish the first European settlement on the continent. Other penal colonies were later established in Van Dieman's Land (Tasmania) in 1803, and Queensland in 1824. The last convict ship, the Hougoumont, left Britain in 1867 and arrived in Western Australia on 10 January 1868. In all, about 164,000 convicts — about 80% men, 20% women — were transported to the Australian colonies between 1788 and 1868 on board 806 ships.

Following their eventual emancipation, most ex-convicts remained in Australia and joined the free settlers, with some even rising to prominent positions in Australian society. Convictism, however, carried a social stigma, and for some later Australians, being of convict descent engendered a sense of shame. But attitudes change and now for many Australians having a convict in one's lineage is a cause for celebration. Regrettably not all attitudes have changed and the racist sentiments of old are still evident in Australian society today.

During Darwin's 1836 stay in Australia, the Indigenous people — including those of Tasmania, and New Zealand — were subject to a calamitous population crash from which the region has never recovered. In Tasmania the British enslaved, slaughtered, and kidnapped the Black people with black men being used for target practice, black women being used as sex slaves, and black babies being roasted.

"Wherever the European has trod, death seems to pursue the aboriginal. We may look to the wide extent of the Americas, Polynesia, the Cape of Good

Hope, and Australia, and we find the same result..."
Charles Darwin (1809–1882), English naturalist, Geologist, and biologist

For native Tasmanians in particular there was no recovery because they were all dead. A combination of disease, starvation, war, and deliberate policies of kidnapping and "reeducating" aboriginal children ensured the decimation of Australia's indigenous population which declined from well over a million in 1788 to just a few thousand by the early twentieth century. The abhorrent European colonial sense of racial superiority without concern or responsibility for the colonised, was expressed in the first verse of Rudyard Kipling's paean to imperialism, *The White Man's Burden*:

TAKE up the White Man's burden —
Send forth the best ye breed —
Go bind your sons to exile
To serve your captives' need;
To wait in heavy harness
On fluttered folk and wild —
Your new-caught sullen peoples,
Half devil and half child.

8

The Persecution of God's Chosen People

In other words, neither oppression nor exploitation as such is ever the main cause for resentment; wealth without visible function is much more intolerable because nobody can understand why it should be tolerated. Antisemitism reached its climax when Jews had similarly lost their public functions and their influence, and were left with nothing but their wealth.

Hannah Arendt (1906-1975), The Jewish German-born American political theorist, The Origins of Totalitarianism, 1968

The politician and lawyer Cicero (106-43 BCE), once reminded a jury of "the odium of Jewish gold" and how they "stick together" and are "influential in informal assemblies." The Roman historian Tacitus (c. 56-120 AD) was contemptuous of "base and abominable" Jewish customs and was deeply disappointed by those of his compatriots who renounced their ancestral gods and converted to Judaism. The Roman poet and satirist Juvenal (c. 55-130) was equally disgusted at the behaviour of converts to Judaism and denounced Jews generally as drunken and rowdy. While such examples may imply the existence of anti-Semitism in antiquity, there is no real evidence to suggest that Jews were the objects of a specific prejudice beyond the generalised contempt felt by Greeks and Romans towards "barbarians" including peoples conquered and colonised.

A much heightened scapegoating of Jews occurred when the great plagues of the fourteenth century were ridiculously blamed on Jews who allegedly caused the contamination of water sources with a mixture of Holy Communion wafers stolen from Christian churches and the menstrual blood of Jewish women. In 1382 the Jewish quarter in Paris was subject to looting and vandalism by raucous rioters. A "Holy War against Jews" fomented by the Archdeacon of Seville in 1391 witnessed the storming of the ghetto, the destruction of synagogues, and the brutal murder of an estimated 41,000 innocent people. During the Black Death, a pandemic that ravaged Europe (1347-1351), 12,000 Jews perished in Bavaria; two thousand were burned in Strasbourg; and 160 were burned in a trench at Chinon in central France.

Such unjust persecution of Jews was encouraged by the Christian Church to divert attention from the emerging idea that a malevolent god was responsible for the plagues which by the end of the century had wiped out almost half of Europe's population. The possible cause of the plague bacillus was at the time believed to have originated on trade ships from China — which is now according to Donald Trump also responsible for the coronavirus pandemic — and then carried on Crusader ships from the Holy Land that supposedly transported millions of Oriental black rats. Rather than attempt to eradicate the problem, resentful Christian authorities — in their panic, fear, and dereliction of duty — chose instead to resort to the extermination of Jews. Such atrocities were then justified by customised myths that portrayed Jews unfavourably: a tactic which incidentally Israel employs to dehumanise Palestinians.

During the Dark and Middle Ages — when the Bible was viewed as being the principal source of knowledge and ultimate arbiter in matters of importance — the Christian Church's stubborn opposition to usury was consequently based on biblical and moral rather than sound commercial considerations. Such opposition was also repeatedly reinforced with legal restrictions to the extent that at the 325 Council of Nicaea — convoked by the Roman Emperor Constantine I — the practice was banned amongst clerics. During Charlemagne's time as Emperor (800–814) the Church extended the ban to include laymen with the assertion "usury was a transaction wherein more was required in return than was given." Centuries later, the 1311 Council of Vienne in Southern France — whose principal function was to withdraw papal support for the Knights Templar on the instigation of Philip IV of France who was in debt to the Templars — declared that persons daring to claim that there was no sin in the practice of usury would be punished as a heretics.

Subsequently in 1139 Pope Innocent II summoned the Second Lateran Council at which usury was denounced as a form of theft requiring restitution from those who practiced it so that during the next two centuries, schemes to conceal usury were strongly condemned. Despite all such pronouncements, however, there was a loophole provided by the Bible's double standard on usury which conveniently permitted Jews to lend money to non-Jews.

> *Thou shalt not lend upon interest to thy brother: interest of money, interest of victuals, interest of any thing that is lent upon interest. Unto a foreigner thou mayest lend upon interest; but unto thy brother thou shalt not lend upon interest; that the LORD thy God may bless thee in all that thou puttest thy hand unto, in the land whither thou goest in to possess it.*
> **Deuteronomy 23:20-21**

Consequently, for long periods during the Dark and Middle Ages, both the Church and civil authorities permitted Jews to practice usury. Many royals, who required substantial loans to finance their lifestyles and the waging of wars, tolerated Jewish usurers in their domains so that European Jews — who had been barred from most professions and ownership of land — found moneylending to be a profitable, though at times, a hazardous profession. Money lending therefore came to be regarded as an inherent Jewish vocation.

So while Jews were legally permitted to lend money to

Christians in need, the Christians themselves resented the idea of Jews making money from their misfortunes by means of an activity biblically prohibited with the threat of eternal damnation to Christians who understandably came to view Jewish usurers with a contempt that gradually nurtured the roots of anti-Semitism. Such contempt and opposition to Jewish usury was frequently violent with Jews being massacred in attacks instigated by members of the nobility who being in debt to Jewish usurers, cancelled their debts through violent attacks on Jewish communities with accounting records being destroyed.

Yet it was from a Jewish ghetto in Frankfurt known as the Judengasse that a humble, poor family of street traders rose to become the richest family in history who as the most successful facilitators of modern capitalism, wielded immense political power and — not always for the benefit of humanity — negatively influenced the lives of innumerable millions. That family was the Rothschilds and any criticism or discussion of their alleged intrigues and irrefutable wealth has more recently been labelled as anti-Semitism by some commentators.

In 1744 in Frankfurt, Mayer Amschel Bauer came into the world and lived above the family shop with up to 30 relatives in severely cramped conditions. His father was Moses Amschel Bauer, an Ashkenazi Jewish moneylender and proprietor of an accounting house. Ashkenazi Jews were descended from the medieval Jewish communities along the

River Rhine from Alsace in the South to the Rhineland in the North. Ashkenaz was the medieval Hebrew name for that German region and consequently Ashkenazim or Ashkenazi Jews were literally "German Jews" and definitely not in any way of Semitic origin.

Many of these Jews migrated, mostly eastwards, to establish communities in Eastern Europe including Belarus, Hungary, Lithuania, Poland, Russia, Ukraine and elsewhere between the 11th and 19th centuries. They took with them and diversified a Yiddish influenced Germanic language written in Hebrew letters which in medieval times had become the lingua franca among Ashkenazi Jews. Although in the 11th century, Ashkenazi Jews comprised only three percent of the world's Jewish population, that proportion had peaked to 92 percent by 1931 and now accounts for about 80 percent of Jews worldwide.

Apart from being unjustly treated, Jewish moneylenders were also made scapegoats for most economic problems for many centuries; were derided by philosophers and condemned to hell by religious authorities; were subject to property confiscation to compensate their "victims"; were framed, humiliated, jailed, and massacred; and were vilified by economists, legislators, journalists, novelists, playwrights, philosophers, theologians, and even the masses. Throughout history major thinkers such as Thomas Aquinas, Aristotle, Karl Marx, J. M. Keynes, Plato, and Adam Smith have invariably regarded moneylending as a major vice. Dante, Dickens, Dostoyevsky, and Shakespeare's "Shylock" character in *The Merchant of Venice*, were but a few of the popular playwrights and novelists who depicted Jewish moneylenders unfavourably.

Moses Amschel Bauer, however, lived at a time and in a place where he enjoyed a degree of tolerance and respect for his business which at its entrance boasted a red, six pointed star that geometrically and numerically represented the number 666 ⬡ six points, six triangles, and a six-sided hexagon. This seemingly innocuous sign, however, was destined to subsequently play an important role in the birth of both Zionist ideology and the state of Israel.

During the 1760s when Amschel Bauer worked for an Oppenheimer-owned bank in Hanover, his proficiency led to his becoming a junior partner and social acquaintance of General von Estorff. On returning to Frankfurt to take over his dead father's business, Amschel Bauer recognised the potential significance of the red sign and accordingly changed his surname from Bauer to Rothschild because "Rot" and "Schild" were German for "Red" and "Sign." The six pointed star, with cunning and determined Rothschild family manipulation, was to eventually end up on the Israeli flag some two centuries later.

On subsequently hearing that his former acquaintance General von Estorff had been attached to the court of Prince William of Hanau, Rothschild with cunning intent renewed their friendship — on the pretext of selling Estorff valuable coins and trinkets at discounted prices — with the confident knowledge that it would lead to an introduction to Prince William himself who was delighted by the prospect of buying such rare items at a discount. By also offering a commission for any other business that the Prince might put his way, Rothschild became a close associate of the Prince and ended up also doing business with other royal court members on whom he invariably lavished nauseating praise to ingratiate himself as he had done with Prince William:

It has been my particular high and good fortune to serve your lofty princely Serenity at various times and to your most gracious satisfaction. I stand ready to exert all my energies and my entire fortune to serve your lofty princely serenity whenever in future it shall please you to command me. An especially powerful incentive to this end would be given me if your lofty princely serenity were to distinguish me with an appointment as one of your Highness' Court Factors. I am making bold to beg for this with the more confidence in the assurance that by so doing I am not giving any trouble; while for my part such a distinction would lift up my commercial standing and be of help to me in many other ways that I feel certain thereby to make my own way and fortune here in the city of Frankfurt.

Rothschild was eventually in 1769 engaged by Prince William to oversee his properties and tax collection with the permission to hang up a business sign that boasted "M. A.

Rothschild, by appointment court factor to His Serene Highness, Prince William of Hanau."

Over two decades later in 1791 in America, Alexander Hamilton — first Secretary of the Treasury, influential member of George Washington's cabinet, and an adroit Rothschild agent — facilitated the setting up of a Rothschild central bank with a twenty-year charter called the Bank of the United States. Hamilton was to be the first of a long line of US politicians who to this day still betray their own country by selling out for a fistful of dollars to serve Jewish interests.

Meanwhile in Europe, Napoleon Bonaparte — French Emperor from 1804 to 1814 — declared his intention in 1806 of removing "the house of Hess-Kassel from rulership and to strike it out of the list of powers." This forced Prince William to flee Germany for Denmark while entrusting an estimated fortune of some $3,000,000 to Rothschild for safekeeping. That same year Mayer Amschel Rothschild's son Nathan Mayer Rothschild married Hannah Barent Cohen, the daughter of a wealthy London merchant and started moving his business interests to London.

When First Baronet Sir Francis Baring and Abraham Goldsmid died in 1810, Nathan Mayer Rothschild by default became the leading banker in England while his brother Salomon Mayer Rothschild departed for Austria to set up the M. von Rothschild und Söhne bank in Vienna.

Back in the US the charter for the Rothschild's Bank of the United States ran out in 1811 and Congress voted against renewal with Andrew Jackson — subsequently to become the 7th US President (1829–1837) — stating "if Congress has a right under the Constitution to issue paper money, it was given them to use by themselves, not to be delegated to individuals or corporations." This led to a displeased Nathan Mayer Rothschild replying "either the application for renewal of the charter is granted, or the United States will find itself involved in a most disastrous war." Jackson countered with "you are a den of thieves, vipers, and I intend to rout you out, and by the Eternal God, I will rout you out." Rothschild's reaction was a promise to "teach those impudent Americans a lesson. Bring them back to colonial status."

When the US declared war on Britain in 1812 — because Britain refused to stop seizing American ships that traded with France — unsurprisingly Britain was backed by Rothschild money with a view to causing a US accumulation of war debt that would force it to surrender and thereby facilitate renewal of the charter for a Rothschild-owned US Bank. That same year Mayer Amschel Rothschild died and his will set out specific instructions for the House of Rothschild to follow including the fact that all key positions in the family business were to be held only by family members; that only male members of the family were allowed to participate in the family business so that the spread of the Rothschild Zionist dynasty without the Rothschild name also became global; that the family was to intermarry with it's first and second cousins so as to preserve the family fortune; that no public inventory of Mayer's estate was to be published; that no legal action was to be taken with regard to the value of the inheritance; and that the eldest son of the eldest son was to become the head of the family, a stipulation that could only be overturned when the majority of the family agreed otherwise. This came into effect immediately and Nathan Mayer Rothschild — one of Mayer's five sons and five daughters — became head of the family while Jacob (James) Mayer Rothschild left for France to set up the de Rothschild Frères bank in Paris.

As to the fate of the $3,000,000 that Prince William of Hanau had given to Mayer Amschel Rothschild for safekeeping, the 1905 edition of the Jewish Encyclopaedia stated the following in Volume 10, page 494:

> *According to legend this money was hidden away in wine casks, and, escaping the search of Napoleon's soldiers when they entered Frankfurt, was restored intact in the same casks in 1814, when the elector (Prince William of Hanau) returned to the electorate (Germany). The facts are somewhat less romantic, and more businesslike.*

The implication being that the money was never returned by Rothschild with the encyclopaedia adding "Nathan Mayer Rothschild invested this $3,000,000 in gold from the East India Company knowing that it would be needed for Wellington's peninsula campaign," with Nathan then making on the stolen money "no less than four profits."

In 1815 the five Rothschild brothers exploited the policy of funding both sides in wars by providing gold for the armies of both Wellington and Napoleon. Because of their ownership of banks throughout Europe, the Rothschilds had a unique network of covert routes and fast couriers who were the only agents permitted to travel through the English and French lines. This meant that they were kept posted on the war's progress which enabled them to buy and sell on the stock exchange in accordance with the intelligence received.

British bonds were at that time called consuls and Nathan Mayer Rothschild instructed his employees to start selling them so as to make other traders believe that the Britain was losing the war and cause them to start panic selling that would see the value of the consul plummet. Rothschild's employees were then instructed to discreetly begin purchasing all available consuls. When it eventually became apparent that Britain had actually won the war, the value of consuls rose to an even higher level than before and the Rothschilds ended up with a return of approximately twenty to one on their investment.

This gave the Rothschilds total control of Britain's economy and with Napoleon's defeat helped London become the financial centre of the world which required the setting up a new Bank of England under the control of Nathan Mayer Rothschild who allegedly boasted "I care not what puppet is placed upon the throne of England to rule the Empire on which the sun never sets. The man who controls Britain's money supply controls the British Empire, and I control the British money supply."

Such control enabled the Rothschilds to replace the method of shipping gold between countries by instead utilising their five European banks to establish the system of paper debits and credits that is still in use today. Having taken control of the British money supply, the Rothschilds proceeded to aggressively pursue renewal of their charter for a central bank in the US. That bank, was to become the Federal Reserve Bank and part of the Federal Reserve System which in effect now controls and implements the monetary policy of the country: a country where a duped people failed to recognise that they were not citizens in a democracy, but rather wretched subjects in a declining plutocracy where the widening divide between the very rich who had made it, and the very poor who never would, had irrevocably damaged American social structures and shattered all illusions of the quintessential American Dream.

It was in 1821 that Kalmann (Carl) Mayer Rothschild was dispatched to Italy where he ended up doing a substantial amount of business with the Vatican which Pope Gregory XVI recognised by conferring upon him the Order of St. George. This was followed-up in 1822 with the emperor of Austria bestowing upon the five Rothschild brothers the title of *Baron*, which Nathan Mayer Rothschild declined to adopt, and in the following year the Rothschilds took over the Catholic Church's worldwide financial operations.

Five years later in 1827 Sir Walter Scott's nine-volume *The Life of Napoleon* was published with a claim in volume two that the French Revolution was orchestrated by Adam Weishaupt's Illuminati and financed by Europe's money changers — an allusion to the Rothschilds.

President Andrew Jackson in 1833 began transferring federal funds from the Rothschild controlled Bank of the US to domestic banks resulting in a subsequent 1835 failed assassination attempt on his life for which he later blamed the Rothschilds. The Rothschilds then acquired the rights to the Almadén quicksilver mines in Spain — quicksilver was vital for refining gold and silver — which being the biggest concession in the world, gave the Rothschilds a virtual world monopoly.

After many years of infighting, President Andrew Jackson finally succeeded in 1837 to rid America of the Rothschilds' central bank by preventing renewal of their charter, and Nathan Mayer Rothschild died with control of his bank being passed on to his younger brother, James Mayer Rothschild. During the following year the Rothschilds sent Ashkenazi Jew August Belmont — who at the age fourteen had joined the banking house in Frankfurt — to America to rescue and resuscitate their banking interests

Despite their setback in America, the Rothschilds managed in 1840 to become the Bank of England's bullion brokers with agencies in California and Australia. In 1841 President John Tyler's veto of the act to renew the Rothschild's

Bank charter for the US resulted in his receiving hundreds of death threats. In 1842 acquisition of the Vítkovice Mining and Iron Corporation — which became a top ten global industrial concern — was completed by Salomon Mayer Rothschild.

Benjamin Disraeli — who would subsequently twice become British Prime Minister — published *Coningsby*, in which Nathan Mayer Rothschild was referred to as being "the Lord and Master of the money markets of the world, and of course virtually Lord and Master of everything else. He literally held the revenues of Southern Italy in pawn, and Monarchs and Ministers of all countries courted his advice and were guided by his suggestions."

In 1845, former President and slave owner Andrew Jackson died. When asked before his death what he regarded as his greatest achievement in office, he unhesitatingly replied in reference to the Rothschilds: "I killed the bank." In the meantime Baron James de Rothschild won the contract to build the first major railway line across France called the Chemin De Fer Du Nord which initially ran from Paris to Valenciennes and then joined with the Austrian rail network built by his brother Salomon Mayer Rothschild.

In 1847 Lionel De Rothschild was elected to the parliamentary seat for the City of London but left his seat vacant for eleven years because as a Jew he was unable to take an oath in the true faith of a Christian so as to enter parliament; Three years later Construction began on Mentmore in England and Ferrières in France, with many other Rothschild manor houses filled with fine works of art being established throughout the world; in 1852 N. M. Rothschild & Sons began refining gold and silver for the Royal Mint, the Bank of England, and other international clients; in 1853 Nathaniel de Rothschild purchased Château Brane Mouton, the Bordeaux vineyard which he renamed Château Mouton Rothschild; Amschel Mayer Rothschild, Salomon Mayer Rothschild, and Kalmann (Carl) Mayer Rothschild died in 1855; and in 1858 the inclusion of new oaths finally enabled Lionel De Rothschild to take his seat in the British parliament and become its first ever Jewish member.

Abraham Lincoln — 16th President of the US from 1860 until his assassination in 1865 — approached Rothschild influenced banks in 1861 for loans to finance the ongoing American Civil War. They agreed on condition that Lincoln renewed the Rothschild Charter for another US central bank and was prepared to pay 24 to 36 percent interest on the loans. Such a high rate of interest, however, outraged Lincoln who took the decision to print his own debt free money and informed the public that it was legal tender for both public and private debts. By April the following year, $449,338,902 worth of Lincoln's debt free money had been printed and distributed which led to his comment "we gave the people of this republic the greatest blessing they ever had, their own paper money to pay their own debts." Sometime later that year *The Times* of London published an article — no doubt

Rothschild instigated — that in part stated:

> *If that mischievous financial policy, which had its origin in the North American Republic, should become indurated down to a fixture, then that government will furnish its own money without cost. It will pay off debts and be without a debt. It will have all the money necessary to carry on its commerce. It will become prosperous beyond precedent in the history of civilised governments of the world. The brains and the wealth of all countries will go to North America. That government must be destroyed or it will destroy every monarchy on the globe.*

Following the unification of Italy in 1863, the Rothschild banking house in Naples closed and the Rothschilds used one of their American agents of influence, John D. Rockefeller, to invest in a Cleveland, Ohio refinery, leading to the 1870 establishment of the Standard Oil company which by the early 1880s controlled some 90 percent of US refineries and pipelines.

Persistent and problematic Rothschild attempts to set up a central bank in Russia were of concern for Tsar Alexander II — who being sympathetic with Abraham Lincoln's similar problem with the Rothschilds — agreed to Lincoln's request for assistance in the American Civil War by dispatching some of his fleet to anchor off New York and California with a warning to the British, French, and Spanish that in the event of any attack against either side, Russia would support US interests.

Much to the annoyance of Rothschild agent August Belmont — who by then was the Democratic Party's National Chairman — President Abraham Lincoln defeated General George McClellan, the Democratic nominee, in the 1864 presidential election; and in 1865 President Lincoln informed Congress that he had "two great enemies, the Southern Army in front of me, and the financial institution in the rear. Of the two, the one in my rear is my greatest foe." Later that year Lincoln was assassinated.

That same year, following a short training period in the Rothschild's London Bank, eighteen year-old Jacob Schiff — His father, Moses Schiff, was a broker for the Rothschilds — arrived in America with the necessary finance and sole purpose of investment in a banking house that would eventually facilitate gaining control of America's money system through the establishment of a central bank; find suitable men, who could be bribed into being Rothschild stooges holding important positions within the federal government, the Congress, Supreme Court, and other federal agencies; engender social conflict amongst minority groups throughout the nation and especially between Whites and Blacks; and establish a movement to undermine religion in America with Christianity being the main target. In 1870 Schiff cofounded the Continental Bank of New York and 1875 joined Kuhn, Loeb & Company.

Jacob Mayer Rothschild in 1868 bought Château Lafite, one of the Premier Grand Cru estates of France, but died shortly afterwards; Nathaniel de Rothschild passed away in 1870; and the Rothschild-Illuminati conspiracy was boosted in 1871 when Freemason Guissepe Mazzini lured into membership the prominent American Freemason, General Albert Pike — the only Confederate military officer or figure to be honoured with an outdoor statue in Washington, DC which in June 2020 was toppled by protesters and set it on fire on Juneteenth, the day marking the end of slavery in the US — whose 1871 "Three World War Letter" was a blueprint for bringing about the One World Order:

> *The First World War must be brought about in order to permit the Illuminati to overthrow the power of the Czars in Russia and of making that country a fortress of atheistic Communism. The divergences caused by the "agentur" (agents) of the Illuminati between the British and Germanic Empires will be used to foment this war. At the end of the war, Communism will be built and used in order to destroy the other governments and in order to weaken the religions.*
>
> *The Second World War must be fomented by taking advantage of the differences between the Fascists and the political Zionists. This war must be brought about so that Nazism is destroyed and that the political Zionism be strong enough to institute a sovereign state of Israel in Palestine. During the Second World War, International Communism must become strong enough in order to balance Christendom,*

which would be then restrained and held in check until the time when we would need it for the final social cataclysm.

The Third World War must be fomented by taking advantage of the differences caused by the "agentur" of the "Illuminati" between the political Zionists and the leaders of Islamic World. The war must be conducted in such a way that Islam and political Zionism mutually destroy each other. Meanwhile the other nations, once more divided on this issue will be constrained to fight to the point of complete physical, moral, spiritual and economical exhaustion . . .

Prior to his death in 1872, Guiseppe Mazzini chose as his successor Adrian Lemmy, another revolutionary who would subsequently be succeeded by Lenin, Trotsky, and Stalin who all had their revolutionary activities financed by the Rothschilds. The following year the loss making Rio Tinto copper mines in Spain — representing Europe's largest source of copper — were purchased by a consortium of foreign financiers including the Rothschilds.

In 1875, Jacob Schiff, by then Solomon Loeb's son-in-law, took control of Kuhn, Loeb & Co. and goes on with Rothschild money to finance John D. Rockefeller's Standard Oil, Edward R. Harriman's Railroad Empire, and Andrew Carnegie's Steel Empire; N. M. Rothschild & Sons launch a share issue to raise capital for the first channel tunnel project between France and England with half of the capital coming from the Rothschild owned Company du Chemin de Fer du Nord; Lionel De Rothschild secretly arranged Rothschild finance for Prime Minister Benjamin Disraeli's British government to acquire a major stake in the Suez Canal; and in 1876 conservative Prussian statesman Otto von Bismarck stated:

> *The division of the United States into two federations of equal force was decided long before the civil war by the high financial power of Europe. These bankers were afraid that the United States, if they remained in one block and as one nation, would attain economical and financial independence, which would upset their financial domination over the world.*

> *The voice of the Rothschilds predominated. They foresaw the tremendous booty if they could substitute two feeble democracies, indebted to the financiers, to the vigorous Republic, confident and self-providing.*

> *Therefore they started their emissaries in order to exploit the question of slavery and thus dig an abyss between the two parts of the Republic.*

In 1881, President James A. Garfield — 20th President of the US for only a hundred Days — stated two weeks before his assassination that "whoever controls the volume of money in our country is absolute master of all industry and commerce . . . and when you realise that the entire system is very easily controlled, one way or another, by a few powerful men at the top, you will not have to be told how periods of inflation and depression originate."

After six thousand feet of tunnel excavations under the English Channel (*la Manche*), the British government in 1883 abandoned the project citing the possible threat to Britain's security; two years later, Nathaniel, son of Lionel De Rothschild, became the first ever Jewish peer and assumed the title of Lord Rothschild; and in 1886 the French Rothschild bank acquired a substantial share of Russian oil fields and formed the Caspian and Black Sea Petroleum Company which rapidly became the second largest producer in the world.

The Rothschilds then moved their attention to Southern Africa in 1887 by financing the despicable Freemason and avowed racist Cecil Rhodes — supporter of the notorious South African Masters and Servants Act which was facetiously nicknamed the "Every Man to Wallop his Own Nigger Bill" — for the amalgamation of South Africa's Kimberley diamond mines into the De Beers company which subsequently in 1893 contracted to sell its entire diamond production to a London diamond syndicate consisting of ten Jewish firms interconnected either through marriage or family ties.

The complete domination of diamond distribution by Jewish companies had been a reality for hundreds of years because the cutting and polishing of diamonds, was one of the few crafts in which medieval European guilds had allowed Jewish participation. So for the majority of Jews there were few vocational options other than gem-polishing or money lending which also involved dealing with diamonds.

Until the early 1700s the world's entire supply of diamonds had been sourced from India by caravan traders who crossed Arabia and exchanged their precious stones for gold and silver from Jewish traders in Aden and Cairo, who in turn sold them on to fellow Jewish merchants in Frankfurt, Lithuania, and Venice. Dealing in diamonds consequently became a hallmark for Jewish traders scattered across central Europe — who also maintained trading centres in the Ottoman Empire through which all Indian diamonds passed — where as moneylenders they were by necessity involved in the assessment, repair, and sale of precious stones that had been tendered as collateral for loans.

When the Portuguese eventually discovered different maritime routes including one to India, the camel caravan routes were gradually replaced by ships and Portugal's mainly Sephardic Jews arranged for ships' officers to buy diamonds directly from the Indian miners in Goa so that Lisbon became Europe's main entry point for the precious stones. Jewish entrepreneurs then established cutting factories in Lisbon and in Antwerp where they employed and exploited the poorer Ashkenazi Jews from eastern Europe to do the cutting and polishing.

Diamonds also proved to be an invaluable asset for the Jews during the Inquisition because unlike most other assets, they could be easily concealed and were readily redeemable for cash in other European countries. For the Jewish people, whose self-imposed "separatism" from the goyim in ghettos and eruvs — designated areas within which observant Jews could carry or push objects on the Sabbath — had resulted in centuries of fear and uncertainty over being expelled so that diamonds became the most favoured investment option for their wealth.

When forced to relocate by the Inquisition, diamond industry Jews fled from Lisbon and Antwerp with their portable diamond cutting tools to resettle in Amsterdam which they quickly established as Europe's diamond centre. They were also instrumental in financing the Dutch East India Company which used its own trade route to India with a stopover at the *Kaap die Goeie Hoop* (the Cape of Good hope) in South Africa where the establishment of Dutch settlements eventually led to the Afrikaner Great Trek of 1836 — to escape British domination and anglicisation of their culture — by more than 12,000 Boers who migrated northwards in separate groups to set up independent republics. The Trek had been regarded as similar to that of the children of Israel who as the chosen people had determined to pursue their own destiny.

As the diamond yielding mines in India began to run dry, an alternative source was sought in Brazil before the eventual first recorded South African discovery of diamonds on 13 October 1867. Fearing that the market would be flooded with South African diamonds, the ten leading London

Jewish merchants immediately set up a syndicate to buy all South African diamonds so as to control the market. Some of these merchants had also acquired substantial stock holdings in Cecil Rhodes' De Beers company which led to one of them, Dunkelsbuhler, to hire Ernest Oppenheimer, a sixteen year old apprentice from Friedberg in Germany, who after proving himself in London, was dispatched in 1902 to run the Kimberly office in South Africa.

Twenty-five years later, in 1927, Ernest Oppenheimer took control of De Beers before going on to found the Anglo American Corporation and thereby consolidate his monopoly over the world's diamond industry (*South Africa Inc.: Oppenheimer Empire*). When Oppenheimer converted from Judaism to Anglicanism in the late 1930s, some observers suggested that the conversion was intended to remove a possible obstacle to the continued sale of industrial diamonds to Hitler's Germany. Oppenheimer's involvement in other controversies included price fixing, antitrust behaviour, and an allegation of not releasing industrial diamonds for the US war effort.

Confirmation that the diamond trade was still dominated by Jewish corporations came from more recent media reports that Tiffany & Co had sourced Blood Diamonds from the Octea Diamond Group, a Beny Steinmetz Group Resources (BSGR) in Sierra Leone where Beny Steinmetz — the Israeli tycoon who dominated the gemstone market — was facing a raft of corruption allegations in one of Africa's poorest countries. The BSGR group of companies had a unique corporate structure and was controlled by a trust fund, the Steinmetz Foundation, of which the Steinmetz family was the beneficiary. Revenue from BSGR companies was being channelled via the Steinmetz Foundation to the Israeli military which stood accused of war crimes and possible crimes against humanity by the UN Human Rights Council. The Foundation had "adopted" a Unit of the Givati Brigade of the Israeli military for which it purchased equipment and provided support during the Israeli assault on the defenceless, besieged residents of Gaza in the winter of 2008/2009 during Operation Cast Lead. On January 22, 2021, Steinmetz was found guilty in Geneva of corruption and was sentenced to five years in prison, and ordered to pay a fine of 50 million Swiss francs.

Dan Gertler, another Israeli businessman in natural resources and founder of the DGI Group of Companies, was at the centre of DR Congo corruption allegations resulting in his coming under scrutiny from the IMF and the World Bank since 2012. When the US initially imposed sanctions on Gertler in 2017 — he made a fortune from his corrupt relationship with DR Congo's former President Joseph Kabila — he hired President Donald Trump's lawyer, dodgy Alan Dershowitz, to get them removed. The sanctions, however, were re-imposed at the start of the Biden administration

In 1891, the British socialist newspaper, *Labour Leader*, referred to the Rothschilds as "this blood-sucking crew has been the cause of untold mischief and misery in Europe during the present century, and has piled up its prodigious wealth chiefly through fomenting wars between States which ought never to have quarrelled. Whenever there is trouble in Europe, wherever rumours of war circulate and men's minds are distraught with fear of change and calamity you may be sure that a hook-nosed Rothschild is at his games somewhere near the region of the disturbance." Such comments — viewed as being anti-Semitic — were of concern to the Rothschilds who by the end of the 1800s had purchased news agencies such as Reuters in London, Havas in France, and Wolf in Germany so as to exert control over what was reported to the general public.

Edmond James de Rothschild visited Palestine in 1895 and financed the first Jewish colonies to initiate the long term objective of creating a Jewish State to serve Rothschild interests. Two years later in 1897 the Rothschilds founded the Zionist Congress with its first meeting being scheduled in Munich, but local Jewish opposition forced a change of venue to Basle in Switzerland.

Since then the Zionist agenda of hijacking Judaism to exploit historical Jewish suffering and the Holocaust; of implementing an appalling Apartheid regime guilty of crimes against humanity and ethnic cleansing despite Jewish familiarity with being the victims of genocide; and of deliberately subverting freedom of expression by seeking to criminalise criticism of Israel's blatant criminality with impunity — has if anything, with the tolerant complicity of most Jews in diaspora — contributed to the continued failure to successfully combat anti-Semitism.

9

The Emergence of Zionism

Though it is Theodor Herzl (1860-1904) — author of *The Jewish State (Der Judenstaat)* in 1896, organiser of the First Zionist Congress in 1897, and founder/first president of the World Zionist Organisation — who is most often cited as being the founder of Zionism, the actual seed for the emergence of the movement was planted in 1870 as a reaction to newer waves of anti-Semitism in Central and Eastern Europe. The movement gained support by branding itself as a Jewish people's movement advocating the re-establishment of, and support for, a Jewish State in the historic Land of Israel (Canaan).The very nature of Zionist ideology was characterised by settler colonialism and the forced displacement of the indigenous population.

Nonetheless, Herzl is still immortalised as the founder of Zionism and the Jewish State. Throughout Israel his name has been lent to streets, boulevards, parks, squares, the city of Herzliya, a forest, a number of restaurants, a museum, and the national cemetery of Mount Herzl; his portrait hangs in the plenum hall of the Knesset; and his birthday is observed as a national holiday on Herzl Day.

Herzl was born in Budapest to parents who were secular, assimilated, German-speaking Jews. He developed an admiration for German culture, philosophy, art, and literature as being the ultimate in Western civilisation. At Vienna University he joined the German nationalist fraternity, Albia — whose motto was Honour, Freedom, Fatherland — but subsequently resigned in protest at the antisemitism he encountered. Like other educated, German-speaking Jews, he also had nothing but contempt for the mass of religious, Torah-abiding, Yiddish-speaking, shtetl-dwelling Eastern European Jews. There is in fact nothing in his writings to suggest any great attachment to either Judaism or its doctrines.

In his book, *Der Judenstaat*, Herzl stated "The Jewish question exists wherever Jews live in perceptible numbers. Where it [antisemitism] does not exist, it is carried by Jews in the course of their migration. We naturally move to those places where we are not persecuted and there our presence produces persecution . . . The unfortunate Jews are now carrying the seeds of anti-Semitism into England; they have already introduced it into America."

In a subsequent chapter, Herzl argued that the immediate cause of antisemitism is "our excessive production of mediocre intellects, who cannot find an outlet downwards or upwards — that is to say, no wholesome outlet in either direction. When we sink, we become a revolutionary proletariat, the subordinate officers of all revolutionary parties; and at the same time, when we rise, there rises also our terrible power of the purse." In other words, he was saying that the responsibility for anti-Semitism lay with Jews who carried its seeds within them, and it was consequently their fault.

Another source of influence during Zionism's formative years, was Ze'ev Jabotinsky (1880-1940) — the Russian Jewish Revisionist Zionist leader whose essay *The Iron Wall (We and the Arabs)* was written after the British Colonial Secretary Winston Churchill prohibited Zionist settlement on the East Bank of the Jordan River — who believed that the Palestinian Arabs would never agree to a Jewish majority in Palestine, and asserted "Zionist colonisation must either stop, or else proceed regardless of the native population. Which means that it can proceed and develop only under the protection of a power that is independent of the native population — behind an iron wall, which the native population cannot breach."

Jabotinsky — a reactionary whose writing was replete with unabashed colonialist and racist platitudes — regarded Zionism as a colonial enterprise similar to the colonisation of Australia and North America. He wrote the following about the Arabs: "culturally they are five hundred years behind us, they have neither our endurance nor our determination." He also pointed out "my readers have a general idea of the history of colonisation in other countries. I suggest that they consider all the precedents with which they are acquainted, and see whether there is one solitary instance of any colonisation being carried on with the consent of the native population. There is no such precedent."

Ironically, Jabotinsky's negative and dehumanising opinion of the Palestinian population was also a feature in the Nazi agenda for solving the "Jewish problem" and preceded the "Final Solution" whose victims were first demeaned and humiliated over a period of years during which time the emphasis was not so much on the elimination of Jews, Gypsies, homosexuals, and other such "sub-humans," but rather on the propaganda that established the categories of "sub-humanity" to be eliminated. Consequently it was only after the concocted threat from the "sub-humans" had been firmly established and sold to the brainwashed general public, that the "final solution" could then be implemented without much if any challenge.

The ploy of using dark psychology to dehumanise certain ethnic and religious groups is so effective that it has been employed repeatedly throughout history. Such racist psychology with discriminatory dehumanisation consists of five basic elements that include alluding to the below par intelligence or morality of the minority group to cause it to be ostracised while boosting the ego of the majority by assuring them of their own superiority; using infestation analogies to make the majority fearful that the minority is a threat to their welfare and security; comparing and referring to the minority as animals with the Nazis having frequently referred to innocent Jewish victims as rats; encouraging the use of violence by the majority who have been brainwashed into accepting that the minority are inhuman; and physically isolating or removing the minority by means of deportation, the formation of ghettos, or the use of concentration camps.

Such thinking with genocidal intent consequently became an essential element of the Zionist agenda so that Jabotinsky's vision of separation by means of an "iron wall" has become a racist reality with Israel still currently building separation walls that confine and condemn Palestinians to the kind of inhumane hardships that only a people — deluded into believing they are god chosen — are capable of hatefully inflicting without conscience. Zionism's plan of action for physically removing Palestinians from Palestine is still a work in progress with racist discrimination, illegal expropriations, and military annexations.

It is astonishing to think that the people who suffered most in the Nazi death camps, are now also responsible for appalling humanitarian catastrophes as for example in Gaza which the blacklisted and much maligned Jewish academic Norman Finkelstein — son of Nazi concentration camp survivors and author of some eleven books including *The Holocaust Industry and Beyond Chutzpah: On the Misuse of Anti-Semitism and the Abuse of History* — has described as "the world's largest concentration camp."

Though the concept of Zionism initially attracted a number aspiring Jewish intellectuals wishing to "jump on the wagon," many more — including Albert Einstein, Sigmund Freud, Hannah Arendt (political scientist), Primo Levi (writer and Auschwitz survivor), Erich Fromm (social psychologist), Henry Siegman (Rabbi and director of the U.S./Middle East Project}, Richard Cohen (US columnist), Rabbi Michael Lerner (editor of Tikkun Magazine), and Uri Avnery, (ex-Israeli army officer) — were opposed to Zionism which after more than a century and contrary to its claim of representing Jews, has actually tarnished their image as a people.

By that time it was already clear that the next prime minster was going to be Golda Meir, a woman whom I frankly detested - a mutual sentiment, I might add. I knew her as an opinionated, obstinate person, primitive in her outlook, rigid in her attitudes, with a genius for reaching and exploiting the deepest fears and prejudices of the Jewish masses. I was certain that with her as prime minister, all peace efforts would come to a total standstill.

Uri Avnery (1923-2018), former member of the Irgun Zionist paramilitary organisation, writer, politician, and founder of the Gush Shalom peace movement.

Zionism's emergence as an effective political entity required increasing its support amongst more diaspora Jews which it achieved by aggressively promoting the combined concepts of a gathering of the exiles, an escape from persecution, and an end to anti-Semitism. Consequently, Zionism's supporters came to regard it as a national liberation movement instead of what it actually was — a colonist, racist, and supremacist ideology that advocated violence in Mandatory Palestine, contrived the forcible expulsion of the indigenous Palestinian population, and subsequently facilitated unrestricted Jewish immigration to Palestine while denying Palestinian refugees the right of return to their lands and property.

> *Between ourselves it must be clear that there is no room for both peoples together in this country. We shall not achieve our goal if the Arabs are in this small country. There is no other way than to transfer the Arabs from here to neighbouring countries — all of them. Not one village, not one tribe should be left.*
> **Joseph Weitz, head of the Jewish Agency's Colonisation Department in 1940.**

It should be noted that the concept of "population transfer" — the only solution to what was referred to as the "Arab Problem" — had the full support of all Zionist leaders who despite being mostly irreligious if not totally apathetic towards Judaism, nonetheless embraced it as a means of pursuing Zionism's agenda by for example citing biblical narratives and falsely claiming to be descendants of Jews who inhabited the land some 2,000 years ago.

Such assertions, however, have recently been refuted by various studies including one published 2006 which declared Ashkenazim were a clear, homogeneous genetic subgroup who came from the same genetic group, irrespective of whether their ancestors were from Poland, Russia, Hungary, Lithuania, or some other place with a historically large Jewish population.

Another study published in 2013 by the scientific journal *Nature Communications* showed that the origins of the matrilineal line for Ashkenazi Jews comes from Europe. This was another contradiction of the much propagated but bogus narrative that European Ashkenazim are descendants of Jews who left Israel and the Middle East some 2,000 years ago. The reality is that most Ashkenazis are descended from local Europeans who converted to Judaism.

The availability of a new genetic map has provided a comprehensive picture of the migration by different Jewish groups across the globe, with some becoming genetically isolated units while others appeared to have mingled and intermarried. Researchers were able to trace the diaspora — historical migration of the Jews — which began in the sixth century BCE when the Kingdom of Judah was conquered by the Babylonians. Though some Jews remained in Judah under Babylonian rule, many fled to Egypt and other parts of the Middle East with Jewish migrations having with varying degrees continued up to the present day.

The expulsion of Jews from Mediterranean regions resulted in the twelfth century migration of Jews to Europe where they began settling in what is now Poland with further migrations to other parts of Europe. This was confirmed by a 2013 study using DNA samples that showed most European Jews were descended from local people who converted to Judaism, and not from individuals who left Israel and the Middle East around 2,000 years ago.

The 2013 study also showed that 80% of Ashkenazim's maternal line comes from Europe with only a few having genes originating in the Near Eastern Countries of the Arabian Peninsula, Cyprus, Egypt, Iraq, Iran, Israel, Jordan, Lebanon, Palestinian territories, Syria, and Turkey. According to Professor Richards this would suggest that, even though Jewish men may indeed have migrated into Europe from Palestine around 2000 years ago, they seem to have married European women who constituted the majority of the European converts to Judaism during the early years of the Diaspora.

The claim by Ashkenazim that they are descended from the Jews who were expelled from the region of Palestine to which they now claim a right to return — a right denied to the indigenous Palestinians brutally expelled during the 1948 Nakba — is therefore lacking in any legitimacy. It is a claim based on concocted narratives that have been questioned, if not discredited by more than a few Jewish and non-Jewish commentators.

> *Appropriations of the past as part of the politics of the present . . . could be illustrated for most parts of the globe. One further example which is of particular interest to this study, is the way in which archeology and biblical history have become of such*

importance to the modern state of Israel. It is this
combination which has been such a powerful factor
in silencing Palestinian history.
Keith W. Whitelam, The Invention of Ancient Israel:
the silencing of Palestinian History, 1996

Apart from its proclivity for shamefaced lies to further its agenda, Zionism also had no qualms about collaborating with the Nazis, embracing the SS, Sacrificing European Jews, opposing asylum for Jews, betraying Jewish resistance, and signing a pact with the Nazis that betrayed Hungarian Jews. Six months after Hitler came to power, the Zionist Federation of Germany — the country's largest Zionist group — submitted a detailed memorandum to the new government that reviewed German-Jewish relations and formally offered Zionist support for "solving" the vexing "Jewish question." It suggested that the first step would require a frank recognition of fundamental national differences:

"Zionism believes that the rebirth of the national
life of a people, which is now occurring in Germany
through the emphasis on its Christian and national
character, must also come about in the Jewish na-
tional group. For the Jewish people, too, national
origin, religion, common destiny and a sense of its
uniqueness must be of decisive importance in the
shaping of its existence. This means that the egotis-
tical individualism of the liberal era must be over-
come and replaced with a sense of community and
collective responsibility . . .

We believe it is precisely the new [National Social-ist] Germany that can, through bold resoluteness in the handling of the Jewish question, take a decisive step toward overcoming a problem which, in truth, will have to be dealt with by most European peoples . . .

Our acknowledgment of Jewish nationality provides for a clear and sincere relationship to the German people and its national and racial realities. Precise-ly because we do not wish to falsify these fundamen-tals, because we, too, are against mixed marriage and are for maintaining the purity of the Jewish group and reject any trespasses in the cultural do-main, we — having been brought up in the German language and German culture — can show an inter-est in the works and values of German culture with admiration and internal sympathy . . .

For its practical aims, Zionism hopes to be able to win the collaboration of even a government funda-mentally hostile to Jews, because in dealing with the Jewish question not sentimentalities are involved but a real problem whose solution interests all peo-ples and at the present moment especially the Ger-man people . . .

Boycott propaganda — such as is currently being carried on against Germany in many ways — is in essence un-Zionist, because Zionism wants not to do battle but to convince and to build . . .

We are not blind to the fact that a Jewish question exists and will continue to exist. From the abnormal situation of the Jews severe disadvantages result for them, but also scarcely tolerable conditions for other peoples.

The Federation's paper, the *Jüdische Rundschau* ("Jewish Review"), proclaimed "Zionism recognises the existence of a Jewish problem and desires a far-reaching and constructive solution. For this purpose Zionism wishes to obtain the assistance of all peoples, whether pro or anti-Jewish, because, in its view, we are dealing here with a concrete rather than a sentimental problem, the solution of which all peoples are interested."

The Haavara Agreement — heskem haavara, or "transfer agreement" — was signed in August 1933 between Nazi Germany and Zionist German Jews resulting in a leading German shipping company starting a direct passenger liner service from Hamburg to Haifa in Palestine. The company provided "strictly kosher food on its ships, under the supervision of the Hamburg rabbinate." The agreement also served as a model for the subsequent 1937 Polish Halifin transfer company, and the signing of further agreements in 1939 by Czechoslovakia, Hungary, Italy, and Romania. Such agreements were a testament to the self-serving arrogance of the signatories — with one side wanting to get rid of the Jews, and the other wanting to grab Palestine — who felt no need to either consider or consult with the indigenous Palestinian population.

Therefore on the basis of them having similar ideologies about ethnicity and nationhood, German National Socialists and Zionists coordinated their efforts in what both sides believed was in their own national interests. As a result, the Hitler government vigorously supported Zionism and Jewish emigration to Palestine from 1933 until 1940-1941, when the Second World War prevented more extensive collaboration.

Meanwhile, even after the Third Reich became more entrenched, the majority of German Jews continued to regard themselves, frequently with considerable pride, as being primarily German. They had little enthusiasm for pulling up roots and starting a new life in a far-away foreign environment. During this period they nonetheless increasingly turned to Zionism which until late 1938, flourished in Germany under Hitler. The circulation of the Zionist Federation's biweekly *Jüdische Rundschau* increased dramatically; numerous Zionist books were published; and the Zionist agenda for Palestine was accelerated so that a Zionist convention held in Berlin in 1936 reflected "in its composition the vigorous party life of German Zionists."

The *Schutzstaffel* (SS) was especially enthusiastic about Zionism with its official newspaper, *Das Schwarze Korps*, proclaiming its support in a May 1935 front-page editorial: "The time may not be too far off when Palestine will again be able to receive its sons who have been lost to it for more than a thousand years. Our good wishes, together with official goodwill, go with them." The sentiment of that article was repeated four months later and included the following quote:

> *The recognition of Jewry as a racial community based on blood and not on religion leads the German government to guarantee without reservation the racial separateness of this community. The government finds itself in complete agreement with the great spiritual movement within Jewry, the so-called Zionism, with its recognition of the solidarity of Jewry around the world and its rejection of all assimilationist notions. On this basis, Germany undertakes measures that will surely play a significant role in the future in the handling of the Jewish problem around the world.*

With such recognition of "Jewish racial separateness," Zionism worked tirelessly to exploit Judaism to further its agenda for Palestine by "reeducating" German Jews into accepting the idea of emigration to the Holy land. American historian Francis Nicosia in his 1985 survey, *The Third Reich and the Palestine Question*, noted: "Zionists were encouraged to take their message to the Jewish community, to collect money, to show films on Palestine, and generally to educate German Jews about Palestine. There was considerable pressure to teach Jews in Germany to cease identifying themselves as Germans and to awaken a new Jewish national identity in them."

At the September 1935 National Socialist Party Congress, the Reichstag adopted the "Nuremberg laws" — for the Protection of German Blood and German Honour — which prohibited marriages and extramarital intercourse between Jews and Germans, and forbade the employment of German females under 45 in Jewish households. This in effect was a declaration that Jews were an alien minority nationality. Instead of being alarmed by such a racist distinction, Zionism rejoiced and a few days later the Zionist *Jüdische Rundschau* editorially welcomed the new measures:

> *Germany . . . is meeting the demands of the World Zionist Congress when it declares the Jews now living in Germany to be a national minority. Once the Jews have been stamped a national minority it is again possible to establish normal relations between the German nation and Jewry. The new laws give the Jewish minority in Germany its own cultural life, its own national life. In future it will be able to shape its own schools, its own theatre, and its own sports associations. In short, it can create its own future in all aspects of national life . . .*

> *Germany has given the Jewish minority the opportunity to live for itself, and is offering state protection for this separate life of the Jewish minority: Jewry's process of growth into a nation will thereby be encouraged and a contribution will be made to the establishment of more tolerable relations between the two nations.*

In an article that appeared in a November 1935 issue of the official *Reichsverwaltungsblatt*, the Interior Ministry's Jewish affairs specialist, Dr. Bernhard Lösener, expressed unconditional support for Zionism:

> *If the Jews already had their own state in which the majority of them were settled, then the Jewish question could be regarded as completely resolved today, also for the Jews themselves. The least amount of opposition to the ideas underlying the Nuremberg Laws have been shown by the Zionists, because they realise at once that these laws represent the only correct solution for the Jewish people as well. For each nation must have its own state as the outward expression of its particular nationhood.*

With cooperation from the German authorities, Zionist groups were able to organise a network of some 40 camps and agricultural centres throughout Germany where prospective settlers were indoctrinated and trained for their new lives in Palestine. Although the Nuremberg Laws forbade Jews from displaying the German flag, Jews were nonetheless guaranteed the right to fly the blue and white flag — at the Zionist camps and centres in Hitler's Germany — that was subsequently adopted by Israel as its national banner.

Further cooperation was also forthcoming form Himmler's security service which helped the Haganah, the Zionist underground military organisation in Palestine. A Haganah official, Feivel Polkes, was paid by the SS agency for information about the situation in Palestine and for assistance in directing Jewish emigration to that country. Haganah-SS collaboration also included secret deliveries of German weapons to Jewish settlers for use in clashes with Palestinian Arabs. Furthermore, Zionism's penchant for spying on those who provide it with assistance and support — as is currently being carried out against Western nations and particularly the US — was also conducted by the Haganah which was kept well informed about German plans by a spy it had managed to plant in the Berlin headquarters of the SS.

Even after the November 1938 "Kristallnacht" also called the "Night of Broken Glass," — when Nazis in Germany torched synagogues, vandalised Jewish homes, schools and businesses, and killed close to 100 Jews — the SS continued to help the Zionist organisation with its work in Germany under more restricted supervision because of the prevailing hostility towards Jewish people. All Zionists nonetheless believed that anti-Semitism was a permanent and inevitable characteristic of most goyim so that creating a Jewish State in Palestine was the only practical solution.

There is also no doubt that both Theodor Herzl and David Ben-Gurion shared the view that anti-Semitism was perversely a useful, if not a vital ally for Zionism. They recognised the fact that every manifestation of anti-Semitism served as an invaluable stimulus for heir cause. While that did not necessarily mean that Zionist leaders were actively encouraging anti-Semitism, they were nonetheless resigned to the reality of its helpful existence and were inevitably willing to make deals with anti-Semites if they thought it would be beneficial to the Zionist agenda.

That agenda was reflected in Ben-Gurion's own craving for the territorial expansion of a Jewish State which he confirmed at the 1937 Zionist congress in Zurich by declaring "our right to Palestine, all of it, is unassailable and eternal" and that he was "an enthusiastic advocate of a Jewish State within the historical boundaries of the Land of Israel." As a strong-willed realist, however, Ben-Gurion was equally aware that, like the Zionist Jews, the Palestinians wanted a state of their own and would not gladly surrender their land. Recognition of that fact led him to believe that achieving Arab-Israeli coexistence within the same territory was an impossibility, He consequently sought to expand Israeli territory only into areas with very small Arab populations.

Such pragmatism characterised Ben-Gurion as a "liberal" Zionist when compared to right wing hawks like Jabotinsky, Menachem Begin and others. In 1954, the IDF General Staff's Planning Department submitted an evaluation titled "Nevo," which amongst other things proposed expanding Israel's Green Line borders with various alternatives for such expansion. This involved setting back Egypt's border preferably to the bank of the Suez Canal; seizing parts of southern Saudi Arabia with a view to possibly controlling the Arabian oil fields; taking over Syrian lands; and moving the border with Jordan far east of the Jordan River.

Despite such proposals, Ben-Gurion was initially opposed to Israel going to war in 1967 because it would result in having to rule over lands populated by Arabs who would be understandably hostile. His opposition, however, was quickly overcome by the euphoria that swept across the nation as a result of the swift victory and conquests. Since then Zionist Israel's illegal and unnecessary land-grabbing antics have continued unabated and include the gradual annexation of the West Bank.

> *The thesis that the danger of genocide was hanging over us in June 1967 and that Israel was fighting for its physical existence is only bluff, which was born and developed after the war.*
> **Israeli General Matityahu Peled, Haaretz, 19 March, 1972**

The extent of Ben-Gurion's pragmatism, however, was not without limitations and he emphatically opposed any possibility of having Israel become binational as in a free and independent state of Palestine/Israel based on the coexistence of two peoples, with equal national and cultural rights, and autonomy guaranteed for both. While proposals for a binational state were intended as a bridge building attempt to engage with Palestinian resistance to being denied a homeland and human rights, Ben-Gurion nonetheless tenaciously clung to the Zionist policy he had been advocating since the 1930s of combatting Palestinian resistance with "aggressive self-defence" that would include driving them out of Palestine.

Such thinking was in keeping with Zionism's European Ashkenazi mindset which regarded the Palestinians as being social and cultural aliens who should not only be avoided and not discussed, but also denied their existence by referring to Palestine as "a land without a people." So instead of trying to coexist with the indigenous Palestinians, the Jewish Israel — as was decreed by Herzl — was to be "a rampart of Europe against Asia, an outpost of civilisation as opposed to barbarism."

Herzl's racially charged view of Orientalism was shared by Ben-Gurion who following the 1929 Arab revolt, stated that the Arabs were "primitive" and that the Jews were facing "an outbreak of the worst instincts of savage masses — inflamed religious extremism, a compulsion for robbery and looting, and a thirst for blood." Any impartial and unbiased person would probably agree that the same could also be said of those Israelis who claim to be immensely civilised and infinitely superior citizens of a state whose ethnic cleansing of the "Promised Land" has surpassed everything that Herzl's Zionist agenda could have desired.

We must expropriate gently the private property on the state assigned to us. We shall try to spirit the penniless population across the border by procuring employment for it in the transit countries, while denying it employment in our country. The property owners will come over to our side. Both the process of expropriation and the removal of the poor must be carried out discretely and circumspectly. Let the owners of the immoveable property believe that they are cheating us, selling us things for more than they are worth. But we are not going to sell them anything back.

An 1895 entry in Herzl's diary

10

The Zionist Hijack of Judaism

Zionism and Judaism is not one thing but two dif-
ferent things. And of course two contradicting one
another. Zionism starts at the place where Judaism
is destroyed . . . one thing is certain, Zionism is not
a continuation or healing of wounded Judaism, but
rather an uprooting.
Chaim Chassas, in the Zionist newspaper, Ha'Arutz,
1943,

Fulfilment of the Zionist agenda for the colonisation of
Palestine required the hijacking of Judaism which with its
biblical narrative of a "chosen people" and "promised land"
could be exploited to legitimise Zionism's revisionist political objective of establishing a Jewish State with a Jewish majority on both sides of the River Jordan.

By hijacking Judaism — and claiming that only a state
controlled by, and exclusive to Jews can protect them against
anti-Semitism and the threat of another Holocaust — Zionism has deviously managed to instigate the gradual erosion
of Judaism's "ethical monotheism" which with the Torah's

commandments and subsequent literature sets out the rules about justice, equality before the law, loving-kindness, social welfare, and the ideals of peace and political freedom: commendable ideals that are not to be found in Zionism's rabid and racist philosophy which with arrogance and impunity reflects the reality of an Apartheid Israeli State.

Fortunately not all Jews have taken the bait with groups such as the Jewish Voice for Peace (JVP) — guided by a vision of justice, equality and freedom for all people — which unequivocally opposes Zionism because it is counter to those ideals. In explaining its "Approach to Zionism," the JVP had the following to say:

> *We know that opposing Zionism, or even discussing it, can be painful, can strike at the deepest trauma and greatest fears of many of us. Zionism is a nineteenth-century political ideology that emerged in a moment where Jews were defined as irrevocably outside of a Christian Europe. European antisemitism threatened and ended millions of Jewish lives — in pogroms, in exile, and in the Holocaust.*

> *Through study and action, through deep relationship with Palestinians fighting for their own liberation, and through our own understanding of Jewish safety and self determination, we have come to see that Zionism was a false and failed answer to the desperately real question many of our ancestors faced of how to protect Jewish lives from murderous antisemitism in Europe.*

While it had many strains historically, the Zionism that took hold and stands today is a settler-colonial movement, establishing an apartheid state where Jews have more rights than others. Our own history teaches us how dangerous this can be.

Palestinian dispossession and occupation are by design. Zionism has meant profound trauma for generations, systematically separating Palestinians from their homes, land, and each other. Zionism, in practice, has resulted in massacres of Palestinian people, ancient villages and olive groves destroyed, families who live just a mile away from each other separated by checkpoints and walls, and children holding onto the keys of the homes from which their grandparents were forcibly exiled.

Because the founding of the state of Israel was based on the idea of a "land without people," Palestinian existence itself is resistance. We are all the more humbled by the vibrance, resilience, and steadfastness of Palestinian life, culture, and organising, as it is a deep refusal of a political ideology founded on erasure.

In sharing our stories with one another, we see the ways Zionism has also harmed Jewish people. Many of us have learned from Zionism to treat our neighbours with suspicion, to forget the ways Jews built home and community wherever we found ourselves to be. Jewish people have had long and integrated histories in the Arab world and North Africa, living among and sharing community, language and custom with Muslims and Christians for thousands of years.

By creating a racist hierarchy with European Jews at the top, Zionism erased those histories and destroyed those communities and relationships. In Israel, Jewish people of colour — from the Arab world, North Africa, and East Africa —have long been subjected to systemic discrimination and violence by the Israeli government. That hierarchy also creates Jewish spaces where Jews of colour are marginalised, our identities and commitments questioned & interrogated, and our experiences invalidated. It prevents us from seeing each other — fellow Jews and other fellow human beings — in our full humanity.

Zionist interpretations of history taught us that Jewish people are alone, that to remedy the harms of antisemitism we must think of ourselves as always under attack and that we cannot trust others. It teaches us fear, and that the best response to fear is a bigger gun, a taller wall, a more humiliating checkpoint.

Rather than accept the inevitability of occupation and dispossession, we choose a different path. We learn from the anti-Zionist Jews who came before us, and know that as long as Zionism has existed, so has Jewish dissent to it. Especially as we face the violent antisemitism fuelled by white nationalism in the United States today, we choose solidarity.

We choose collective liberation. We choose a future where everyone, including Palestinians and Jewish Israelis, can live their lives freely in vibrant, safe, equitable communities, with basic human needs fulfilled. Join us.

Despite the concern and noble sentiments of organisations such as the JVP, however, the majority of the world's people and in particular in the West — have after more than seventy years of being paralysed into silence by the accusatory Zionist venom of anti-Semitism and Holocaust denial — failed to condemn incalculable cheating, lying, stealing, murdering, and ruthless violation of the legal and natural human rights of the Palestinian people by a Zionist Apartheid Jewish State devoid of conscience, humanity, or any of the noble principles of the religion to which it claims to belong.

This country exists as a fulfilment of a promise made by God Himself. It would be ridiculous to ask it to account for its legitimacy.
Golda Meir (Israeli Prime Minister 1969-1974), Le Monde, 15 October 1971

The concept of legitimacy cannot be claimed on the basis of some Biblical narrative written thousands of years ago by scribes (ancient Jewish record-keepers) intent on inventing a Jewish people and creating a Jewish nation. Genuine legitimacy, like respect, cannot be feigned, fabricated, purchased or purloined: it has to be earned with commendable conduct and well intentioned cooperation in the affairs of all humanity.

Genuine legitimacy for a Zionist Apartheid Israel, therefore, cannot be established by the silencing of demands for accountability for contemptible and illegal behaviour with impunity; cannot be established by devilish duplicity, rambunctious denial of obvious criminality, or the deprivation of human and political rights for others; and cannot be established by numerous self-serving false flag operations such as the 1954 Lavon Affair when Israeli agents working in Egypt planted bombs in several buildings, including a US diplomatic facility, and left evidence behind implicating Egyptians. The ruse would have worked, had not one of the bombs detonated prematurely, resulting in the capture of one of the bombers that subsequently led to the round up of an Israeli spy ring. As to be expected, Israel's response to the scandal was to claim that there was no spy ring, and that it was all a hoax perpetrated by "anti-Semites."

There was also the 1967 USS Liberty Incident when during the Six-day War unmarked Israeli jet fighter aircraft and Israeli Navy motor torpedo boats attacked the USS Liberty — a US Navy technical research ship — killing 34 crew members and wounding 171 others with a view to blaming the Egyptians for the attack. Israel's barefaced lie on that occasion was that the USS Liberty had been mistaken for an Egyptian vessel. The incident was covered up and investigations shut down by a subservient American government and a spineless President Lyndon Johnson who may have feared suffering the same fate as his predecessor, JFK.

> *Certain facts are clear. The attack was no accident. The Liberty was assaulted in broad daylight by Israeli forces who knew the ship's identity . . . The President of the United States led a cover-up so thorough that years after he left office, the episode was still largely unknown to the public — and the men who suffered and died have gone largely unhonored.*
>
> **Paul Findley (1921-2019), American writer and politician, They Dare to Speak Out, 1985**

Israel's ultimate false flag operation, however, was undoubtedly the September 11, 2001 attacks on the US when two planes were flown into the twin towers of the World Trade Center in New York City; a third plane hit the Pentagon just outside Washington, D.C.; and a fourth plane crashed in a field in Shanksville, Pennsylvania. Almost 3,000 people were killed and over 25,000 injuries sustained during the attacks which triggered the US War on Terror, a war that fulfilled Israel's widest dreams. Despite overwhelming evidence of Israeli complicity, the attacks were nonetheless blamed on the Al-Qaeda terrorist group.

Members of of the Architects & Engineers for 9/11 Truth — check their website — have demonstrated that it was impossible for plane crashes and jet fuel fires to trigger the collapse of the Twin Towers which literally exploded, pulverised concrete, and laterally launched at high speeds pieces of steel beams weighing several hundred tons for hundreds of meters. The pyroclastic dust — similar to that from a volcano — that cascaded through the streets, indicated a high temperature mixture of hot gasses and relatively dense solid particles, an impossible phenomenon in a simple collapse. Equally impossible was the collapse of a 47-storey skyscraper —into its own footprint at near free-fall speed — which had not been hit by a plane

> *Although 9-11 is disguised and interpreted by the government and media as an act of terrorism carried out by Islamic fanatics, the evidence indicates that it was a carefully planned false-flag attack carried out by the Israeli military after years of planning and preparation.*
> **Christopher Lee Bollyn, Solving 9-11: The Deception That Changed the World**

Israel's legitimacy cannot be established by a Fascist ideology based on the "supremacy" of a "chosen people" whose Apartheid colonial objectives include the savage military ethnic cleansing of the indigenous Palestinians; the continual bribing and corrupting of the elected representatives of other nations; and by forever committing crimes against humanity to legitimise the illegitimate because the time will certainly come — as it did for the Nazis — when there has to be a reckoning that demands justice and retribution.

The time for that reckoning, however, must be relentlessly pursued. People everywhere — including all those Americans who are either illiterate, politically naive, simply oblivious to, or disinterested in what is happening not only in America, but also the rest of the world — have to be resolute in deciding that goodwill towards Israel and tolerance for its crimes against humanity can no longer be permitted because of regret over the Holocaust. Jews do not have a monopoly on suffering as is witnessed by the fact that — and that is not counting the millions of injuries and fatalities resulting from Israeli-instigated conflicts — some twelve million children under the age of five die annually from preventable diseases and malnutrition in what is equivalent to a double Jewish "holocaust." People must determine that the vow of "never again" shall be applicable not just to Jews, but to all peoples including Palestinians; that Israelis, like the Nazis, must be made accountable for the crimes they commit; and that collective cowardice, criminal cooperation, and culpable complicity regarding Israel are an irresponsible betrayal of all humanity.

The collective cowardice resulting from the fear of being stigmatised as anti-Semites or Holocaust deniers is an irrational and immoral reaction to the well financed and orchestrated Zionist campaign for the promotion of guilt-inducing reminders of the Holocaust, otherwise known as the Holocaust industry. Current and future generations cannot be held hostage in perpetuity by Zionist Israel for crimes committed by past generations. Furthermore, past persecutions of the Jewish people does not grant Zionism the automatic right to now ethnically cleanse the Palestinian people. Shrill and constant cries of anti-Semitism to silence criticism of Apartheid Israel are now so commonplace that they have — like the boy in *Aesop's Fables* who repeatedly cried "wolf" falsely only to be ignored when there actually was one — have become monotonous and meaningless.

Criminal cooperation is the provision to Israel of preferential access to US and European Union markets including the latter's failure to enforce laws prohibiting the import of Israeli goods produced in the Occupied Territories; criminal cooperation is the direct foreign investment in Israel which averaged US $8,365.44 million from 1995 until 2020, reaching an all time high of US $52,368 million in the fourth quarter of 2019 and a record low of US $10,028.10 million in the third quarter of 2010; and criminal cooperation is the acceptance by politicians of pro-Israel political action committee contributions which in the US alone are quite astronomical. Israel's ability to bribe and corrupt politicians does not extend to the people, therefore it is up to the people to show their disapproval in the only possible and peaceful way: they must effectively boycott Israeli goods by joining the BDS campaign; they must boycott companies who invest in Israel; they must crusade against individuals or organisations that associate with, or support Israel; and they must continually lobby their politicians especially those that have accepted the accursed Israeli new shekel and demand justice and respect for the human rights of Palestinians.

Culpable complicity with Israel's barbarous criminality takes many forms including nations who either abstain or vote against UN resolutions condemning Israel's persistent persecution of the Palestinians with the US having used more vetoes on behalf of Israel than it has on behalf of itself; culpable complicity includes the provision of military-related equipment to Israel with the knowledge that it will be used to continue brutally oppressing the Palestinians in the illegally Occupied Territories; and culpable complicity includes the hypocritical double standards by which Israel's criminality is either leniently judged or just completely ignored as compared to other less useful international law violators whom Western nations neither respect nor regard as being of value either politically or for having natural resources. This is particularly true of the US, the UK, Canada, France, and Germany.

Apart from highjacking Judaism and exploiting its adherents, Zionism in pursuit of its racist agenda has also with deceitful and deliberate intent to varying degrees hijacked and undermined the political scope of other nations to prevent justified criticism of its own continuous criminality. It would appear that the majority of Jewish people are either unaware of what Zionist Israel is doing to save them from another Holocaust — by ethnically cleansing the Palestinian people — or are with conscious callousness indifferent to the suffering of others so long as they are not Jews.

Israel has been controlling Gaza and the West Bank for over fifty years through repression, institutionalised discrimination, and systematic abuses of the Palestinian population's rights. Such control involves at least five categories of major violations of international human rights law and humanitarian law including unlawful killings, forced displacement, abusive detention, the closure of the Gaza Strip and other unjustified restrictions on movement, the development of illegal settlements, and all the accompanying discriminatory policies that disadvantage Palestinians.

There is irrefutable documented evidence that Israeli troops killed more than 2,000 Palestinian civilians during the last three Gaza assaults in 2008-09, 2012, and 2014. Many of those attacks amounted to violations of international humanitarian law due to a failure to take all feasible precautions to spare civilians. Some amounted to war crimes, including the calculated targeting of civilian structures such as schools, hospitals, and essential public utilities.

Though Israeli security forces In the West Bank have routinely used excessive force that seriously wounds or kills civilians — with some Israeli officials backing a "shoot-to-kill" policy against demonstrators, rock-throwers, and suspected assailants — official Israeli investigations into such security force abuses have been perfunctory with a consistent failure to punish those who are responsible.

The open-fire policy — which allows unjustified use of lethal force — conveys Israel's deep disregard for

*the lives of Palestinians and facilitates Israel's con-
tinued violent control over millions of Palestinians.*
**B'Tselem, The Israeli Information Centre for Human
Rights in the Occupied Territories**

Another aspect of Zionism's "selfless" policy to save Jews from another Holocaust had by 2017 established 237 settlements that housed some 580,000 settlers who enjoy Israeli civil law affording them legal protections, rights, and benefits while providing them with infrastructure, services, and subsidies. Palestinians living in the same territory, however, are subject to Israeli military law that denies them the privileges enjoyed by illegal Jewish settlers thereby creating and sustaining a separate and unequal system of laws, rules, and services: and that is definitely Apartheid!

The establishment of such settlements required the expropriation of thousands of acres of Palestinian land to facilitate Jewish settlement and supporting infrastructure. Discriminatory burdens, including making it nearly impossible for Palestinians to obtain building permits in East Jerusalem and in the 60 percent of the West Bank where Palestinians have been forced to leave their homes or to build at the risk of seeing their "unauthorised" buildings bulldozed and razed to the ground. The demolition of Palestinian homes on the pretext of not having permits has been ongoing for decades despite the law of occupation which prohibits destruction of property except for military necessity, or punitively as collective punishment against families of Palestinians suspected of attacking Israelis.

Zionism's zeal for the "protection" of Jewish citizens has also since 1967 resulted in the incarceration of hundreds of thousands of Palestinians following "trials" in military courts, which have near to a 100 percent conviction rate. Even more outrageous, is that on average, hundreds every year are placed in administrative detention — with some simply for nonviolent activism — based on secret evidence without charge or trial. Israel also jails Gaza and West Bank Palestinian detainees inside Israel to satisfy its racist penchant for making life as difficult as possible by creating onerous restrictions on family visits and violating international law requiring that they be held within the occupied territory. Many detainees, including young children, face harsh conditions and ill treatment.

Israel's policy on accountability evinces its profound disregard for the lives, physical wellbeing and property of Palestinians. The state has also made it clear that, for its part, it bears no responsibility for the consequences of its control over the Palestinian population, neither as the occupying power in the West Bank nor an external entity exerting control over the Gaza Strip. Israel's powers as ruler, which it is quick to enforce when it serves its own purposes, vanish into thin air when it has to answer for its actions.

In this way, Israel manages to do as it pleases in the Occupied Territories without anyone holding it to account for its actions: the military law enforce-

ment system whitewashes violations (in the sphere of criminal justice), and the state ensured for itself a nearly blanket exemption from paying compensatory damages for harm caused by its security personnel (in the sphere of civil justice). Without deterrence and oversight mechanisms, the road to serious human rights abuses lies wide open. This ongoing state of affairs is one of the cornerstones of the occupation and of Israel's control of the Palestinian population. Years of experience have shown that Palestinian victims stand a slim chance of seeing justice done and that the chance that Israelis be held to account for their actions is similarly slim —certainly in the case of senior ranking officials responsible for designing policy. At the same time, virtually all Palestinians in the Occupied Territories are painfully aware of how vulnerable they are to injury, abuse or even death at the hands of Israeli security forces and, moreover, that it is highly unlikely that anyone will be held to account for the harm or that the Palestinian will receive compensation for the harm sustained.

B'Tselem, whose work confirms that the pangs of the collective Jewish conscience have not completely perished

When on December 20, 2019, The International Criminal Court's chief prosecutor announced that a full investigation into alleged war crimes in the Palestinian Territories would be launched, Israel's response was as usual hypocritical and vitriolic with its foreign ministry stating: "The prosecutor has been influenced by Palestinian manipulation, which aims to weaponise the court." An even more hypocritical response came from Prime Minister Netanyahu — a man whose barefaced lies and inherent corruption are hardly qualifications for commenting on truth and justice — who with hypocritical bombast claimed "This is a dark day for truth and justice. It is a baseless and outrageous decision."

There can be no denying — even by the most biassed, blinkered, and racist of Jews — that traditional Judaism has been hijacked by the political ambitions of revisionist Zionism which in pursuit of its agenda has implicated Jews everywhere.

Zionism is racist. It demands political, legal and economic power for Jews and European people and cultures over indigenous people and cultures. Zionism is not just racist but anti-Semitic. It endorses the sexist European anti-Semitic imagery of the effeminate and weak "diaspora Jew" and counters it with a violent and militarist "new Jew," one who is a perpetrator rather than a victim of racialised violence.

Zionists disseminate the myth that Israel is a democracy. In truth, Israel has established and enforces internal policies and practices that discriminate against Jews of Mizrahi descent and exclude and restrict Palestinian people. Moreover, Israel, in collaboration with the United States, undermines any Arab movements for social change and liberation.

Zionism perpetuates Jewish exceptionalism. In defence of its crimes, Zionism tells a version of Jewish history that is disconnected from the history and experiences of other people. It promotes the narrative that the Nazi holocaust is exceptional in human history — despite it being one of many holocausts from Native Americans North and South to Armenia and Rwanda. It sets Jews apart from the victims and survivors of other genocides instead of uniting us with them.

Through a shared Islamophobia and desire for control of the Middle East and broader West Asia, Israel makes common cause with Christian fundamentalists and others who call for Jewish destruction. Together they call for the persecution of Muslims. This shared promotion of Islamophobia serves to demonise resistance to Western economic and military domination. It continues a long history of Zionist collusion with repressive and violent regimes, from Nazi Germany to the South African Apartheid regime to reactionary dictatorships across Latin America.

Zionism claims that Jewish safety depends on a militarised Jewish State. But Israel does not make Jews safe. Its violence guarantees instability and fear for those within its sphere of influence and endangers the safety of all people, including Jews, far beyond its borders. Zionism colluded willingly in creating the conditions that led to violence against Jews in Arab countries. The loathing aroused by Israeli vio-

lence and military domination toward Jews living in Israel and elsewhere is used to justify further Zionist violence.

Excerpts from the Charter of the International Jewish Anti-Zionist Network which is available in full on its website.

11

The Ploy of Playing the Victim Card

You cannot continue to victimise someone else just because you yourself were a victim once — there has to be a limit.
Edward W. Said (1935 - 2003), a Palestinian American professor of literature at Columbia University

In her book — *Emotional Blackmail: When the People in Your Life Use Fear, Obligation, and Guilt to Manipulate You* — psychotherapist Doctor Susan Forward devised the acronym FOG to sum up the strategies typically used by manipulators as being Fear, Obligation, and Guilt. Manipulators can resort to employing all three strategies together, or rely on just one or a combination of two. The playing of the "victim card" or self-victimisation — casting oneself in the role of a victim — is the fabrication or exaggeration of victimhood for various reasons including justification for the abuse, exploitation, or manipulation of others as a coping strategy, or for seeking attention.

It is common knowledge that the "poor me" strategy is

often used by young children who will shed crocodile tears, pout pathetically, or sulk sadly if they fail to get what they want, as and when they want it. Exploitation of the "poor me" strategy by supposedly mature adults to stimulate the sympathy of others, however, is a symptom of some personality disorder, is inexcusable, and is liable to be regarded as being disingenuous, dishonest, and downright insufferable.

Consequently endless "poor me" reminders of the Holocaust to either justify and mitigate Apartheid Israel's illegal and violent expropriation and occupation of Palestinian land, or to silence criticism of those abhorrent transgressions, is a disgraceful exploitation of what was a cataclysmic event for Jewish people in general, and a betrayal of the memory those Jews who perished in the Nazi death camps in particular. And yet it is those same people who while claiming to have a covenant with god, are the ones responsible for unaccountable war crimes and crimes against humanity that defy any "poor me" exhortations by them and their supporters.

The exploitation of Fear, Obligation, and Guilt was particularly useful while the Israeli government was zoning as "open green space" virtually all unbuilt-upon land of Palestinian East Jerusalem following the 1967 invasion while preventing Palestinians from living in Jewish West Jerusalem where there was already insufficient space to accommodate all the Jews even without having Palestinian homes appropriated or demolished to make room for Jewish settlers. This policy of deliberate displacement of Palestinians ⊠ despite the Fourth Geneva Convention stating "the Occupying Power shall not deport or transfer parts of its own civilian population into the territory it occupies" — was described in the book *Separate and Unequal: The Inside Story of Israeli Rule in East Jerusalem* by Amir Cheshin who as a former Israeli army colonel and Advisor on Arab Affairs was one of the architects of the post-1967 policy:

> . . . *Israel's leaders adopted two basic principles in their rule of East Jerusalem. The first was to rapidly increase the Jewish population in East Jerusalem. The second was to hinder growth of the Arab population and to force Arab residents to make their homes elsewhere. It is a policy that has translated into a miserable life for the majority of East Jerusalem Arabs . . . Israel turned urban planning into a tool of the government, to be used to help prevent the expansion of the city's non-Jewish population. It was a ruthless policy, if only for the fact that the needs (to say nothing of the rights) of Palestinian residents were ignored. Israel saw the adoption of strict zoning plans as a way of limiting the number of new homes built in Arab neighbourhoods, and thereby ensuring that the Arab percentage of the city's population — 28.8 in 1967 — did not grow beyond this level. Allowing 'too many' new homes in Arab neighbourhoods would mean "too many" Arab residents in the city. The idea was to move as many Jews as possible into East Jerusalem, and move as many Arabs as possible out of the city entirely. Is-*

raeli housing policy in East Jerusalem was all about this numbers game.

Palestinian continuity, heritage, and rightful claims to East Jerusalem were, and still are, being gradually undermined by the illegal placement of interspersed, fortified, and guarded Jewish enclaves which are then expanded and linked as part of the plan to displace indigenous Palestinians and establish Jewish presence in all of Jerusalem. Apart from Israel's demographic considerations, Silwan's Palestinian population of approximately 45,000 was also victim to an Israeli reinvention of the area as "The City of David" with a visitors' centre having been built to provide some legitimacy for an assertion that lacked any archaeological or historical evidence.

Israel's unscrupulous "creative tactics" for helping Jewish settlers take over Palestinian land ranged from audacious fraud and forgery to military seizures for "security needs" or the "public good" to the use of outdated Ottoman laws. In order to facilitate the transfer of Palestinian land to Jewish settlers without having to purchase the land, Israel created and institutionalised a number of official ploys including "seizing land for military needs" which saw over 40 settlements being established on thousands of acres of privately owned Palestinian land following the 1967 war; use of expropriation orders for "the public good"; enforcement of Ottoman land laws which stipulated that land not worked continuously for three straight years would automatically return to the state;

funding of land takeovers, wherein the money is generally transferred through the World Zionist Organisation's Settlement Division or local and regional settler councils; and by not enforcing laws against settlers and institutions which illegally and forcibly take over private Palestinian land. The hypocrisy and inhumanity of the "poor me" Jewish State was highlighted by Human Rights Watch in a 2020 report which included the following:

The Israeli government continued to enforce severe and discriminatory restrictions on Palestinians' human rights; restrict the movement of people and goods into and out of the Gaza Strip; and facilitate the transfer of Israeli citizens to settlements in the occupied West Bank, an illegal practice under international humanitarian law.

Israel's twelve-year closure of Gaza, exacerbated by Egyptian restrictions on its border with Gaza, limits access to educational, economic and other opportunities, medical care, clean water and electricity for the nearly 2 million Palestinians who live there. Eighty percent of Gaza's population depend on humanitarian aid.

Israeli forces stationed on the Israeli side of fences separating Gaza and Israel continued to fire live ammunition at demonstrators inside Gaza who posed no imminent threat to life, pursuant to open-fire orders from senior officials that contravene international human rights standards. According to the Palestinian rights group al-Mezan, Israeli forces killed 34 Palestinians and, according to Gaza's Health Ministry, injured 1,883 with live ammunition during these protests in 2019 as of October 31.

Closure

Israel imposes sweeping restrictions on the movement of people and goods into and out of the Gaza Strip. A general travel ban excludes only what Israel calls "exceptional humanitarian cases," meaning mostly medical patients and their companions, as well as prominent businesspersons who can obtain permits. In the first nine months of 2019, the army denied or failed to respond in a timely manner to 34 percent of permit applications from Palestinians with scheduled medical appointments outside Gaza, according to the World Health Organisation (WHO). The rejection or delay rate for applications for those injured in demonstrations along the fences separating Israel and Gaza is 82 percent.

In the West Bank, including East Jerusalem, Israeli security forces killed 23 Palestinians and wounded at least 3,221, including those suspected of attacking Israelis, but also passersby and demonstrators, as of November 11. In many cases, video footage and witness accounts strongly suggest that Israeli forces used excessive force. As of November 11, attacks by Israeli settlers killed two Palestinians, injured 84, and damaged property in 234 incidents, according to OCHA. Israel maintained onerous restrictions on the movement of Palestinians in the West Bank.

Israeli Actions in Gaza

As of November 11, lethal force by Israeli forces resulted in the killing of 71 and injuring 11,453 Palestinians in Gaza, OCHA reported. An additional 33 were killed and 114 injured, according to al-Mezan, during escalated fighting between November 12 and 14. Many of the killings took place in the context of protests, when Israeli forces fired on people who approached or attempted to cross or damage fences between Gaza and Israel, using live ammunition in situations where lesser measures could have been used, in contravention of the international human rights law standard for policing situations that lethal force be used only as a last resort to prevent an imminent threat to life. The gunfire maimed many people, including 128 between the start of protests in March 2018 and September 2019 whose limbs had to be amputated.

Israeli Actions in the West Bank

In the West Bank, including East Jerusalem, Israeli security forces killed 23 Palestinians and wounded at least 3,221, including those suspected of attacking Israelis, but also passersby and demonstrators, as of November 11. In many cases, video footage and witness accounts strongly suggest that Israeli forces used excessive force. As of November 11, attacks by Israeli settlers killed two Palestinians, injured 84, and damaged property in 234 incidents, according to OCHA.

Settlements, Discriminatory Policies, Home Demolitions

Israel continued to provide security, infrastructure administrative services, housing, education, and medical care for more than 642,867 settlers residing in unlawful settlements in the West Bank, including East Jerusalem.

Freedom of Movement

OCHA documented 705 permanent obstacles such as checkpoints across the West Bank in July. Israeli-imposed restrictions designed to keep Palestinians far from settlements forced them to take time-consuming detours and restricted their access to their own agricultural land.

The separation barrier, which Israel said it built for security reasons but 85 percent of which falls within the West Bank rather than along the Green Line separating Israeli from Palestinian territory, cuts off many Palestinians from their agricultural lands and isolates 11,000 Palestinians who live on the western side of the barrier but are not allowed to travel to Israel and must cross the barrier to access their own property and other services.

Arbitrary Detention and Detention of Children

As of October 31, according to Prison Services figures, Israeli authorities held 4,731 Palestinians in custody for "security" offences, including 2,840 convicted prisoners, 1,061 pretrial detainees, and 460 in administrative detention based on secret evi-

dence without charge or trial. Excluding Jerusalem residents, West Bank Palestinians were tried in military courts, including those charged with nonviolent speech or protest activity. Those courts have a near-100 percent conviction rate. Israel incarcerates many West Bank and Gaza Palestinian detainees and prisoners inside Israel, complicating family visits and violating the provisions of international humanitarian law that prohibit their transfer outside the occupied territory.

As of August 31, Israel was detaining 185 Palestinian children, many suspected of criminal offences under military law, usually stone-throwing. Israel denied Palestinian children arrested and detained in the West Bank legal protections granted to Israeli children, including settlers, such as protections against nighttime arrests and interrogations without a guardian present. Israeli forces frequently used unnecessary force against children during arrest and physically abused them in custody.

Following that very brief look at "the only democracy in the Middle East" with its "most moral army in the world," it is now necessary to consider that other "kosher" claim that the Jewish State is just "defending itself." Anyone believing that load of "poor me" malarkey, should seriously bear in mind the atrocities committed by Israel during just two of its numerous operations: Operation Cast Lead (27 December 2008 - 18 January 2009) and Operation Protective Edge (8 July - 26 August 2014).

Cast Lead

On Saturday (Jewish Sabbath) 27 December 2008, while spineless and hypocrisy-ridden western nations were still preoccupied with their glutinous Christmas overindulgence and goodwill towards all men, Israel yet again proceeded to "defend" itself against 1.8 million virtually unarmed Palestinian civilians who were still waiting for a state of their own as opposed to an open prison.

> *Israel, I am convinced, can and should survive as a peaceful, prosperous society — but within the essential borders of 1967. That much we owe them, but no more. We do not owe them our support of their continued occupation of Arab lands . . . The Palestinians have as much right to a homeland as the Jewish people.*
> **Former US Senator William J. Fulbright (1905-1995)**

So it was against those Palestinians who lacked a single warplane, warship, or battle tank — and regarded as beasts and snakes by god's chosen "poor me" people — that without warning, the war criminal state of Israel unleashed an offensive codenamed Operation Cast Lead which began with a "shock and awe" campaign by 64 of Israel's fleet of approximately 300 US-supplied F-16 warplanes. Israel's stated intention was to end rocket attacks into Israel by armed Palestinian factions who unlike the Israelis did not have a right to defend themselves.

If Israel has the right to defend itself by launching air strikes that have destroyed Palestinian homes and schools, then surely Palestinians have the right to protect themselves from the brutal and escalating Israeli violence, which has led to a death toll of more than 80 over the past few days alone, along with hundreds of injured civilians. Israel has long used illegal tactics of collective punishment in Gaza, effectively laying siege to an area home to 1.7 million people while periodically shelling homes and schools, to say nothing of Israeli activities in the West Bank.

The Brookings Institution which provide the highest quality research, policy recommendations, and analysis on a full range of public policy issues

It would, of course, be anti-Semitic to suggest that if Israel were to give the Palestinians back their lands and desist from ethnically cleansing them, then the rocket attacks might cease. Apart from an inherent hate for Palestinians, the Israeli attack was also timed to send a clear message to incoming President Obama — "I will bring peace to the Middle East if I become US President" — that it was Israel and not the US which determined the course of events in the Middle East.

Every time we do something you tell me America will do this and will do that . . . I want to tell you something very clear: Don't worry about American

pressure on Israel. We the Jewish people control America, and the Americans know it.
A warning from Prime Minister Ariel Sharon — the war criminal responsible for the 1982 Sabra and Shatila massacres in Lebanon — to Foreign Minister Shimon Perez in October 2001.

In addition to its warplanes, Israel deployed US-made AH-64 Apache attack helicopters and AH-1F Cobra gunships while its naval fleet of Super Dvora-class fast patrol boats directed cannon and machine gun fire along the coast. Following the destruction of all preselected targets, Israeli ground forces — with help from UAVs (drones) with attack and ISTAR (intelligence, surveillance, target acquisition, and reconnaissance) capabilities — crossed into Gaza on 3 January 2009 to occupy open areas and encircle towns and refugee camps. Apart from infrared and digitally enhanced zoom cameras capable of identifying body heat signatures from a height of 10,000 feet, some UAVs were equipped with two AGM-114 Hellfire guided missiles and two domestically produced missiles.

The Eitan UAV carrying more than a ton of weapons — which had been developed and war game tested in the Aegean in July 2008 for strikes against Iran — also made its combat debut by firing Spike missiles. Human rights organisations subsequently noted that despite the imaging and targeting capabilities of these UAVs, their missiles — including one that dispersed tiny, sharp-edged cubes of purpose-made shrapnel — were responsible for a high number of Palestinian civilians deaths whose use as guinea pigs for testing newly developed Israeli weaponry, had been a regular occurrence.

Israeli ground forces were supported by one of the world's most technologically advanced artillery corps — towed/ self-propelled howitzers and multiple rocket launchers — connected to sophisticated radar and navigation networks that maximised accuracy. Apart from 100,000s of US-supplied artillery shells, there were also high explosive munitions for bunker destruction, illumination, armour-piercing, and anti-personnel fragmentation devices containing more than 1,200 fragments that exploded above targets so as to create a wide area of coverage within a 350-foot radius.

Ground assaults were led by hundreds of APCs — armoured personal carriers -- and some 300 tanks armed with grenades, heavy machine guns, TOW/Spike missiles, and precision guided shells capable of being fired into windows from a distance of a mile (1.5 km). Further troop assistance was provided by 100 armoured (with bulletproof windows) CAT D9 bulldozers which with US help had been modified for demolition, route creation, barrier/fortification building, and mine/booby trap clearing. Also employed were Viper miniature robots, electronic jamming devices, special weapons systems including some that were controversial and in some cases even illegal. Following initial denials, Israel, in the face of irrefutable evidence, subsequently admitted using white phosphorous which causes immediate, deep, excruciating, chemical burns with delayed healing.

Because of the glaring disparity between the blockaded, ill-equipped Palestinians and the US backed and financed Israelis, it would be preposterous to attempt any comparison between their respective weaponry and resources. Equally preposterous would be the suggestion that Israel was "defending" itself.

In a 2001 secretly filmed interview with an Israeli family that is still available on YouTube — *I Deceived the US to Destroy Oslo Accords* — a less than reputable Benjamin Netanyahu makes it clear that far from being defensive, Israel's harsh military repression had been specifically designed as part of " . . . a broad attack on the Palestinian Authority. To bring them to the point of being afraid that everything was collapsing." When asked about the world's reaction to such an attack, Netanyahu arrogantly replied "the world won't say a thing. The world will say we're defending."

The world had said it about previous Israeli atrocities; said it about Operation Protective Edge; and will continue saying it as Israel ceaselessly pursues its agenda of brutalising the Palestinian people. Operations Cast Lead and Protective Edge — chillingly described by Israeli generals as "mowing the lawn" — were symbolic of the Israeli mindset which rejects diplomacy in favour of brute military force: not as a last resort but as the first and only option which is relentlessly pursued on the basis of "If force doesn't work, use more force!"

- According to investigations by independent Israeli and Palestinian human rights organisations, between 1,385 and 1,419 Palestinians were killed during Cast Lead, a majority of them civilians, including at least 308 minors under the age of 18. More than 5000 more were wounded. Thirteen Israelis were also killed, including 3 civilians.

- According to the UN, 3,540 housing units were completely destroyed, with another 2,870 sustaining severe damage.

- More than 20,000 people, many of them already refugees — some two or three times over — were made homeless.

- According to the Israeli advocacy group Gisha, attacks on Gaza's electricity infrastructure caused an estimated $10 million in damage.

- According to an assessment by the Private Sector Coordination Council, a Palestinian economic group, 268 private businesses were destroyed with another 432 damaged at an estimated cost of more than $139 million. A separate report found that 324 factories and workshops were damaged during the war.

- According to the UN Relief Works Agency (UNRWA), which provides services to Palestinian refugees, the offensive damaged almost 20,000 metres (approx. 12

miles) of water pipes, four water reservoirs, 11 wells, and sewage networks and pumping stations. Israeli shelling also damaged 107 UNRWA installations.

- Eighteen schools, including 8 kindergartens, were destroyed, and at least 262 others damaged. Numerous Palestinian government buildings, including police stations, the headquarters of the Palestinian Legislative Council, and part of Palestinian President Mahmoud Abbas' compound, were also destroyed.

- After an investigation of the destruction of civilian infrastructure in Gaza, Human Rights Watch accused the Israeli military of violating the international ban on "wanton destruction" as mentioned in the Fourth Geneva Convention.

Protective Edge

Another barbaric and deadly assault on Gaza that wreaked further havoc, punishment and devastation on an already blockaded population whose children — yet again caught in the crossfire — even if they escaped death or injury, still suffered staggering stress, trauma, and long term psychological damage.

- According to the United Nations Office for the Coordination of Humanitarian Affairs (UNOCHA), as of August 25 at least 2,076 Palestinians, over 70% of them civilians, were killed by Israel during Operation Protective Edge.

According the Al Mezan Center for Human Rights, this includes 521 children. An additional 10,224 people were injured during the attacks.

- During the same period a total of 69 Israelis, including 5 civilians (one a child and one a foreign national), were killed.

- As of August 25, it was estimated that 17,200 housing units had been severely damaged or completely destroyed. A further 37,650 had been damaged to the extent that they were uninhabitable. This temporarily displaced at least 475,000 people and more than 100,000 will remain displaced for an extended period.

- At least 58 hospitals and 216 schools were damaged or destroyed. As many as 360 factories were also damaged with at least 126 of them completely destroyed. Most farms and agricultural land also have been destroyed or severely damaged. This has left the Gaza economy in ruins.

- During the attack the main Gaza electrical plant was destroyed. As a result, electricity is now available in Gaza on average for only six hours per day. In many areas, running water also is not available as a result of damaged and destroyed infrastructure.

- The attack on Gaza caused widespread fear and trauma in Gaza, particularly among children. This trauma will require psycho-social support for adults and children alike.

While centuries of past persecution of the Jewish people may have justified the playing of the "victim card," such justification is no longer valid when those former victims are either part of, or support an Apartheid State — flaunting the belief of being god chosen, superior, and not accountable for its criminal transgressions — that since its establishment has persisted in the perverse persecution of an innocent, indigenous population. Furthermore, the disingenuous portrayal of Israel as a poor little Jewish State "defending itself" is no longer compatible with the fact that Israel — with its nuclear weapons stockpile and more than $10 million a day of US aid — is the dominant military power in the Middle East; has invaded neighbouring Arab countries; and has illegally occupied the lands of the Palestinian people while deliberately displacing them and denying them their legal and human rights.

Israel's heinous crimes against humanity which are perpetrated with an arrogant impunity facilitated by endless reminders of the Holocaust and the constant portrayal of Jews as the perennial victims — deserving of the well over $100 billion already received in compensation and some $150 billion in foreign aid from the US alone — who have morphed from the victims of the Nazi persecution, into Fascist persecutors with an added illusory conviction of "chosenness" as opposed to a racially pure Nazi "master race." The preposterous idea of a "chosen people" has inevitably led to some dark humour that may be construed, by those so inlined, as being anti-Semitic.

> *I love being a victim, but I think you actually need to be Jewish to make money out of it.*
> **Dmitry Dyatlov. author of The fact that you have un-limited texts does not necessarily mean that you can-not stop talking: Meditations for recovery from the compulsive behaviour of your choice, 2017**

12

Statehood on Stolen Land

There is the Jewish Agency, which gets a lot of money from the United States, from American Jews, whose sole job it is to create settlements. It enlists people all over the world - especially in Russia, and in the United States, by the way - to come and settle in the Occupied Territories as a kind of religious statement, a kind of nationalist statement: "This is a country given to us by God." A lot of Israelis who do not believe in God believe that God has given us this country.

Uri Avnery

While European monarchs were instigating anti-Jewish pogroms and expulsions of Jews, Ottoman Muslim rulers had by comparison exercised religious tolerance; protected both Christian and Jewish holy sites; permitted pilgrims of both faiths to visit Jerusalem; graciously welcomed Jewish victims of the Spanish Inquisition expelled from Spain in 1492; and even encouraged Jewish settlement throughout their empire.

Every honest Jew who knows the history of his peo-

ple cannot but feel a deep sense of gratitude to Is-
lam, which has protected the Jews for 50 genera-
tions, while the Christian world persecuted the Jews
and tried many times "by the sword" to get them to
abandon their faith.
Uri Avnery, Muhammed's Sword September 27, 2006

It is also a fact that Jews had never actually completely disappeared from Palestine because at least 5,000 were
part of a 300,000 population in 1517 with Ottoman taxation
registers in 1553 listing 1,958 Jews in Jerusalem alone. Jewish numbers gradually increased over time and following a
surge in East European and Yemenite Jewish immigration,
the Jewish population in 1895 had risen to 47,000 (8%) out
of 522,000. So even before Theodor Herzl published his book
Der Judenstaat (The Jewish State) which gave impetus to the
Zionist movement in 1896, there was already a significant
number of Jews in Palestine living peacefully amongst Christian and Muslim Palestinians.

At Basel I founded the Jewish State. If I said this out
loud today, l would be greeted by universal laughter.
In five years perhaps, and certainly in fifty years,
everyone will perceive it.
Theodor Herzl, President of the Jewish Congress, 3
September 1897

The First Zionist Congress held in Basel, Switzerland
on 29-31 August 1897 was attended by 208 delegates who
— without consulting Palestine's indigenous inhabitants —

announced that "Zionism aims at establishing for the Jewish people a publicly and legally assured home in Palestine," and revealed the following program for achieving their goal:

> *The promotion of the settlement of Jewish agriculturists, artisans, tradesmen and manufacturers in Palestine.*

> *The organisation and uniting of all Jews by means of appropriate local and international institutions, in accordance with the laws of the various countries.*

> *The strengthening and fostering of Jewish national sentiment and national consciousness.*

> *Preparatory steps toward obtaining the consent of governments, where necessary to achieve the Zionist purpose*

Such preparatory steps included utilising both fair and foul tactics on a global scale which even included a group of Rothschild backed Zionist Jews who in 1905 — along with Georgi Apollonovich Gaponl, a Russian Orthodox priest and working class leader — attempted to overthrow Tsar Nicholas II of Russia in a Communist Coup known as the Bloody Sunday incident. The coup's failure, however, forced them flee from Russia for refuge in Europe.

Following his 1913 inauguration, US President Woodrow Wilson, received a visit from the Ashkenazi Jew lawyer, Samuel Untermyer, who tried to blackmail him for $40,000 over an affair Wilson had at Princetown University with a fellow professor's wife. As Wilson was unable to make the payment, Untermyer offered to pay off the woman on the condition that Wilson promised to appoint to the next vacancy on the US Supreme Court a nominee recommended by Untermyer, an arrangement to which Wilson agreed. Consequently in June 1916, Ashkenazi Jew Louis Dembitz Brandeis was appointed to the Supreme Court by Wilson in accordance with settlement of his blackmail agreement. Justice Brandeis had been the elected leader of the Executive Committee for Zionist Affairs since 1914.

Brandeis was followed by seven more Jewish Supreme Court justices with the last three being Ruth Bader Ginsburg (1993-2020), Stephen Breyer (1994-), and Elena Kagan (2010-). During her fifth visit to Israel in July 2018, Ginsburg was given a lifetime achievement award from the Genesis Prize Foundation — while being lauded as "an outstanding Jewish jurist whose fearless pursuit of human rights, equality and justice for all stems from her Jewish values." — but omitted to mention either the Palestinians or the injustice of their brutal persecution. Her omission reflected the double standard perception of universal justice by many westerners, Israelis, and diaspora Jews.

The only stable state is the one in which all men are equal before the law.
Aristotle (384–322 BCE)

Zionist chicanery was also employed during the First World War in which Germany — despite being in the process of winning — offered Britain and France a negotiated peace deal. The Rothschild bankers, however, wanted to prevent that from happening because apart from making money from the war, they also had an endgame of getting Palestine for a militarised Jewish State that could be used to promote and protect their worldwide business interests. That being the case, Rothschild agent Dembitz Brandeis sent a Zionist delegation to Britain with the promise to bring the US into the war on condition that Britain gave Palestine to the Zionists.

Meanwhile, in spite of being reelected on the back of a promise to keep the US out of the war, President Wilson obliged the Rothschilds and Zionism by having the US join and prolong the conflict. Of the 4.7 million Americans who served, 116,516 died and some 320,000 became sick or were wounded. The sacrifice of American lives to fulfil Zionist policies continues to this day in keeping with Israel's desire for the division, destruction, or political subservience of neighbouring Arab countries.

Before that war ended on November 11, 1918, the Rothschilds prevailed on the British government to issue the following letter in November 1917 which was subsequently and erroneously dubbed as the Balfour Declaration:

Foreign Office
November 2nd, 1917

Dear Lord Rothschild,
I have much pleasure in conveying to you, on behalf

*of His Majesty's Government, the following decla-
ration of sympathy with Jewish Zionist aspirations
which has been submitted to and approved by the
Cabinet.*

*His Majesty's Government view with favour the es-
tablishment in Palestine of a national home for the
Jewish people and will use their best endeavours
to facilitate the achievement of this object it being
clearly understood that nothing shall be done which
may prejudice the civil and religious rights of existing non-Jewish communities in Palestine or the
rights and political status enjoyed by Jews in any
other country.*

*I should be grateful if you should bring this decla-
ration to the knowledge of the Zionist Federation."*

Signed
Arthur James Balfour

The letter's stipulation of "it being clearly understood
that nothing shall be done which may prejudice the civil and religious rights of existing non-Jewish communities
in Palestine," was reiterated in 1919 when President Wilson
dispatched the King-Crane Commission to areas of the former Ottoman Empire to seek opinions on their future governance. In the section concerning Palestine and Zionism, the
report explicitly stated the following:

*If the strict terms of the Balfour statement are ad-
hered to, it can hardly be doubted that the extreme*

Zionist program must be greatly modified. For a "national home for the Jewish people" is not equivalent to making Palestine into a Jewish State; nor can the erection of such a Jewish State be accomplished without the greatest trespass upon the "civil and religious rights existing non-Jewish communities in Palestine." The fact came out repeatedly in the Commission's conference with Jewish representatives, that the Zionists looked forward to a practically complete dispossession of the present non-Jewish inhabitants, by various forms of Purchase.

The non-Jewish population of Palestine, nearly nine-tenths of the whole, are emphatically against the entire Zionist program. To subject a people so minded to unlimited Jewish immigration, and to steady financial and social pressure to surrender the land, would be a gross violation of the peoples' rights. No British officer, consulted by the Commissioners, believed that the Zionist program could be carried out except by force of arms . . . Decisions, requiring armies to carry out, are sometimes necessary, but they are surely not gratuitously to be in the interests of a serious Injustice. The initial claim, often submitted by Zionist representatives, that they have a right to Palestine, based on an occupation of two thousand years ago, can hardly be seriously considered.

In view of all these considerations, and with a deep sense of sympathy for the Jewish cause, the Commissioners feel bound to recommend that only a greatly reduced Zionist program be attempted, and even that, only very gradually initiated. This would have to mean that Jewish immigration should be definitely limited, and that the project for making Palestine distinctly a Jewish commonwealth should be given up.

On 26 November 1947, when it became apparent to Zionists and their supporters that the UN vote on the Partition of Palestine would be short of the required two-thirds majority in the General Assembly, they filibustered for a postponement until after Thanksgiving thereby gaining time to get the US to threaten the loss of aid to nations such as Greece — which planned on voting against — into changing their votes. US President Truman — also threatened with loss of Jewish support in the upcoming Presidential election — later noted:

The facts were that not only were there pressure movements around the United Nations unlike anything that had been seen there before, but that the White House, too, was subjected to a constant barrage. I do not think I ever had as much pressure and propaganda aimed at the White House as I had in this instance. The persistence of a few of the extreme Zionist leaders — actuated by political motives and engaging in political threats — disturbed and annoyed me.

On 29 November 1947 the UN voted for a modified Partition Plan — despite Arab opposition on grounds that it violated UN charter principles of national self-determination — recommending the creation of independent Arab and Jewish States with a Special International Regime for the City of Jerusalem. The resolution's adoption prompted the 1947–48 conflict including atrocities by Zionist terror gangs whose genocidal brutality was responsible for the murder of thousands of unarmed Palestinian civilians and the forced exodus — a reality and not a myth like the exodus of the Israelites from Egypt — of more than 750,000 others.

At the time, the general consensus of opinion was that Israel's contentious creation had been permitted as a conscious and wilful act of Holocaust compensation which included toleration of the crimes committed against humanity. Since then, Israel has steadfastly adhered to that successful tactic of blackmail, bribery, and bullying to suppress and silence — with accusations of anti-Semitism and/or Holocaust denial — any criticism of its blatant violations and arrogant disregard for international Law.

On May 14, 1948, on the day in which the British Mandate over Palestine expired, the Jewish People's Council gathered at the Tel Aviv Museum, and approved the following proclamation — read by David Ben-Gurion — declaring the establishment of the State of Israel. The new state was recognised that same evening by the US and three days later by the USSR.

The Land of Israel was the birthplace of the Jewish people. Here, their spiritual, religious, and national

*identity was formed. Here, they achieved indepen-
dence and created a culture of national and universal significance. Here, they wrote and gave the Bible
to the world . . . In the year 1897, the First Zionist Congress, inspired by Theodor Herzl's vision of
the Jewish State, proclaimed the right of the Jewish
people to national revival in their own country . . .
This right was acknowledged by the Balfour Declaration of November 2, 1917 . . . The Nazi holocaust, which engulfed millions of Jews in Europe,
proved anew the urgency of the reestablishment of
the Jewish state . . . The survivors of the European
catastrophe, as well as Jews from other lands, proclaiming their right to a life of dignity, freedom and
labor, and undeterred by hazards, hardships, and
obstacles, have tried unceasingly to enter Palestine
. . . Accordingly, we, the members of the National
Council, representing the Jewish people in Palestine
and the Zionist movement of the world, met together
in solemn assembly today, the day of the termination
of the British Mandate for Palestine, and by virtue
of the natural and historic right of the Jewish people
and of the resolution of the General Assembly of the
United Nations, hereby proclaim the establishment
of the Jewish State in Palestine, to be called Israel
. . . The State of Israel will be open to the immigration of Jews from all countries of their dispersion;
will promote the development of the country for the
benefit of all its inhabitants; will be based on the
precepts of liberty, justice, and peace taught by the*

Hebrew Prophets; will uphold the full social and political equality of all its citizens, without distinction of race, creed, or sex; will guarantee full freedom of conscience, worship, education, and culture; will safeguard the sanctity and inviolability of the shrines and Holy Places of all religions; and will dedicate itself to the principles of the Charter of the United Nations . . .

The declaration, laced with blatant deceptions gratifyingly gift wrapped with well-intentioned promises — including the one that it "will promote the development of the country for the benefit of all its inhabitants" — trademarked a strategy of deliberate deception with outrageous chutzpah that Zionism has pursued in the name of all Jews to this day. That strategy — hardly in keeping with the Jewish concept of *"Tikkun olam"* (Hebrew for "world repair") which connotes social action and the pursuit of social justice — has since been addressed in August 2016 by the Centre For Constitutional Rights in an item titled *The Genocide of the Palestinian People:An International Law and Human Rights Perspective.*

While there has been recent criticism of those taking the position that Israel is committing genocide against Palestinians, there is a long history of human rights scholarship and legal analysis that supports the assertion. Prominent scholars of the international law crime of genocide and human rights authorities take the position that Israel's policies toward the Palestinian people could constitute a form of genocide. Those policies range from the 1948 mass killing and displacement of Palestinians to a half-century of military occupation and, correspondingly, the discriminatory legal regime governing Palestinians, repeated military assaults on Gaza, and official Israeli statements expressly favouring the elimination of Palestinians . . . Francis Boyle, a professor of international law, testified in 2013 that: "The Palestinians have been the victims of genocide as defined by the 1948 Convention on the Prevention and Punishment of the Crime of Genocide."[17] He argued that:For over the past six and one-half decades, the Israeli government and its predecessors in law — the Zionist agencies, forces, and terrorist gangs — have ruthlessly implemented a systematic and comprehensive military, political, religious, economic, and cultural campaign with the intent to destroy in substantial part the national, ethnical, racial, and different religious group (Jews versus Muslims and Christians) constituting the Palestinian people.

A further example of Israeli violations occurred on February 6, 2017, when the Knesset plenum approved the Law for the Regulation of Settlement in Judea and Samaria. The law covered Israeli settlements that were built "in good faith" or with "the consent of the state" and in effect retroactively legalised illegal Israeli settlements in the West Bank Area C as designated in the Oslo Accords. Though the law was struck down in June 2020 by Israel's Supreme Court with a nearly unanimous decision that the Regulation Law was "unconstitutional" — on the grounds that it "violates the property rights and equality of Palestinians, and gives clear priority to the interests of Israeli settlers over Palestinian residents" — the Likud Party called the ruling "unfortunate" and vowed to "work to legislate a new law."

The overturning of that law, however, will not affect the reality of Apartheid Israeli discrimination against Palestinians because in July 2018, the Israeli Knesset passed the highly controversial nation-state law which strictly speaking merely gave expression to existing realities. The law was criticised for discriminating against minorities, running counter to democratic values, and undermining the principle of equality. It was also evident that the law's main supporters on the government side had some hidden and more far-reaching intentions which included placing Jewish collective rights above individual rights and freedoms. The law was also a further indication of the government's deliberate policy of leading Israel away from a more liberal democracy, and towards a majoritarian democracy: a policy that affects the Supreme Court as a defender of liberal principles.

Basic Law: Israel as the Nation-State of the Jewish People

1 — Basic Principles

A. The land of Israel is the historical homeland of the Jewish people, in which the State of Israel was established.

B. The State of Israel is the national home of

the Jewish people, in which it fulfils its natural, cultural, religious, and historical right to self-determination.

C. *The right to exercise national self-determination in the State of Israel is unique to the Jewish people.*

2 — Symbols of the State

A. *The name of the state is "Israel".*

B. *The state flag is white, with two blue stripes near the edges and a blue Star of David in the centre.*

C. *The state emblem is a seven-branched menorah with olive leaves on both sides and the word "Israel" beneath it.*

D. *The state anthem is "Hatikvah".*

E. *Details regarding state symbols will be determined by the law.*

3 — Capital of the State

Jerusalem, complete and united, is the capital of Israel.

4 — Language

A. *The state's language is Hebrew.*

B. *The Arabic language has a special status in the state; Regulating the use of Arabic in state institutions or by them will be set in law.*

C. This clause does not harm the status given to the Arabic language before this law came into effect.

5 — Ingathering of the Exiles

The state will be open for Jewish immigration and the ingathering of exiles.

6 — Connection to the Jewish people

A. The state will strive to ensure the safety of the members of the Jewish people and of its citizens in trouble or in captivity due to the fact of their Jewishness or their citizenship.

B. The state shall act within the Diaspora to strengthen the affinity between the state and members of the Jewish people.

C. The state shall act to preserve the cultural, historical, and religious heritage of the Jewish people among Jews in the Diaspora.

7 — Jewish Settlement

The state views the development of Jewish settlement as a national value and will act to encourage and promote its establishment and consolidation.

8 — Official Calendar

The Hebrew calendar is the official calendar of the state and alongside it the Gregorian calendar will be used as an official calendar. Use of the Hebrew calendar and the Gregorian calendar will be determined by law.

9 — Independence Day and Memorial Days

A. *Independence Day is the official national holiday of the state.*

B. *Memorial Day for the Fallen in Israel's and Holocaust and Heroism Remembrance Day are official memorial days of the State.*

10 — Days of Rest and Sabbath

The Sabbath and the festivals of Israel are the established days of rest in the state; Non-Jews have a right to maintain days of rest on their Sabbaths and festivals; Details of this issue will be determined by law.

11 — Immutability

This Basic Law shall not be amended, unless by another Basic Law passed by a majority of Knesset members.

A global chorus of criticism regarding the law was led by the EU stating that the legislation would complicate a two-state solution — something Israel never planned on having, nor will ever willingly accept — to the Israel-Palestinian conflict. The EU joined Israeli Arab political leaders, Israeli opposition politicians, and liberal Jewish groups in the US in flagging up concern, with some saying the law amounted to "apartheid," which incidentally has been a reality since 1948. The expression of deep concern by the international community was as usual — whenever Israel is concerned — just a lot of hot air that quickly cooled with nothing positive being accomplished.

> *Actually — and this was where I began to feel seriously uncomfortable — some such divine claim underlay not just "the occupation" but the whole idea of a separate state for Jews in Palestine. Take away the divine warrant for the Holy Land and where were you, and what were you? Just another land-thief like the Turks or the British, except that in this case you wanted the land without the people. And the original Zionist slogan — "a land without a people for a people without a land" — disclosed its own negation when I saw the densely populated Arab towns dwelling sullenly under Jewish tutelage. You want irony? How about Jews becoming colonisers at just the moment when other Europeans had given up on the idea?*
> **Christopher Hitchens (1949-2011), English-American intellectual, philosopher, and social critic, Hitch 22: A Memoir**

13

State Intelligence Agencies

As well as its rapacious land grabbing and illegal annexations, Israel — a relatively small nation with a Jewish population of around 7.2 million — nonetheless has a national intelligence agency (Mossad) that directly employs over 7,000 people with a budget of 10 billion shekels (US $2.73 billion), making it the second-largest Western espionage agency after America's Central Intelligence Agency (CIA). Though Mossad came into being following the end of the British Mandate in 1948 when the State of Israel was created in Palestine, its intelligence and security roots dated back to 1940 when Shai, an acronym for *Sherut Yediot*, was established.

During the Second World War the British Special Operations Executive (SOE) provided the Haganah with weapons, training, and funding in return for linguistic experts and operatives. Shai, which as Haganah — the intelligence arm of the Zionist terrorist paramilitary force during the time of the British Mandate — had begun operating on a worldwide basis when the Jewish Agency was founded in 1929 at the Zionist Congress in Zurich, Switzerland. The Jewish Agency ⊠ which then consisted of Zionists, non-Zionists, and a substantial number of American Jews, was effectively under Zionist control ⊠ having been ostensibly created to aid and sustain Jewish communities in Palestine, actually served as a cover for Shai's extension of covert operations in Western Europe and the US.

Shai's objectives between 1923 and 1948, were to promote the establishment of an independent Jewish State; to penetrate Mandatory installations in order to keep the Zionist leadership informed about British viewpoints and intended future actions; to gather political intelligence that would be useful for Zionist propaganda; to infiltrate Arab and anti-Zionist organisations in Palestine and neighbouring nations; to monitor and control all extremist Jewish groups in Palestine and abroad; to provide security for smuggled arms and illegal immigration programs; and to obtain information about Nazi Germany so as to provide security for Jewish underground and escape channels throughout Europe before, during, and after World War Two.

The service components of the Shai organisation included Political Intelligence; Counterespionage and Internal Security; Military Intelligence; Police Branch of Military Intelligence; and Naval Intelligence and Security, which all worked independently on behalf of the different ministries to which they were attached. The independence of these various service units ⊠ with all of them represented in the main West European capitals ⊠ coupled with postwar chaos, inevitably meant that they often acted independently with competition being rife between them.

By April 1951, the Israeli Prime Minister David Ben-Gurion and his cabinet — profoundly concerned by the prevalent covetousness, mutual mistrust, and escalating costs of uncoordinated efforts between the different service units — decided on a complete overhaul of Israel's intelligence and security community. Consequently, under the forceful direction of Reuven Shiloah, Mossad's first Director, the services were reorganised according to functions and responsibilities with an established mechanism to coordinate operations. The Naval Intelligence and the Security Service were integrated; the embryonic air intelligence unit became a part of Military Intelligence; the Ministry of Foreign Affairs retained the Research Division; Shin Bet (the internal security service) remained intact apart from internal changes; and the Political Intelligence Service became independent from the Ministry of Foreign Affairs and was reorganised as the Secret Intelligence Service or Mossad.

Israel's intelligence services consequently coalesced into the three-pronged community that has more or less survived to this day: Aman, the military intelligence arm that supplies information to the Israeli Defence Force; the Shin Bet, responsible for internal intelligence, counter-terror and counter-espionage; and the Mossad, which deals with covert activities beyond the country's borders. It was a coalescence that prioritised having a strong army and intelligence services over diplomacy. Ben-Gurion kept tight control over the agencies thereby creating a concentration of covert and political, power.

This was all officially kept hidden from the Israeli public with officials being forbidden by Ben-Gurion from acknowledging or revealing the existence of that sprawling web of official organisations. Mentioning the names Shin Bet and Mossad in public was actually prohibited until the 1960s. Because of their existence being finally acknowledged, Ben-Gurion prevented the creation of any legal basis for examining the conduct of operations by those agencies. This enabled "state security" to initiate questionable actions and conduct numerous operations that under democratic control, supervision, accountability, and oversight would have been subject to criminal prosecution and lengthy incarceration. The most notable example of such impunity, was Ben-Gurion giving himself the authority to order targeted killings — extra-judicial executions — despite Israeli law not having a death penalty.

Mossad

Mossad's initial principal objectives had included targeting the Arab states with regards to their capabilities and intentions toward Israel; their relations with the USSR and other major powers; their official facilities and representatives throughout the world; their leaders and their internal and inter-Arab politics; general morale, military preparedness, unit formations, and equipment for the military forces; obtaining information on secret US policies or decisions that might affect Israel; acquiring (stealing) scientific intelligence from the US and other developed countries; ascertaining the nature of East European government policies toward Israel and their position on Jewish emigration; close monitoring of anti-Zionist activity throughout the world; and getting political and economic intelligence in other areas of possible interest such as in Africa. Extra special efforts were also made to counter Arab propaganda and to neutralise anti-Zionist activity. More recently, extra operational activity ⊠ covert political, economic and paramilitary action programs ⊠ had been devoted to combating Arab terrorism which was the result of Israel's illegal and repressive occupation of the Palestinian Territories.

The main thrust of Mossad's activity was concerned with the acquisition of positive foreign intelligence, the initiation of robust political action, and the employment of ruthless counterterrorist operations. Mossad's acquisition of positive intelligence required conducting agent operations against Arab nations, their official representatives, and their installations throughout the world with particular emphasis on Western Europe and the US where Arab national interests in the Near East were in conflict with those of Israel. Collection of information was not only on the disposition, morale, armaments, equipment and quality of leadership of every Arab Army that may become involved in future conflicts, but also on Arab commercial activity regarding the purchase of Western weaponry and the recruitment of economic, military, and political experts. As to the Arab recruitment of experts, Mossad endeavoured to recruit such experts as Israeli intelligence agents or at least dissuade them from either helping the Arabs or to establish their precise functions.

A further Mossad responsibility was to instigate squabbles and rancour amongst the Arabs so as to reduce Western sympathy for them; to monitor and counteract Arab propaganda; to detect and thwart Arab terrorism; and to go on the offensive against terrorists especially in the Near East and Western Europe. Having a mixed Christian, Druze and Moslem population consequently made Lebanon an attractive arena for Israel's mischievous intelligence and military operations where covert assets were employed to assist with mounting paramilitary and executive action operations against Palestinian freedom fighters and their leaders, personnel, and installations in Lebanon. Israel also provided support ⊠ as was the case in the Sabra and Shatila massacre of Palestinian refugees ⊠ for Christian rightists in the Lebanese civil war.

Israel's historic animosity towards Lebanon has its roots in a covetous desire for the waters of the Litany River — scarcity of water has further helped to heighten regional tensions in the Arab-Israeli conflict — which is why Israel has repeatedly endeavoured to occupy parts of southern Lebanon while periodically punishing the Lebanese with what can only be described as terrorist atrocities. The recent August 4, 2020, alleged explosion of 2,750 tons of ammonium nitrate stored at the port of Beirut — obliterating the city's main commercial hub and damaging large swathes of the Lebanese capital — was unlikely to have been an accident as claimed and probably involved Israel in some way. The blast, the most destructive in the country's conflict-ridden history, killed some 180 people, wounded more than 6,000, made an estimated 300,000 homeless, and caused some $15 billion worth of damage.

This brings to mind the March 2, 2007, interview with Democracy Now's Amy Goodman, when US General Wesley Clark, the former Europe Head of NATO, listed a total of seven countries including Iraq, Syria, Lebanon, Libya, Somalia, Sudan and Iran that had to be "taken out" with Israel's help. A short video of the interview can be viewed on YouTube: *General Wesley Clark Reveals Middle East Invasion Was Pre-Planned & Iran is NEXT*. Such thinking was in keeping with that of the Project for the New American Century (PNAC) — founded in 1997 by William Kristol and Robert kagan and stacked with other neoconservative Jewish Americans — "to promote American global leadership." Of the twenty-five people who signed PNAC's founding statement of principles, ten went on to serve in the Bush administration, including Dick Cheney, Donald Rumsfeld, and Paul Wolfowitz who all played key roles in shaping US foreign policy including support for the Iraq War because of Saddam Hussein's alleged possession of "weapons of mass destruction" which did not exist.

In addition to its operations against the Arabs, Mossad acquired economic, political, and scientific intelligence in both the Eastern and Western worlds with a view to protecting the State of Zionist Israel in particular, and as an afterthought, Jews in general. Counterintelligence efforts — including the use of tactics to silence anti-Israel criticism and factions in the West — were concentrated in the Soviet Union, the United States, Europe, and at the United Nations where negative policy decisions could hinder Israel's Zionist goals.

Mossad's initial stages of training for candidates incorporated a compulsory Basic Operations course for recruits and lower ranking personnel; an Operations course; and a Field Operations course. Completion of the entire training program took almost two years and was usually given to classes of around twelve recruits. Most of the training occurred within Tel Aviv and surrounding areas with a combination of instructors consisting of some on permanent assignment, intelligence officers on temporary tours of duty, and personnel from headquarters including the Director of Mossad and department directors, who occasionally gave lectures on their areas of expertise.

An advanced services school in Jerusalem offered specialised two to three month courses on world political affairs, Israel's economic and political objectives, newly developed technical operational aids, and up to date information on foreign intelligence services. Some of the younger officer recruits — who were not up to scratch in certain areas of higher education or languages — were sent to universities abroad, where their pursuit of advanced degrees also served as cover for their extracurricular Mossad activities. One of the established requirements for Mossad intelligence officers was fluency in Arabic with a nine-month, intensive Arabic language course being available. Mossad officers who were destined for Arab operations received further training with work in the Administered Territories — such as the Sinai where they combined running Bedouin agents into Egypt with Military Intelligence — for several years so as to hone their language skills before being posted abroad.

Other tasks of vital importance for Mossad were its establishment of special relationships with both highly placed individuals and government offices in every country of importance to Israel; liaising with Zionists and other sympathisers — who could support Israeli intelligence efforts — within Jewish communities throughout the world; carefully grooming such contacts to serve as channels for information, disinformation, propaganda, and other functions; directing covert operations throughout Africa, Europe, the Far East including Southeast Asia, the Near East, North America, and South America. Covert operations were generally conducted through official and semiofficial Israeli establishments, deep cover companies and organisations of which some were especially created or adapted for specific objectives, and infiltration of non-Zionist national and international Jewish organisations such as the International Jewish Anti-Zionist Network (IJAN).

Responsibilities for intelligence officers working under cover of diplomatic establishments included facilitating exchange of information with local service officials, managing communications, providing accommodation addresses and finance channels, and identifying targets of interest for agents. Official organisations used for cover included Israeli Purchasing Missions, Israeli Government Tourism, El Al and Zim offices (shipping agents), Israeli construction companies, industrial groups, and international trade organisations. For activities in which the Israeli Government can never admit involvement, use was made of deep cover or illegal individuals who employed a more subtle and distant approach infiltrating their targets. This was particularly true in Arab countries because many Israelis had come from Arab countries where they were born and raised and consequently appeared more Arab than Israeli in attitude, demeanour, and speech. By providing well researched backgrounds and CVs, forged passports, and identity papers from Arab and Western nations, Mossad had managed to successfully operate with agents in Arab nations with Israelis disguised and documented as Arabs or citizens from European nations.

Because of Israel's "Law of Return" there was no shortage of Jewish emigrants to Israel with both language skills and knowledge of their former countries of residence who could be useful to Mossad in helping to analyse intelligence information that would contribute to the overall operational efficiency of its agents. Such people were equally useful for passing themselves off as citizens of their respective nations of origin with the assistance of Israel's penchant for counterfeiting and forging identity documents.

Mossad was also dependent on a variety of Jewish communities and organisations overseas for the recruitment of agents and the gathering of relevant information. Zionism's aggressive ideology ⊠ which stressed that all Jews belonged to Israel to which they must return ⊠ had created some difficulty for getting support for Mossad's intelligence operations from anti-Zionist Jews, but this had been mostly countered by ensuring that Mossad agents operated with discreet and utmost tact within Jewish communities so as to avoid either embarrassment or repercussions for Israel.

One important role played by Mossad was to assist Israel to quickly accelerate development of its technological, scientific, and military capabilities by exploiting scientific exchange programs with naive and trusting nations such as the US. Apart from the overt large-scale acquisition of published scientific papers and technical journals from all over the world, Israel also devoted considerable intelligence resources to covertly obtain scientific and technical information by gaining access to various classified defence projects in the US and other Western nations.

Another major Mossad target for infiltration ⊠ using diplomatic and journalistic cover ⊠ was the United Nations which not only sponsored international exchanges in all fields, but was also of importance in the settlement of disputes between Israel and Arab nations. Agent recruitment was almost exclusively from people of Jewish origin despite the occasional conflict between individual dedication to the Zionist State of Israel and loyalty to a Jewish homeland. Recruitment of goyim dupes was a comparative rarity.

Assistance from Arabs — whether directly or indirectly — was usually due to some financial inducement which caused the Israelis to regard such sources as being unreliable. Mossad found it easier to recruit Palestinians over whom they had more control either because of unjustly imprisoned relatives under Administrative detention orders, or of bank assets frozen by Israel following the Nabka in 1948. In such cases the release of relatives or bank assets was made in exchange for providing information or other assistance to Mossad.

The agency was also always ready to exploit any weakness or motivation of potential agents or collaborators with blackmail, bribery, and bullying being standard methods of persuasion; by taking advantage of vulnerabilities such as fear, jealousy, rivalry, and political dissension; and even by false-flag recruitment tactics whereby citizens of Western European nations under the cover of a national NATO intelligence organisations are employed for operations in Arab target countries.

With no apparent constraints on Mossad's covert but nonetheless audacious criminality — because of it being separate from Israel's democratic institutions — there is nothing to define its purpose, objectives, roles, missions, powers, and budget; it is exempt from the State's constitutional laws; and is consequently regarded as a dangerous deep state now credited with over 2,700 assassination operations (not counting the failed attempts or ones unacknowledged as was the case with Yasser Arafat's death in 2004) which by far exceed those carried out by any other intelligence service the West. Between 2010 and 2012, four Iranian nuclear scientists were assassinated with another being wounded in a failed attempt. In November 2020 another such scientist, Mohsen Fakhrizadeh, was also assassinated.

The command-and-control systems, war rooms, information gathering technology, and pilotless drone aircraft that now serve the US and its allies were all to a greater extent developed in Israel and field tested on Palestinian "guinea pigs." The inhumanity of such field testing is hardly befitting a much touted and supposedly civilised democracy, let alone a people claiming to have been chosen by "god himself." The moral and legal concerns raised by state-sponsored killing — including the existence of legal systems for secret agents that is separate from that applicable to the rest of Israel's population — are also a further indication of Israel's continued moral decline.

Mossad is a crime organisation with a license which made working for it the fun part.
Tamir Pardo, former Mossad chief (2011-2015)

Shin Bet

Though it is Mossad that is more renowned globally, Shin Bet — known by its Hebrew acronym "Shabak — with its past links to violent Zionist paramilitary groups before Israel's creation, is nonetheless one of the most powerful security organisations in the world. The agency is infamous for torturing and killing Palestinian detainees with the UN Committee Against Torture having condemned it for using violent interrogation techniques.

However, the methods of interrogation, which were described by nongovernmental organisations on the basis of accounts given to them by interrogatees and appear to be applied systematically, were neither confirmed nor denied by Israel. The Committee, therefore, must assume them to be accurate. These methods include: (1) restraining in very painful conditions, (2) hooding under special conditions, (3) sounding of loud music for prolonged periods, (4) sleep deprivation for prolonged periods, (5) threats, including death threats, (6) violent shaking, and (7) using cold air to chill; and are in the Committee's view breaches of article 16 and also constitute torture as defined in article 1 of the Convention. This conclusion is particularly evident where such meth-

ods of interrogation are used in combination, which appears to be the standard case.
One of the conclusions from the UN Torture Convention/Israel special report

An October 7, 2019, article in *+927 Magazine* — headlined "How Israeli doctors enable the Shin Bet's torture industry: From approving brutal interrogation techniques to writing false medical reports, doctors in Israel have taken an active role in the torture of Palestinian prisoners" — raised the question of Israeli medical ethics. Such concerns have also been dealt with by the Physicians for Human Rights – Israel (PHRI) which was founded in 1988 by a group of Israeli physicians led by Dr. Ruchama Marton. PHRI "stands at the forefront of the struggle for human rights — the right to health in particular — in Israel and the Occupied Palestinian Territory" and "works to promote a just society where the right to health is granted equally to all people under Israel's responsibility."

Since being established, Shin Bet has continued to the present day using violent interrogation methods on prisoners while denying them even the most basic of human rights, preventing them getting legal representation, and deliberately disregarding due process. The agency pays particular attention to Palestinians activists with known political connections. Shireen Essawi, a human rights lawyer, who was one of its targets, was arrested at an Israeli checkpoint in 2010, detained and subjected to violent and degrading treatment which became increasingly harsh with psychological torture becoming particularly prevalent. In 2013, on reflection, she said it had been an unforgettable ordeal.

> *They tied my hands and legs and blindfolded me, and repeatedly dragged me along the floor, slamming me against the wall.*
> **Shireen Essawi**

The Issawi family has not been fully reunited for over sixteen years because of their children's political activism which has resulted in repeated harassment and arrests. In 2014, Shireen was again arrested along with her brothers Shadi and Medhat. They were accused of "cooperating with actors working against Israel." Shireen's arrest was part of a crackdown by the Israeli authorities on lawyers who had defended Palestinian prisoners. Medhat's activism had already caused him to receive a twenty-year prison sentence. He was subsequently released in late 2013 — a few days before the release of his brother Samer — following a 266-day hunger strike. During their administrative detention, they were brought several times before a court that continuously postponed hearing their case sine die and without any reason.

Even though in October 2017 Shireen was released from an Israeli prison after being arbitrarily detained for over three and a half years, efforts to prevent her from practicing her profession continued with what could be described as psychological torture until January 2019 when, in her own words, "The so-called [Israeli] Court of Appeal handed me an order preventing me from practicing in the legal professional for the rest of my life . . . Even where our livelihoods are concerned, they declare a racist war against us . . . When the occupation intelligence services arrested me in 2010 and investigator shouted during the investigation asking: 'How did they allow a vandal from a family of vandals become a lawyer? I will come after you until I ban you from work and the bar expels you.'"

> *[Shin Bet] use psychological torture a lot. When [a Palestinian detainee] realised they'd tortured his father and wife the same way they'd tortured him, he tried to commit suicide.*
> **Ishai Menuchin, Public Committee Against Torture In Israel**

An example of Shin Bet's contempt for due process occurred in April 1984, when four armed Palestinians hijacked an Israeli bus and forced it to drive towards the Egyptian border. The hijackers were subsequently captured in the Gaza Strip by Shin Bet agents who shot and killed them in cold blood, and initially denied the killings despite eyewitness accounts. In the wake of what came to be known as the Bus 300 incident, Israel's Knesset established the Landau Commission to examine Shin Bet's activities. The commission concluded the organisation used violent methods, but that "a moderate measure of physical pressure cannot be avoided." Israeli authorities, for some inexplicable reason, seem to think that the extrajudicial killing of Palestinians is equivalent to "a moderate measure of physical pressure."

So absolute is the prohibition on torture that it is considered *jus cogens* in international law, meaning that it is and no other law can supersede it. By failing to pass any domestic legislation prohibiting torture, Israel and its courts have allowed for torture to be used in cases of "necessity," thereby giving interrogators free rein to torture Palestinian political prisoners. If that is justice according to god's chosen people, just try imagining what due process by satan's followers would be like.

Aman

Israel's Military Intelligence Directorate, or Aman, consists of a number of tactical intelligence units maintained by the individual branches of the Israeli Defence Force. A central agency collates, processes, and provides military intelligence information, as well as coordinating operations with the other intelligence agencies. Aman, nonetheless, as an independent agency produces reports for military and government use, acts as liaison between the military and government, coordinates the flow of information between civilian and military intelligence agencies, and assesses the threat of war. Following the 2006 Lebanon War — which severely damaged Lebanese civil infrastructure, and displaced approximately one million Lebanese — Aman carried out a systematic "intelligence soak" of the Gaza Strip that identified over 600 allegedly Hamas-related targets for the Israeli Air Force in the subsequent Operation Cast Lead assault on Gaza in 2008-2009.

Aman consists of three main units designated 8200, 9900, and the 504. 8200 is the largest and main information gathering unit and is charged with developing and utilising information gathering tools, analysing, processing and sharing of the gathered information to relevant officials. 8200 operates in all zones including wartime by joining combat field headquarters in order to enable a faster flow of information.

In an article that appeared on September 12, 2014, in the *Guardian* newspaper — "Any Palestinian is exposed to monitoring by the Israeli Big Brother: Testimonies from people who worked in the Israeli Intelligence Corps tell of a system where there were no boundaries" — the following excerpt was part of the testimony:

> *As a soldier in Unit 8200, I collected information on people accused of either attacking Israelis, trying to attack Israelis, desiring to harm Israelis, and considering attacking Israelis. I also collected information on people who were completely innocent, and whose only crime was that they interested the Israeli security system for various reasons. For reasons they had absolutely no way of knowing. All Palestinians are exposed to non-stop monitoring without any legal protection. Junior soldiers can decide when someone is a target for the collection of information. There is no procedure in place to determine whether the violation of the individual's rights is necessarily justifiable. The notion of rights for Palestinians does not exist at all. Not even as an idea to be disregarded.*

Any Palestinian may be targeted and may suffer from sanctions such as the denial of permits, harassment, extortion, or even direct physical injury. Such instances might occur if the individual is of any interest to the system for any reason. Be it indirect relations with hostile individuals, physical proximity to intelligence targets, or connections to topics that interest 8200 as a technological unit. Any information that might enable extortion of an individual is considered relevant information. Whether said individual is of a certain sexual orientation, cheating on his wife, or in need of treatment in Israel or the West Bank – he is a target for blackmail.

Throughout the duration of my service no one in my unit ever asked, at least not out loud, if there is anything wrong with this well-oiled system — whether the transformation of any individual into a target is a legitimate act.

When I joined Unit 8200 I was highly motivated. I passed a course and became an Arabic translator. There were things that I felt uncomfortable with in the work framework, though the importance of my role and our missions within the unit in which I served overshadowed these feelings.

There is also an elite unit, Sayeret Matkal. which is considered the best combat unit in the Israeli army and one of the best special forces units in the world. It is not part of any regional command and only responds to orders from the

Chief of General Staff. It is primarily a field intelligence-gathering unit that conducts deep reconnaissance behind enemy lines to obtain strategic intelligence as well as being tasked with counter-terrorism and hostage rescue operations beyond Israel's borders. Chief among such operations was Operation Thunderbolt (later renamed Operation Jonathan) where they stormed the airport terminal in Entebbe, Uganda on July 4, 1976, to rescue 106 Jewish and French hostages of an Air France flight hijacked by Palestinian and German terrorists. While commanding that rescue mission, Yonatan "Yoni" Netanyahu — older brother of Benjamin Netanyahu — was killed in action. Yonatan's involvement and death in that operation probably provided brother Benjamin's career with some undeserved impetus.

14

Israel's Self-Defence Claim: a Cynical Justification for Ethnic Cleansing the Palestinian People

The world must know that the Jewish people have a right to self defence like any other people.
Menachem Begin (1913-1992), head of the Zionist paramilitary organisation, the Irgun, and Prime Minister of Israel (1977-1983)

Slobodan Milosevic — who in 1999 was charged by the International Criminal Tribunal for the former Yugoslavia (ICTY) and died while on trial for crimes against humanity — was the first politician to use the term "ethnic cleansing" in April 1987 to characterise the murderous violence towards Serbs that was committed by Kosovar Albanian commanders. "Ethnic cleansing" consequently became the euphemism — initially used by the perpetrators, and later by commentators — to describe individual and mass killings, arbitrary extra-judicial executions, mass rapes, starvation, destruction of residences and religious institutions, and expulsions. Before Srebrenica, Serbian commanders used the military code-words of *"etnicko ciscenj"* ("cleansing of the region") and *"ciscenje prostor"* or *"terena"* ('cleaning the territory') for leaving nobody alive.

By July 1991, journalists and politicians had adopted the term "ethnic cleansing" so that in due course it became the official language of diplomacy and international law as applied to scenarios that somehow failed to meet the legal requirement for proof of intent to commit genocide. In 1993 the UN referred to this "new term" as *la purification ethnique, nettoyage ethnique,* or *épuration ethnique* in official French translations and used it in seven subsequent Security Council Resolutions. The UN's adoption of Milosevic's euphemism was despite its never having been formally defined or recognised as a term with specific legal status and mandated obligations, as genocide had been since the 1948 Genocide Convention.

Genocides during the twentieth century were the result of a fatal combination of social Darwinism (survival of the fittest), racist genetic theory, and fervent nationalism. Such genocides began with the Ottoman Empire's 1915 genocide of Armenians which signalled the emergence of mass murder committed by xenophobic totalitarian regimes on an unprecedented scale. The Young Turk regime in 1915 referred to the genocide of Armenians as the eradication of "dangerous microbes"; the Nazi term for "Jew-free" was *"Judenrein"*; and the Russian term for "purges" was *"chitki,"* and now for "ethnic cleansing" it is *"chischenie."*

Victim groups were initially stigmatised as carriers of

filth and disease, and then classified as "the disease" to be eradicated. Hitler referred to Jews as parasites, a plague, cancers, tumours, bacilli, bloodsuckers, blood poisoners, lice, vermin, bedbugs, fleas and racial tuberculosis on the German body. Israelis now use similar terms to describe Palestinians. From 1937 to 1949, Stalin and his secret police chief, Lavrentiy Beria, used the term "purge" when deporting ("*korenizatsiia*") over two million stigmatised members of ethnic minorities to slave labour camps in Siberia, resulting in hundreds of thousands of deaths: deaths that were in effect a calculated genocide.

The three main rationales for genocide include belonging to the "right" religion, race, or political belief; claiming to represent progress or a higher level of civilisation; and self-defence which can be used as an excuse for lethal retaliation such as that used by Apartheid Israel and its brainwashed supporters in the West who cite it as justification for the barbaric ethnic cleansing/genocide of Palestinians.

One of Israel's most successful Hasbara — propaganda portraying Israel positively on the world stage — falsehoods was the acceptance of its premise that Jews are the victims of Palestinian aggression, not only by the Israeli public, but also Jews in diaspora, Western governments, and the mainstream media who with grovelling insincerity declare with regular monotony "Israel has a right to defend itself." Israeli public relations campaigns aggressively promoting the concept of self-defence have been instrumental in helping Israeli officials avoid accountability following each of the six major assaults on Gaza since Israel withdrew its settlers from the Gaza Strip in September 2005.

> *The receptivity of the masses is very limited, their intelligence is small, but their power of forgetting is enormous. In consequence of these facts, all effective propaganda must be limited to a very few points and must harp on these in slogans until the last member of the public understands what you want him to understand by your slogan.*
> **Adolf Hitler.**

Israel has claimed that its recent attacks on Gaza are justified under international law while invoking Article 51 of the UN charter which clearly recognises the right to self-defence as an "inherent" right of States. In a statement delivered before the Security Council following the assaults on Gaza, Israel's Ambassador to the UN, Gabriela Shalev, invoked Article 51 by claiming with an inherent Israeli capacity and competence for lying, "In its military operation, Israel exercised its inherent right to self-defence, enshrined in Article 51 of the United Nations Charter. Any other State would have acted in the same manner faced with similar terrorist threats."

> *Nothing in the present Charter shall impair the inherent right of individual or collective self-defence if an armed attack occurs against a Member of the United Nations, until the Security Council has taken*

measures necessary to maintain international peace and security. Measures taken by Members in the exercise of this right of self-defence shall be immediately reported to the Security Council and shall not in any way affect the authority and responsibility of the Security Council under the present Charter to take at any time such action as it deems necessary in order to maintain or restore international peace and security.

Article 51

In response to Shalev's disingenuous assertion, opponents argued that while the right to self-defence is an inherent right of States, it was nonetheless subject to the customary rules of proportionality and necessity. They noted that Israel's massive military operations in Gaza did not meet those two conditions — the military operations being excessively violent compared to the alleged attacks that provoked them — and concluded that they were therefore illegal under international law. Israelis obviously believe that as a god chosen people they have a right to be selective about which articles of international law they want to invoke.

If you tell a lie big enough and keep repeating it, people will eventually come to believe it. The lie can be maintained only for such time as the State can shield the people from the political, economic and/ or military consequences of the lie. It thus becomes vitally important for the State to use all of its powers to repress dissent, for the truth is the mortal ene-

my of the lie, and thus by extension, the truth is the greatest enemy of the State.

Joseph Goebbels (1897-1945), Reich Minister of Propaganda of Nazi Germany

Global acceptance of Israel's frequently repeated "self-defence" justification is tantamount to complicity that allows Israel to continue adding to its illegal acts of criminal dispossession while simultaneously managing to avoid being made accountable for refusing to allow Palestinian refugees to return to their homes, expelling the Bedouin from the Negev desert, expelling Bedouin from the Jordan Valley, establishing ranches for Jews in the Negev, discriminating in budgets in Israel, and shooting at Gaza's fishermen to prevent them from earning a living. Thousands of such continuous crimes against humanity which stretch from 1948 to the present day have become the realty of everyday life for Palestinians whether they are blockaded in Gaza, divided in isolated pockets of land, citizens of Israel, living in exile, or imprisoned in refugee camps

Despite the overwhelming evidence of war crimes committed by Israeli forces, the impressive success of Israel's "self-defence" PR campaigns has continued providing its officials with the impunity and licence to use military force as and when it pleases them. Begin's contention of "a right to self defence like any other people," is apparently not applicable to the Palestinian people who in any case — as many god chosen and humane Israeli leaders are more than happy to frequently remind us — "do not exist." Regardless of such racist Israeli arrogance, the Palestinian people do exist — and it is they as a people subject to a brutal occupation — who have "a right to self defence like any other people."

Importance of the universal realisation of the right of people to self-determination and of the speedy granting of independence to colonial countries and peoples for the effective guarantee and observance of human rights.

> 1. *Calls upon all States to implement fully and faithfully the resolutions of the United Nations regarding the exercise of the right to self-determination and independence by peoples under colonial and foreign domination;*
>
> 2. *Reaffirms the legitimacy of the struggle of peoples for independence, territorial integrity, national unity and liberation from colonial and foreign domination and foreign occupation by all available means, including armed struggle;*

UN General Assembly, Resolution 37/43

Despite evidence to the contrary, Israel still holds onto its disingenuous claims that all Israel's wars, including 1967 when Israel attacked Egypt without just cause; the invasion and occupation of southern Lebanon from 1982-2000 which amongst other considerations included Israel's desire for the water of the Litani River; and the three Gaza conflicts in 2008, 2012 and 2014, were all wars of self-defence. Meanwhile Western banks and financial institutions hold billions of dollars worth of shares in companies that sell weapons, military equipment and technology to Israel thereby enabling, enhancing, and encouraging Israel's propensity for the brutal racial oppression of Palestinians.

A fourth generation of Palestinian children is now being brought up in refugee camps inside and outside Palestine, living in chronic poverty and denied the right to return to their family homes.

Hundreds of thousands more Palestinians suffer discrimination over access to public services, land rights and employment within Israel itself.

Israel's siege of Gaza has condemned its 1.9 million inhabitants to poverty and psychological violence on a daily basis as movement is restricted and there is an ever present threat of military force.

In the West Bank, the expansion of Israeli settlements, the continued construction of the apartheid wall, the military closure of the Jordan Valley and the annexation of East Jerusalem are creating an irreversible reality of permanent occupation.

This brutal occupation, the building of the apartheid wall and ongoing military oppression can only be continued with the support of countries and companies that continue to back Israel through business and investment.

War On Want

Part of Israel's "self-defence" has for decades also been reliant on the Shin Bet torture of Palestinians despite their right to not be subjected to ill-treatment or torture be it physical or psychological. As one of the few human rights considered absolute, torture may never be balanced against other rights and values and cannot be suspended or limited, including in difficult circumstances. Even Israel's High Court of Justice (HCJ) in 1999 ruled that Israeli law did not empower security agencies to use physical means of interrogation such as the specifically discussed methods of painful binding, shaking, placing a sack over a person's head for prolonged periods of time, and sleep deprivation. The justices did, however, state that interrogators who exceeded their authority and use such "physical pressure" may not necessarily bear criminal responsibility for their actions, if they are later found to have used these methods in a "ticking bomb" situation as a necessity for defence purposes. As far as Israelis are concerned, the mere existence of any Palestinian is a "ticking bomb" situation.

Needless to say the High Court's ruling was ignored by Shin Bet interrogators who as a god chosen people continued with impunity to detain their Palestinian victims in inhuman conditions within narrow, windowless cells that are sometimes mouldy, foul-smelling and constantly lit with artificial lighting painful to the eyes. Some detainees reported being held in solitary confinement and completely cut off from their surroundings; others reported exposure to extremes of heat and cold, as well as sleep deprivation; and many described abominable hygienic conditions with prison authorities not allowing them to shower, change clothes, brush their teeth, or even use toilet paper. The food was deliberately lacking in both quality and quantity with detainees losing weight while in custody. During interrogations they are forced to sit bound to a chair without moving for hours, and sometimes even for days on end. Detainees were subjected to shouting, violence, and threats that included harm to themselves and their relatives. The perpetrators of such inhumanity can hardly be regarded as "people," let alone ones chosen by god.

The majority of psychologically or physically abused Palestinians during interrogations had no means of complaining until the interrogations were over because they were invariably denied the right to consult with counsel, and HCJ petitions against the denial of this right have been repeatedly dismissed. Furthermore, detainees are usually not afforded the opportunity of coming before a judge in a remand hearing and in any case most hearings are cursory with detainees being denied legal representation. While detainees may approach the judge on their own initiative, they tend to avoid revealing what they had undergone for fear of reprisals from their interrogators. Even when they do come forward, the Israeli authorities take no action as has been monitored and substantiated by human rights organisations. Since 2001, not a single criminal investigation has been launched into complaints against Shin Bet interrogators despite hundreds of complaints being lodged with relevant authorities. The following article of the UDHR is one that Israel chooses to disregard.

> *No one shall be subjected to torture or to cruel, in-human or degrading treatment or punishment.*
> **Article 5 of the Universal Declaration of Human Rights**

Instead of endless, disingenuous whining about being victims defending themselves while with unbelievable inhu-mane barbarity oppressing Palestinians, Israeli Jews should start taking responsibility for their dehumanisation of Pales-tinians; stop exploiting the Holocaust as justification for that dehumanisation, and recognise that Palestinians — whose opposition is not motivated by anti-Semitism but by the hei-nous crimes being inflicted upon them — were also created *"b'tselem Elohim,"* in the image of god.

The irrational depiction of Palestinians as compulsive Jew-haters is due more to Jewish trauma than to the be-haviour of Palestinians. The late Israeli scholar Yehuda Elka-na observed, that what "motivates much of Israeli society in its relations with the Palestinians is . . . a particular interpre-tation of the lessons of the Holocaust . . . But this Holocaust lens distorts how Palestinians actually behaved: not like genocidal Jew-haters, but rather like other peoples seeking national rights."

Elkana — who was a Holocaust survivor, historian, phi-losopher of science, and former rector of the Central European University in Budapest — in an article published in *Haaretz* in 1988 that challenged the role of memories of the Holocaust, which he called "the central axis of our national experience," in Israeli identity. He was critical of the custom of repeatedly taking schoolchildren to Yad Vashem — Israel's official memorial to the victims of the Holocaust — because he believed that Holocausts could happen to any people, and the message was universal.

It is paradoxical that Benjamin Netanyahu — confirming how racist hyper-nationalism plagues mainstream Israeli politics — chose Effi Eitam in December 2020 to lead Israel's Holocaust museum which before the pandemic was getting over a million visitors annually and was a mandatory stop for visiting world leaders. Apart from living in an illegal settlement in the Golan, Eitam has also long advocated the ethnic cleansing of Palestinians and called for the quashing of basic civil rights for non-Jews.

Elkana claimed that where "anomalous incidents" were reported about things done to Palestinians, the initial reaction of his acquaintances, was to either deny that such things had happened, or to simply dismiss them as symptomatic of a reciprocal hatred between Israelis and Palestinians. His own view was that:

There is no "anomalous incident" that I have not seen with my own eyes. I mean this literally: I was an eye-witness to incident after incident; I saw a bulldozer bury people alive, I saw a rioting mob tear away the life-support system from old people in the hospital, I saw soldiers breaking the arms of a civilian population, including children. For me all this is not new. At the same time I do not generalise: I do not think that they all hate us; I do not think that all Jews hate the Arabs; I do not hate those responsible for the "anomalies" — but that does not mean that I condone their acts or that I do not expect them to be punished with the full severity of the law

Elkana also confessed that his personal conviction was that:

The deepest political and social factor that motivates much of Israeli society in its relations with the Palestinians is not personal frustration, but rather a profound existential "Angst" fed by a particular interpretation of the lessons of the Holocaust and the readiness to believe that the whole world is against us, and that we are the eternal victim.

With that in mind, Elkana came to the conclusion that this was "the tragic and paradoxical victory of Hitler." Elkana believed that "any philosophy of life nurtured solely or mostly by the Holocaust leads to disastrous consequences," and that Thomas Jefferson was correct in his view that democracy and worship of the past were incompatible. While it may be the duty of the world to remember the Holocaust, he argued, "we" must learn to forget, for the penetration of such memories deep within Israeli national consciousness, in his view, was the greatest threat to the state of Israel.

15

Erasure of a People's History and Denial of Their Existence

I remember how it all began. The whole state of Israel is a millimetre of the whole Middle East. A statistical error, barren and disappointing land, swamps in the north, desert in the south, two lakes, one dead and an overrated river. No natural resource apart from malaria. There was nothing here. And we now have the best agriculture in the world? This is a miracle: a land built by people.
Shimon Peres (1923-2016), former Prime Minister and President of Israel, Maariv, 14 April 2013

Perpetuation of this concocted criminal narrative is typical of the "integrity" that has come to be expected from Israeli leaders including Shimon Peres who epitomised the disparity between Israel's image of "principled and pious innocence" in the West and the reality of its bloody, colonial, ethnic cleansing policies in Palestine. Despite the violent displacement of the Palestinians being a matter of irrefutable historical record, Peres always insisted that Zionist forces "upheld the purity of arms" during the establishment of the

State of Israel while disingenuously claiming that before Israel existed, "there was nothing here." Though regarded by many as being a war criminal — short video on YouTube: *Shimon Peres: Peacemaker Or War Criminal?* — Perez was nonetheless hypocritically awarded the Nobel Peace Prize for his role in the negotiations that led to the 1993 Oslo Accords which true to form, Israel completely ignored.

Peres, who during seven decades served as prime minister twice and as president without actually ever winning a national election outright, was also a member of 12 cabinets and had spells as defence, foreign, and finance minister. Between 1953 and 1965 — while serving first as director general of Israel's defence ministry and then as deputy defence minister — Peres, on account of his responsibilities at the time, was regarded as "an architect of Israel's nuclear weapons programme" which, to this day, Israel has managed to keep beyond the scrutiny of the International Atomic Energy Agency (IAEA), while insisting that Iran should be sanctioned for having nuclear facilities and trying to instigate the US into launching a war against the Iranians.

In 1975, as was subsequently revealed by secret minutes, Peres met with South African Defence Minister P. W. Botha and offered to sell nuclear warheads to the Afrikaner Apartheid regime despite sanctions. Peres also authorised the 1986 Mossad operation to lure nuclear whistle-blower Mordechai Vanunu from London to Rome where he was kidnapped and smuggled to Israel. Vanunu served 18 years in prison — with more than 11 being spent in solitary confinement — and after his release in 2004, he was further subjected to a broad range of restrictions on his speech and movement, was arrested several times for violations of his parole terms such as giving interviews to foreign journalists, and attempting to leave Israel. In December 2019 Israel's high court rejected a petition from Vanunu to be permitted to leave the country.

Peres also played a key role in the military regime that was imposed on the Palestinian people — with the Israeli authorities perpetrating mass land theft and displacement — and in 2005 as Vice Premier in the cabinet of Ariel Sharon, Peres reinvigorated his attack on Palestinians with plans to encourage Jewish Israelis to move to the Galilee with a "development" plan covering 104 communities. During that same year, in secret talks with US officials, Peres claimed Israel had "lost" 1,000 square kilometres of Negev land to the Bedouin, and that the "development" of the Negev and Galilee would relieve what he described as "a demographic threat." This was in spite of the fact that the Bedouin had been living on that land for centuries before Israel was even established.

In order to legitimise the unlawful appropriation of Palestinian land and property and justify illegal settlement by Jewish immigrants, Zionism invoked cleverly crafted policies to indigenise Jewish settlement — through associations with archaeology and biblical history — while simultaneously denying the history of Palestinian existence in the land that Zionism coveted. The Zionist strategy of expelling Palestinians from their land has been a slow and deliberate process that according to Israeli historian Ilan Pappé, included Zionist leaders and military commanders meeting regularly from March 1947 to March 1948, to finalise plans for ethnically cleansing Palestine.

The subsequent escalation of Zionist attacks on the British and Arabs ended up with the British deciding to hand over their responsibility for Palestine to the newly founded United Nations which betrayed the Palestinians and has continued to leave them stateless. As a result of the Zionists commencing and continuing their ethnic cleansing campaign against the Palestinians, war broke out between the budding Jewish State and neighbouring Arab countries with the UN appointing Count Folke Bernadotte, a Swedish nobleman and diplomat, as its mediator to Palestine. Recognising the plight and suffering of the Palestinians and wanting to bring about a peaceful solution that would halt the ongoing ethnic cleansing, however, made him a target for the Zionists who assassinated him in September 1948. Thus began the Zionist State's long history of assassinating anyone who got in the way of its agenda.

Bernadotte was replaced by his American deputy, Ralph Bunche, whose treacherous negotiations between Israel and the Arab states resulted in the latter conceding even more Palestinian land to the newly founded Zionist State. In May 1949, Israel was admitted to the UN and its grip over 78 percent of historic Palestine was consolidated. The remaining 22 percent became known as the West Bank and the Gaza Strip, with the former being gradually and illegally annexed, and the latter being eventually subject to an inhumane blockade.

In the meantime hundreds of thousands of Palestinian became refugees whose existence as a people is still being denied along with their right to return home. According to a recent report released by the Israel Central Bureau of Statistics, Israel — since its creation in 1948 — has facilitated the unfettered immigration to some 3.3 million Jews to Israel while simultaneously denying the Palestinian refugees the right of return to what has been their homeland for centuries. This was made possible when in 1950 Jewish immigration to Israel was legalised with the Knesset's Law of Return, which determined the right of every Jew to immigrate to Israel and become an Israeli citizen. Moreover, a child or a grandchild of a Jew, a Jew's spouse and the spouse of the child or grandchild of a Jew, who were not Jewish themselves, also became entitled to this right as a result of an amendment to the Law of Return in 1970.

Almost two-thirds of the 3.3 million immigrants who arrived in Israel since 1948 were from Europe and America with no connection to Palestine whatsoever; over half of those were from the former Soviet Union (USSR); and the remaining third originated from parts of Asia and Africa. In a special governmental operation — as part of a desperate attempt to outnumber the indigenous Palestinians — Operation Solomon (Mivtza Shlomo) was a covert Israeli military operation to airlift Ethiopian Jews to Israel from May 24 to May 25, 1991. Non-stop flights of 35 Israeli aircraft, including Israeli Air Force C-130s and El Al Boeing 747s, transported 14,325 Ethiopian Jews to Israel in 36 hours. Between then and 1999, 39,000 others were also transported so that with further emigration there are now some 150,000 Ethiopian Jews in Israel: Ethiopian Jews who have since disgracefully suffered systematic discrimination, racism, and treatment as "second-class citizens" by those civilised Ashkenazi Jews of European descent.

> *Some of us remember the dramatic rescue efforts in the last four decades by the State of Israel to bring this ancient group of Beta Israel "home," which instilled pride in Jews around the world. Yet there has been the heartbreak not only of those who perished along the way on the perilous journey by foot through deserts and hostile lands, but the suffering among the subsequent generations of Ethiopian Jews in Israel. Many of them lack decent wages, housing and educational opportunities.*
> **The New York Jewish Week, July31, 2019**

As part of its strategy to remove the Palestinians from their land, the Zionist State also worked tirelessly at erasing Palestinian heritage and culture as a means of completely wiping the existence of Palestine — and hence that of its indigenous population — off the world map.

De-Arabizing the history of Palestine is another crucial element of the ethnic cleansing. 1500 years of Arab and Muslim rule and culture in Palestine are trivialised, evidence of its existence is being destroyed and all this is done to make the absurd connection between the ancient Hebrew civilisation and today's Israel. The most glaring example of this today is in Silwan, (Wadi Hilwe) a town adjacent to the Old City of Jerusalem with some 50,000 residents. Israel is expelling families from Silwan and destroying their homes because it claims that King David built a city there some 3,000 years ago. Thousands of families will be made homeless so that Israel can build a park to commemorate a king that may or may not have lived 3,000 years ago. Not a shred of historical evidence exists that can prove King David ever lived yet Palestinian men, women, children and the elderly along with their schools and mosques, churches and ancient cemeteries and any evidence of their existence must be destroyed and then denied so that Zionist claims to exclusive rights to the land may be substantiated.

Miko Peled, Israeli peace activist and author

It was for example no secret that Moshe Dayan, the former much revered Israeli military leader, defence minister, and prodigious thief of archeological artefacts, used the strength of the Israeli army to pillage over 1,000 artefacts from Gaza — dating from the Ottoman era to the time before Christ — in an effort to erase Palestinian history. One such example was the ancient Christian Tell Umm El-'Amr or Saint Hilarion Monastery — located on coastal dunes some 10 kilometres south of Gaza City — and considered to be one of the most important in the Middle East. The monastery, which spanned more than four centuries dating from the late Roman Empire to the Umayyad period, was comprehensively plundered by the Israeli occupation.

People from the region have testified that the occupation moved everything to Israel in 1993, before the Palestinian Authority was established. In a study entitled "Looting and Salvaging the Heritage of Palestine," the Institute for Palestine Studies stated that in Palestine there once existed 12,216 archaeological sites, of which thousands were plundered and destroyed because of the occupation. Gaza represents what was once an open-air museum of different civilisations including heathens, Christians and Muslims who all enriched the city with antiquities. The first documented human settlements in the Gaza Strip date back to 6000 years and as such have been part of the Iron, Bronze, Stone, Roman, Byzantine, Islamic, Ottoman, and Modern ages. Since the 1948 establishment of Israel, the Strip has been subject to endless attacks targeting its antiquities and tangible heritage as noted by Emek Shaveh on its website.

Emek Shaveh is an Israeli NGO working to defend cultural heritage rights and to protect ancient sites as public assets that belong to members of all communities, faiths and peoples. We object to the fact that the ruins of the past have become a political tool in the Israeli-Palestinian conflict and work to challenge those who use archaeological sites to dispossess disenfranchised communities. We view heritage site as resources for building bridges and strengthening bonds between peoples and cultures and believe that archaeological sites cannot constitute proof of precedence or ownership by any one nation, ethnic group or religion over a given place.

The archaeological artefact tells a complex story which is independent of religious dictates and traditions. Listening to this story and bringing it to the wider public can enrich our culture and promote values of tolerance and pluralism. We believe that the cultural wealth of this land belongs to the members of all its communities, nations and faiths. An archaeological site is comprised not only of its excavated layers, but also its present-day attributes — the people living in or near it, their culture, their daily lives and their needs.

We view the practice of archaeology as an endeavour that can benefit the common good. The various means of involving local communities in work on the site in or near which they live, whether it is managing its heritage, engaging in joint excavations, developing the site, or devising tours that combine visits to the site with an introduction to the local community — strengthen a community's relationship to its wider environment, yield economic dividends and can bring about significant social change.

We believe that becoming familiar with the complex and diverse history revealed through archaeological research can teach us something essential about ourselves, and cultivate an appreciation of this country's vast cultural diversity, in the past and present.

Emek Shaveh

According to Emek Shaveh, the West Bank is an area rich in antiquity sites that reflect the long and varied history of the region in which Israel began taking an interest immediately following its occupation in 1967 and has since used archaeology as a vital means of tightening its control over the West Bank in defiance of international law which stipulates that archaeological sites and antiquities are cultural assets and the property of the occupied territory. Consequently the activities permissible for the Staff Officer for Archaeology (SOA) — who administers the territory on behalf of the Military Commander — and those acting on his behalf are limited to efforts for rescue and preservation of the antiquities. Israel's interpretation of protecting archaeological assets, however, deviates from the restrictions imposed on it as an occupying power and includes violations of international law.

As the SOA has control over every aspect of excavations, that control "gives Israel the power to shape the historical narrative, which it presents through archaeological discoveries. The archaeological activity is intended to prove and to strengthen the historical, religious and cultural affinity of the

Jewish people and the State of Israel to the West Bank in an attempt to appropriate history and efface the heritage and historical narratives of other peoples and cultures."

Emek Shaveh further asserts "Israel continues to use its position as the administrator of archaeological sites in the West Bank as a means to deepen its control over West Bank land, to expand the settlement enterprise, and extend the policy of dispossession of Palestinians from their lands and cultural assets. Although the takeover of land through archaeology is not the main method of achieving Israeli control over land, it is significant because of its symbolic aspects and impact on public awareness."

The Zionist agenda of expelling the Palestinian people and expropriating their land was formulated neither before nor after Israel's inception, but was actually conceived as early as June 1895 when Theodor Herzl noted the following in his diary: "We shall try to spirit the penniless population [Palestinians] across the border by procuring employment for it in the transit countries, while denying it any employment in our own country. Both the process of expropriation and the removal of the poor must be carried out discreetly and circumspectly."

Ten years later, Israel Zangwill, an ardent adherent of Zionism in Britain and top level organiser, propagandist — and coiner of the slogan "a land without a people for a people without a land" — subsequently acknowledged during a Manchester speech that Palestine was in fact populated by

Arabs: "[We] must be prepared either to drive out by the sword the [Arab] tribes in possession as our forefathers did or to grapple with the problem of a large alien population, mostly Mohammedan and accustomed for centuries to despise us." In 1905, Palestine had approximately 645,000 Muslims and Christians, and only 55,000 mainly non-Zionist or anti-Zionist Jews in the Orthodox neighbourhoods of Jerusalem and other cities.

In pursuit of its goal for the creation of a Jewish State, Zionism recognised that its main objective of getting Palestinian land and solving the "Palestinian problem" could be achieved by denying the rights of the Palestinian population, by out-populating them, or simply by displacing them. This resulted in the adoption of a three-pronged strategy consisting of large-scale Jewish immigration resulting in a Jewish majority; denying work to Palestinian farmers and labourers, thereby encouraging their migration out of Palestine; and lobbying the relevant world powers for sponsorship of a Jewish State as was the case in Britain's infamous Balfour Declaration. Though the simultaneous pursuit of these three strategies achieved variable degrees of success, it was ultimately the barbaric forced expulsions — the Naqba — that was instrumental in securing the necessary land for a Jewish State.

One of the main reasons for toleration of the atrocities perpetrated by Zionism, was the massive waves of migration caused by the 1881 pogroms in Russia which were followed by the spread of flagrant anti-Semitism throughout Eastern Europe towards the end of nineteenth century and into the start of the twentieth. In the US for example, in 1880, there were about 250,000 Jews, but by the end of World War One, there were four million. Consequently the massive waves of Jewish migration created circumstances that favoured the legitimisation of Zionism — especially in Britain and the US — and its proposal for the establishment of a Jewish State whereby Western nations with still lingering sentiments of anti-Semitism could be rid of their Jews.

Despite it becoming evident that Zionists were hellbent on delegitimising the Palestinians — something on which they were, and still are, very proficient at by either getting rid of them, denying them jobs, or simply resorting to use of forcible expulsion — the rest of the world failed miserably to act and prevent the still prevailing and brutal treatment of Palestinians by a god chosen people. Theodor Herzl was fully aware that while delegitimising the Palestinians was of vital importance, it was equally important to legitimise the Jewish presence in Palestine. To do so he began with an overture to Sultan Abdul Hamid — whose Ottoman Empire exercised ultimate control over Palestine — but was repulsed by the Sultan even after travelling to Constantinople in 1896 to ask for the sultan's grant of land in Palestine in return for helping the empire restore its depleted treasury with aid from Jewish financiers.

*Take no further steps in this matter. I cannot alien-
ate a single square foot of land, for it is not mine
but my people's. My people fought for this land and
fertilised it with their blood . . . Let the Jews keep
their millions.*

Sultan Abdul Hamid

In a subsequent approach to Germany and Kaiser Wil-
helm II, Herzl put it bluntly: "We need a protectorate and the
German would suit us best," pointing out that Zionist leaders
were German-speaking Jews and that the language used at
the First Zionist Congress the previous year had been German. Consequently a Jewish State in Palestine would intro-
duce and promote German culture. The Kaiser, however, was
not prepared to risk either provoking the Ottoman Empire
which was a major purchaser of German arms, or angering
Christians at home.

Though an attempt to recruit Britain as a sponsor of Zionism's agenda was initially unsuccessful with the British being also reluctant to upset the Ottomans, a connection was
established that eventually led to that Declaration which betrayed the Palestinian people and condemned them to a fate
of ogreish oppression that bedevilled them to this day: a fate
imposed by a people transformed from being the oppressed,
to being the hate-filled and vicious oppressors.

*The overarching goal [of each home invasion] was
to instil a sense of persecution among the Palestinians . . . It's a rolling trauma.*

An admission by Israeli soldiers — looking back with regret on the acts they carried out, night after night, at the behest of their state — in testimonies compiled in a new human rights report "A Life Exposed: military invasions of Palestinian homes in the West Bank," from Breaking the Silence, Yesh Din, and Physicians for Human Rights.

16

The Right of Return

It is also important to note that under the ICCPR the right to return does not depend on a person's status as a refugee. Every individual who has maintained "genuine and effective links" with the territories in question should enjoy the right to return, regardless of whether he or she is a refugee, that is, someone who fled persecution.

The International Covenant on Civil and Political Rights (16 December 1966)

In 1950, members of the Israeli Knesset unanimously passed a law — based on Zionism's support for, and espousal of the establishment of a Jewish State in the territory disingenuously described as the historic Land of Israel, or in reality, Palestine — giving any Jew the right to live in Israel and obtain Israeli citizenship. The members, however failed to define who was actually a Jew because it may have seemed inconceivable to them that anyone who was not a Jew, would claim to being one.

Every Jew has the right to come to this country as an Oleh [an immigrant who has made aliyah, or move to Israel].
The Law of Return, 5710 - 1950

The law was amended in 1955 and again in 1970 when the Knesset extended aliyah rights to people with one Jewish grandparent while also offering the same rights to the immigrant's spouse and children, regardless of whether those individuals were considered Jewish according to halacha (religious law). Halacha recognises as Jewish someone whose mother was Jewish or was converted to Judaism by Orthodox authorities.

Apart from being prejudiced and overly discriminatory, the law also raised questions about the moral credentials of a nation that robustly claims to be the "only democracy" in the Middle East while also bombastically asserting its army is the "most moral" in the world. To begin with, there is an obvious psychopathic absence of guilt, remorse, and shame over the discriminatory denial of a right to return for 7.2 million Palestinians who constitute the largest and longest suffering group of refugees in the world.

In his book *The Bible and Zionism: Invented Traditions, Archaeology and Post-Colonialism in Palestine-Israel*, historian Nur Masalha shows how the biblical language of a "chosen people" and "promised land" has been used by many Christian and Jewish Zionists as the "title deeds" for Israel, thereby justifying ethnic divisions and violence.

The zealously promoted Zionist premise that Jews are returning to their "promised land," is too preposterous to even consider because Ashkenazi Jews who constitute one of the largest Jewish ethnic divisions in Israel and are the most affluent and influential, were mostly descended from Jews who lived in Europe for many centuries, and not from individuals who left Israel and the Middle East around 2,000 years ago.

In 2013, Professor Martin Richards — head of the Archaeogenetics Research Group based at the University of Huddersfield — co-authored an article entitled "A substantial prehistoric European ancestry amongst Ashkenazi maternal lineages." By having an entire mitochondrial genome — transmitted exclusively through the female germ line — available for study, it was possible to draw up family trees with a much finer resolution than previously achieved. The trees showed that the four major Ashkenazi lineages in fact formed clusters within descent lines that were established in Europe some 10,000 to 20,000 years ago. The professor and his colleagues thus concluded "the great majority of Ashkenazi maternal lineages were not brought from the Levant, as commonly supposed." The researchers also estimated that overall, at least 80 percent of Ashkenazi maternal ancestry comes from women indigenous to Europe, eight percent from the Near East, and the rest being uncertain.

According to Doctor Harry Ostrer, a pathology, paediatrics, and genetics professor at the Albert Einstein College of Medicine in New York — author of *Legacy: A Genetic History of the Jewish People* — the expulsion of Jews from Mediterranean regions resulted in the twelfth century migration of Jews to Europe where they began settling in what is now Poland. On average, all Ashkenazi Jews are genetically as closely related to each other as fourth or fifth cousins.

Ashkenazim are Jewish individuals who initially built religion-based communities in Central and Eastern Europe where one of their characteristics was the use of Yiddish — a High German dialect written in the Hebrew alphabet with influence from classical Hebrew, Aramaic, and several modern languages. It is still spoken by some 200,000 people mainly in America, Israel, and Russia. Ashkenazim are now playing a leading role in Zionism's Hasbara, a word masquerading as public relations — supposedly disseminating positive information abroad about Israel — but which is actually an Israeli euphemism for energetic peddling of persistent propaganda, blatant lies, and false news.

> *"With the help of a clever persistent propaganda, even heaven can be represented to the people as hell, and the most wretched life as paradise,"*
> **Adolf Hitler, Mein Kampf, 1925**

Apart from denying Indigenous Palestinians the right to return to their centuries-old homeland, in 2018 an Israeli Basic Law was enacted specifying the nature of the State of Israel as the nation state of the Jewish people without any mention of the Palestinians:

Basic Law: Israel as the Nation State of the Jewish People

1 — Basic principles

A. *The land of Israel is the historical homeland of the Jewish people, in which the State of Israel was established.*

B. *The State of Israel is the national home of the Jewish people, in which it fulfils its natural, cultural, religious and historical right to self-determination.*

C. *The right to exercise national self-determination in the State of Israel is unique to the Jewish people.*

The racist nature of this contentious law — passed by 62 votes to 55 after a heated eight-hour debate during which opposition and Arab MKs tore up the printed text of the law, waved black flags and shouted "apartheid" — was described by Prime Minister Benjamin Netanyahu as merely enshrining into law the country's existing characteristics: "We enshrined in law the basic principle of our existence. Israel is the nation state of the Jewish people, that respects the individual rights of all its citizens . . . This is our state — the Jewish State. In recent years there have been some who have attempted to put this in doubt, to undercut the core of our being. Today we made it law: this is our nation, language and flag."

There is no crueler tyranny than that which is perpetuated under the shield of law and in the name of justice.

Charles De Montesquieu (1689-1755), French judge, man of letters, and political philosopher

During the debate, Avi Dichter, a sponsor of the law and the Knesset's Foreign Affairs and Defence Committee chairman — in the final address before voting — turned to the Arab MKs and said: "We were here before you, and we will be here after you." The law's eleven articles included the statement that Jews have the right to self-determination in Israel; appointed the contested city of Jerusalem as Israel's capital; and asserted Israel's role in preserving the cultural heritage of the Jewish diaspora.

Though the EU — along with Israeli Arab political leaders, Israeli opposition politicians and liberal Jewish groups in the US — led the mealy-mouthed chorus of irresolute criticism by adding that the legislation would complicate a two-state solution to the Israel-Palestinian conflict with some saying the law amounted to "apartheid," no tangible measures were taken and the Apartheid State got away with the lie in Section 1 of the law which defined Israel as being the historical homeland of the Jewish people and exclusively granted the Jewish people the right to national self-determination in the country. The understanding of "Jewishness" referred to the character of Judaism as a nation, as formulated by Zionism. That Zionist formulation was evident in Article 7 of the law which stressed that Jewish settlement of the land represented a national value and should, therefore, be promoted.

Approximately 750,000 Palestinians were displaced and became refugees as a result of the 1948 war which led to the founding of Israel. None of these displaced persons were ever allowed to return to the homes or communities from which they were displaced and the Palestinian refugee population has continued to grow in the time that has passed since 1948. Today there are more than 7 million Palestinian refugees scattered around the world. The reality of Palestinian forced displacement is at the core of the Palestinian experience and the Palestinian refugee issue is at the heart of the Palestinian-Israeli conflict. This paper provides background information on the history of the Palestinian refugee issue and the politics of the right of return.

American Friends Service Committee: Palestinian refugees and the right of return

So while any Jew — with no connection whatsoever to Palestine — has a right to settle in illegally Occupied Palestinian Territories, over seven million Palestinian refugees have no such right to return to the land of their forefathers. This is despite the fact that the right of return for refugees is a universal right, enshrined in international law through the Universal Declaration of Human Rights and the Geneva Convention. UN resolution 194 affirms that Palestinians have a right of return to their homes.

Everyone has the right to leave any country, including his own, and to return to his country.

Universal Declaration of Human Rights Article 13/2

As a god chosen people whom god "gave" Palestine, however, Israeli Jews are apparently not bound by the international laws that apply to inconsequential, unchosen goyim. Nor do they give a damn that their failure to respect the right of return for Palestinians refugees who were forcibly expelled from their homes in 1948 is a flagrant violation of international law and has fuelled decades of suffering on a mass scale for those "imprisoned" in camps spread across Jordan, Lebanon, Syria, the West Bank, and the Gaza Strip.

A decision taken by the US and instigated by pro-Israel organisations and wealthy Jewish individuals in 2018 to cut funding to the UN Relief and Works Agency for Palestine Refugees (UNRWA) — which provides essential services to millions of Palestinian refugees — has added to the strain on their lives and created an untenable situation: a situation that is getting closer to breaking point with the suffering, deprivation, and discrimination imposed by the Israel being ignored and unpunished because Israelis are always unconditionally exempted by virtue of their guilt-inducing reminders of the Holocaust.

> *Israel has reached an unimaginable peak of evil. And indeed many people all over the world find it hard to imagine that this is so . . . The only possible conclusion must be that Israeli evil has nothing to do with Judaism and that what is manifested in Israeli behaviour is not Jewishness . . .*
> **Nurit Peled-Elhanan, award-winning Israeli professor, author, and human rights activist at the Closing Session of the Russell Tribunal on Palestine**

WILLIAM HANNA

May this Tribunal prevent the crime of silence . . .
**Lord Bertrand Russell (1872-1970), defining the spirit
and objective of the International War Crimes Tribunal constituted in 1966**

17

The Weaponisation of Anti-Semitism

An anti-Semite used to mean a man who hated Jews.
Now it means a man who is hated by Jews.
Joseph Sobran (1946-2010), hard-hitting American
conservative writer and moralist

Is criticism of Israel actually anti-Semitism or simply a justifiable demand that Israel grants the Palestinian people the same legal and human rights that Israeli Jews demand for themselves? Even daring to ask such valid questions is liable to invite — by conflating Zionist Israel with Judaism — shrill accusations of anti-Semitism and Holocaust denial: two of the defamatory weapons in Zionism's armoury to silence criticism of its Apartheid State, and to discredit pro-Palestinian activism including Jewish organisations — such as the Jewish Voice for Peace — even to the extent of Jewish communities excommunicating those Jews with a conscience who support freedom for the Palestinian people.

> . . . *[T]he most vitriolic hatred directed towards me comes from the Jewish community. It has come be-*

tween me and my family. Over the past ten years, I have regularly received death threats, sexually threatening emails, voicemails and even letters delivered to my home. I have been barred from traveling to Israel. I almost was kicked out of rabbinical school. I have been called a kapo more times than I can count. I have developed a thick skin. One has to in order to keep doing this work . . . I always maintained it didn't seep in. But did it? Does it? . . .

Rabbi Alissa Wise in an interview — who recently stepped down as deputy director of the Jewish Voice for Peace — in an interview with Arielle Angel, Editor-in-Chief of Jewish Currents, April 1, 2021

Appropriation of the word "Semite" to be used exclusively in reference to Jews, required the Anti-Defamation League (the ADL was formed in 1913) and other Jewish groups to financially contribute, to politically coerce, and to calculatingly con the mainstream media into perpetuating the totally false premise that only Jews are semites. Use of the word "semite" and its subsequent use in the term "anti-Semite" has with malicious intent silenced critics of Israel even to the extent of wrecking their careers, their social standing, and their lives. Consequently people in politics, the media, and other public service professions cringe at the thought of being labeled, "anti-Semitic" and unfortunately — even against their own better judgment — unconscionably succumb to publicly presenting themselves as diehard supporters of an Apartheid Jewish State.

"Israelis and American Jews fully agree that the memory of the Holocaust is an indispensable weapon — one that must be used relentlessly against their common enemy . . . Jewish organisations and individuals thus labor continuously to remind the world of it. In America, the perpetuation of the Holocaust memory is now a $100-million-a-year enterprise, part of which is government funded."

According Moshe Leshem, the Israeli author of Balaam's Curse: How Israel Lost Its Way, and How It Can Find It Again, the expansion of Israeli power is commensurate with the expansion of the "Holocaust" propaganda.

So what exactly is a Semite? Diligent, impartial research will reveal that the word "Semite" has no relation with any particular religious group or ethnicity, but with a group of semitic languages: Amharic (spoken by Ethiopians and Eritreans in lands formerly known as Abyssinia); Arabic (spoken by Arabs and others in Muslim countries because it is the language of the Qur'an); Aramaic (spoken mostly by the Chaldeans of Iraq, some Catholics, and Maronite Christians at least liturgically if not socially); Hebrew (spoken by Israelis, some Jews, and others outside of Israel); and Syriac (spoken by some in various parts of Syria and the Middle East). Linguistic experts also point out that Abraham — who in biblical memory was the father of Christians, Jews, and Muslims — would have not spoken Hebrew, but Aramaic which was then the language of the land.

Furthermore, actual genetic Jews are from Spain, Portugal, North Africa and the Middle East and are known as "Sephardic," a word derived from the Hebrew "Sepharad," which relates to Spain. Sephardic Jews, because of familiarity with their own history and the true meaning of the word "semite," tend to avoid using the term "anti-Semite" because it is utter nonsense. Alternatively, Ashkenazi Jews who as recent studies have illustrated, have a maternal lineage derived largely from Europe which contradicts the notion that European Jews are mostly descendants of people who left Israel and the Middle East some 2,000 years ago.

Zionist Israeli leaders and likeminded Jews in Israel and in diaspora no longer view anti-Semitism as resulting from the bogies of the past including fear of shadowy Jewish power; of Jewish control of capitalism; or simply an ethnic nationalism that refuses to accept Jews as social equals. Consequently, anti-Semitism had to be redefined — to suit Zionism's agenda — as being any opposition to Israeli policies such as the ethnic cleansing and illegal settlement programs on land captured during the Israeli-Arab wars. The "old" antisemitism therefore, had to be repackaged — by conflating opposition to Apartheid Israel's Zionist policies with hatred of Jews — and sold to the world as the "new anti-Semitism."

The process of changing from the "old" to the "new" anti-Semitism seriously began In 1973 when then Israeli Foreign Minister Abba Eban declared, "one of the chief tasks of any dialogue with the gentile world is to prove that the distinction between anti-Zionism and anti-Semitism is not a distinction at all." In 1974, ADL — one of Zionism's rabid attack dogs — published a book titled The New Anti-Semitism that argued while it was easy to identify and comprehend Fascist anti-Semitism, there was now a new and far more dangerous form of anti-Semitism threatening Jews globally: and that threat was the criticism of Israel.

Examples of Zionism's success in weaponising anti-Semitism to silence any criticism of Israel in the European Union (EU) include the November 2018 EU declaration which called on "member states that have not done so yet to endorse the non-legally binding working definition of anti-Semitism employed by the International Holocaust Remembrance Alliance (IHRA)." The IHRA defined anti-Semitism as "a certain perception of Jews, which may be expressed as hatred toward Jews," and listed eleven examples to illustrate its meaning, several of which refer to criticism of the Israeli State.

In February 2015, French President Francois Hollande promised that his government would soon announce a raft of tough criminal laws that crack down on "anti-Semitism, racism, homophobia, and Holocaust denial." His announcement was made in a speech to CRIF, France's main Jewish communal body and Israel lobby group. Hollande added that the Internet needed to be "regulated" to suppress videos and even search results deemed to be "anti-Semitic" with an appropriate model being the laws used to prevent the dissemination of child pornography. Criminalising criticism of Israel restricts the right to the freedom of speech that was much vaunted following the January 2015 attack on the Charlie Hebdo French satirical weekly magazine. The concept of free speech in a country whose national motto is Liberté, égalité, fraternité — liberty, equality, fraternity — is, however, not applicable where Israel is concerned with pro-Palestinian activists being arrested and prosecuted for wearing T-shirts advocating a boycott of Israel. While taking part in an April 2015 ceremony at the site of Natzweiler-Struthof in Alsace — the only Nazi concentration camp on French soil — to mark 70 years since Allied troops liberated the last Nazi camps at the end of World War Two, Hollande reaffirmed not only his undying support for Apartheid Israel by urging vigilance against anti-Semitism and racism, but also his presidential hypocrisy by failing to mention that despite the lessons learnt from the Second World War, concentration camps still exist today with the world's largest being the ruthlessly blockaded Gaza Strip.

Such staunch French government support for Apartheid Israel — despite undeniable evidence of the Jewish State's crimes against humanity — has been the double standard policy of recent presidents Sarkozy, Hollande, and Macron with the latter having described anti-Zionism as "a reinvented form of anti-Semitism."

In December 2019, the French parliament adopted a controversial law linking anti-Semitism with anti-Zionism.

Critics of the law denounced the association made by the new legislation between anti-Zionism and anti-Semitism. The Final vote ended with 154 MPs in favour of the legislation, 72 against, and with many MPs, however, choosing to leave before the vote. This was in contrast to the 550 MPs who were present for the earlier vote on the social security budget. Fewer than a third of the ruling party members supported the new law, with 26 against, and 22 abstaining.

Evidence of Israel's Hasbara activities emerged in January 2017 with an Al Jazeera undercover investigation revealing — in a four-part series titled The Lobby and readily available on YouTube — how an Israeli embassy official in London was at the centre of plots to influence British student movements, lobbying groups, and politicians. Despite that revelation of attempts to subvert British democracy, Israel's Ministry of Foreign Affairs and the Ministry of Strategic Affairs had not only continued with their underhand tactics to create favourable perceptions of Israel, but had actually intensified their efforts to discredit pro-Palestinian activists, sympathisers, and politicians with accusations of anti-Semitism that eventually destroyed Labour Party leader Jeremy Corbin and had him replaced in April 2020 by the avowed Zionist Keir Starmer who refused to reveal the names of those who donated to his campaign.

At the end of October 2020, Corbin was suspended from the Labour party pending an investigation following his response to a damning report published by the Equality and

Human Rights Commission into the problem of anti-Semitism in Labour: a problem surreptitiously kindled and overtly stoked by Friends of Israel parliamentary parties, pro-Israel lobby groups, and a muzzled, mainstream media that has lost its way and betrayed the Charter for a Free Press

> *"One antisemite is one too many, but the scale of the problem was also dramatically overstated for political reasons by our opponents inside and outside the party, as well as by much of the media."*
> **Jeremy Corbin**

Jewish lobby influence had already been reconfirmed in February 2016 when it was announced that local councils, public bodies, and even some university student unions were to be banned by law from boycotting "unethical" companies, as part of a controversial government crackdown. Under the plan all publicly funded institutions were to lose the freedom to refuse buying goods and services from companies involved in the arms trade, fossil fuels, tobacco products, or Israeli settlements in the occupied West Bank. Government ministers stressed that public bodies continuing to pursue boycotts would face "severe penalties."

In April 2020, however, pro-Palestine activists secured the right to boycott Israel following a UK Supreme Court decision that ruled the government could not ban public authority pension schemes from engagement in ethical divestment policies targeting Israel. The decision reversed a 2016 government ban preventing local councils from taking part in the BDS campaign and other boycotts that run contrary to UK foreign and defence policies. This Supreme Court decision is nonetheless final.

Anti-boycott legislation — which has become a common feature in many EU countries — has alarmed concerned commentators because it could be exploited as an instrument to suppress legitimate criticism of Israel's occupation and severe violations of Palestinian human rights. That concern was expressed in an open letter by 34 Jewish historians and other scholars, including some from Yale University in the US and Tel-Aviv University in Israel:

To Europe we say: don't conflate criticism of Israel with anti-Semitism

In the context of its EU Presidency, the Austrian government will hold a high-level conference on November 21st, titled "Europe Beyond Anti-Semitism and Anti-Zionism — Securing Jewish Life in Europe."

We fully embrace and support the EU's uncompromising fight against anti-Semitism. The rise of anti-Semitism worries us. As we know from history, it has often signalled future disasters to all mankind. The rise of anti-Semitism constitutes a real threat and should be a major concern in contemporary European politics.

However, the EU also stands for human rights and has to protect them as forcefully as it fights an-

ti-Semitism. This fight against anti-Semitism should not be instrumentalised to suppress legitimate criticism of Israel's occupation and severe violations of Palestinian human rights.

Israeli Prime Minister Netanyahu was to address the conference in Austria, until he cancelled to stabilise his government. He has worked hard to conflate criticism of the state of Israel with anti-Semitism.

To our great concern, we see this conflation also in the official announcement of the conference by the Austrian government. It says: "Very often, anti-Semitism is expressed through exaggerated and disproportionate criticism of the state of Israel.

These words echo the anti-Semitism definition of the International Holocaust Remembrance Alliance (IHRA). Several examples of contemporary anti-Semitism attached to this definition, relate to harsh critique of Israel. As a result, the definition can be dangerously instrumentalised to afford Israel immunity against criticism for grave and widespread violations of human rights and international law — criticism which is considered legitimate when directed at other countries. This has a chilling effect on any critique of Israel.

Moreover, the conference announcement identifies anti-Zionism with anti-Semitism. However, Zionism, like all other modern Jewish movements in the 20th century, was harshly opposed by many Jews, as well as by non-Jews who were not anti-Semitic. Many victims of the Holocaust opposed Zionism. On the other hand, many anti-Semites supported Zionism. It is nonsensical and inappropriate to identify anti-Zionism with anti-Semitism.

We must also not forget that the state of Israel has been an occupying power for more than 50 years. Millions of Palestinians under occupation lack basic rights, freedom and dignity. As the Israeli occupation is now transforming into annexation, it is essential, more than ever, that Europe rejects efforts to restrict free speech and to silence criticism of Israel on the false ground of equating it with anti Semitism.

Europe also needs to do so for the credibility and effectiveness of its fight against anti-Semitism. Extending this fight to protect the state of Israel from criticism feeds misconceptions that Jews equal Israel – and are thus responsible for what Israel does.

As Israeli scholars, most of whom research and teach Jewish history, we say to Europe: Relentlessly fight anti-Semitism to protect Jewish life in Europe, and allow it to thrive. Do so while maintaining a clear distinction between criticism of the state of Israel, harsh as it may be, and anti-Semitism. Don't mix anti Zionism with anti-Semitism. And preserve free speech for those who reject the Israeli occupation and insist that it ends.

In the US criticism of Israel — especially in the mainstream media — is strictly forbidden as is apparent from a study released by 416Labs — a Toronto-based consulting and research firm — which confirms that US newspapers consistently portray Palestine in a more negative light than Israel; prioritise, privilege, and legitimise Israeli sources; and omit vitally important facts — including those expressed by Palestinian sources — that help to understand the illegal Israeli occupation. Based on the analysis of nearly a hundred thousand headlines dating back to 1967 in the top five US dailies — *The New York Times, Washington Post, Wall Street Journal, Chicago Tribune, and the Los Angeles Times* — the study examined the frequency of using certain words evoking a particular view or perception and came up with the following key conclusions:

"Since 1967, use of the word "occupation" has declined by 85% in the Israeli dataset of headlines, and by 65% in the Palestinian dataset; since 1967, mentions of Palestinian refugees have declined by an overall 93%; Israeli sources are nearly 250% more likely to be quoted as Palestinians; the number of headlines centring on Israel were published four times more than those centring on Palestine; words connoting violence such as "terror" appear three times as much as the word "occupation" in the Palestinian dataset; explicit recognition that Israeli settlements and settlers are illegal rarely appears in both datasets; since 1967, mentions of "East Jerusalem," distinguishing that part of the city occupied by Israel in 1967 from the rest of the city, appeared only a total of 132 times; The Los Angeles Times has

portrayed Palestinians most negatively, followed by The Wall Street Journal, Chicago Tribune, Washington Post, and lastly The New York Times; and Coverage of the conflict has reduced dramatically in the second half of the fifty-year period."

Apart from the US mainstream media's biased condemnation of criticism of Israel, the entire weight of the American establishment recently descended on Minnesota Representative Ilhan Omar for her criticism of Israel, branding her as an anti-Semite for daring to draw attention to the influence that AIPAC had on American government policy.

According to Human Rights Watch, many US states have recently begun using anti-boycott laws and executive orders to punish companies refusing to do business with illegal Israeli settlements in the West Bank. Currently more than 250 million Americans, some 78 percent of the population, live in states with anti-boycott laws or policies. Twenty-seven states have adopted laws or policies that penalise businesses, organisations, or individuals engaging in or calling for boycotts against Israel. The laws or policies in 17 of those states explicitly target not only companies refusing to do business in or with Israel, but also those refusing to do business in illegal Israeli settlements. Some states whose laws do not explicitly apply to settlements have also penalised companies that cut settlement ties.

One of the finest examples of a double standard hypocrisy occurred in July 2017 when Jewish Senator Ben Cardin —

who has throughout most of his life been an active supporter of boycotts including anti-Apartheid boycotts of Afrikaner South Africa as a means of achieving racial, social and economic justice — introduced an AIPAC-sponsored amendment to a trade bill that sought to derail the growing BDS movement.

Cardin's unstinting humanitarianism, however, does extend to the Palestinian people whose legal and human rights are undeserving of god chosen people consideration. Cardin's amendment was designed to pressure the EU — at a time it was negotiating the Transatlantic Trade and Investment Partnership (T-TIP) with the US — to abandon steps taken in recent years to oppose Israeli settlements. Such steps have included new guidelines to prevent either individuals or organisations operating within Israeli-occupied territories from receiving EU funding and a requirement that settlement products entering the EU must be labelled accordingly. As presented, the legislation would conflate Israel with the Occupied Palestinian Territories and directly contradict decades of official US policy by in part stating that "the term actions to boycott, divest from, or sanction Israel means actions by states, non-member states of the United Nations, international organisations, or affiliated agencies of international organisations that are politically motivated and are intended to penalise or otherwise limit commercial relations specifically with Israel or person doing business in Israel or in Israeli-controlled territories."

The Bill of [so-called] Rights of the US Constitution protects the basic freedoms of US citizens including freedom of speech, freedom of religion, the right to keep and bear arms, the freedom of assembly, and the freedom to petition.

Freedom of Speech / Freedom of the Press

The most basic component of freedom of expression is the right to freedom of speech. Freedom of speech may be exercised in a direct (words) or a symbolic (actions) way. Freedom of speech is recognised as a human right under article 19 of the Universal Declaration of Human Rights. The right to freedom of speech allows individuals to express themselves without government interference or regulation. The Supreme Court requires the government to provide substantial justification for the interference with the right of free speech where it attempts to regulate the content of the speech. Generally, a person cannot be held liable, either criminally or civilly for anything written or spoken about a person or topic, so long as it is truthful or based on an honest opinion and such statements.

From the First Amendment of the US Constitution

A followup documentary by *Al Jazeera, The Lobby USA*, was not allowed to air as a result of being censored by Qatar — the gas-rich Gulf emirate that funded *Al Jazeera* — coming under intense Israeli lobby pressure not to air the film. All four parts of the video, however, are available on YouTube, and a full list of the numerous Israel lobby groups in the US is available on the If America Knew website.

The documentary reveals how The Israel Project, a major advocacy group based in Washington, is running a secret influence campaign on Facebook with underhanded tactics by anti-Palestinian groups being planned and executed in collusion with the Israeli government. The director of The Israel Project admitted to *Al Jazeera's* undercover reporter "there are also things that we do that are completely off the radar. We work together with a lot of other organisations . . . We produce content that they then publish with their own name on it."

The main object and major part of the operation was apparently to create a network of Facebook "communities" that focused on the environment, feminism, history, and world affairs that were well camouflaged so that while appearing to have no connection to pro-Israel advocacy, were actually disseminating a pro-Israel and anti-Palestinian propaganda multimillion dollar funded campaign with the truth being relentlessly suppressed by means of distortions, omissions, and vilification.

The film also exposes how Israel and its lobbyists surreptitiously spy on, gratuitously smear, and openly intimidate US citizens whose consciences as decent human beings demand support for Palestinian human rights such as that spearheaded by BDS and the Israeli Information Centre for Human Rights, B'Tselem. The latter's name (literally meaning "in the image of"), was chosen by a late Member of the

Knesset and was an allusion to Genesis 1:27: "and God created humankind in His image. In the image of God did He created them." The name expressed the Jewish and universal moral edict to respect and uphold the human rights of all people.

Also exposed were semi-covert black-ops by Israel's government agency, the Ministry of Strategic Affairs in collusion with an extensive network of US-based organisations including the Israel on Campus Coalition, The Israel Project, and the Foundation for Defence of Democracies, whose name confirms that its members do have — even though it may appear sick and warped — a sense of humour.

The documentary also reveals efforts on US university campuses by pro-Israel advocacy groups who employ aggressive information warfare tactics with regularly invented smears — including false accusations of sexual assault — to discredit professors and students who espoused equal rights for Palestinians. Also targeted was the non-violent BDS movement which endeavoured to use economic pressure on Israel's government to make it comply with international law, end the military occupation of the West Bank, and halt the decades-long blockade of the Gaza Strip. Equally evident was that such smear campaigns were very well-funded to the tune of millions of dollars and involved coordination with Israel's Ministry of Strategic Affairs.

Apart from the distortion of facts and smearing BDS supporters, the documentary provides evidence that employees and volunteer pro-Israel campus groups were instructed to denounce BDS as a "racist hate group" and were asked to produce multimedia content such as memes that were considered to be dishonest and "bigoted" even by their own employees.

A further revelation has an Israeli embassy employee describing her typical work day as "mainly gathering intel, reporting back to Israel . . . to report back to the Ministry of Foreign Affairs, the Ministry of Strategic Affairs." She also discusses how the Israeli government is "giving our support" to front groups "in that behind-the-scenes way," and using fake Facebook profiles to infiltrate the circles of Palestine solidarity activists on campus. One employee of the Israel Project featured in the documentary, confessed to the *Al Jazeera* undercover reporter that much of the pro-Israel advocacy work she had been asked to do made her feel somewhat "uneasy" and "uncomfortable" because it smeared Palestinian rights activists as "anti-Semites" and "racists" for criticising Israeli government policy.

Also apparent from the film was that U.S.-based groups coordinated their efforts directly with the Israeli government and particularly with the Ministry of Strategic Affairs — in charge of Israel's global campaign of covert sabotage targeting the BDS movement — which was run by a former military intelligence officer who claimed to have mapped Palestinian rights activism "globally" . . . "not just the United States, not just campuses, but campuses and intersectionality and labour unions and churches."

The film also has pro-Israel lobby leaders speaking (actually boasting) openly about how they use money to influence the political process in such blunt terms that if the comments were made by critics of Israel, they would definitely be categorised as being anti-Semitic. David Ochs, founder of HaLev, which helps to send young people to AIPAC'S annual conference, admits that AIPAC and its donors organise fundraisers outside the official umbrella of the organisation, so that the money doesn't show up on disclosures as coming specifically from AIPAC. He describes one group organising fundraisers in both Washington and New York as being "the biggest ad hoc political group, definitely the wealthiest, in DC," adding that it had no official name, but was clearly tied to AIPAC. "It's the AIPAC group. It makes a difference; it really, really does. It's the best bang for your buck, and the networking is phenomenal."

> *Congress is "terrorised" by AIPAC . . . In practice, the lobby groups function as an informal extension of the Israeli government.*
> **Paul Findley (1921-2019), American writer and politician, They Dare to Speak Out: People and Institutions Confront Israel's Lobby**

Not to be outdone by its southern neighbour or most European nations, Canada, as a follow-up to the February 2009 London Declaration on Combating Anti-Semitism, the Canadian Parliamentary Coalition for Combating Anti-Semitism (CPCCA) hosted the second such conference — with the boast that it was "the largest ever international parliamentary gathering on anti-Semitism" — not only to confirm Canada's increasingly pro-Israeli policy, but also to further the curtailment of free speech by conflating legitimate criticism of Israel with anti-Semitism. The Independent Jewish Voices (IJV) Canada, in a petition that was signed by over 1,500 people and addressed to Canadian Parliament members, stated "the CPCCA's goal is to criminalise criticism of Israel and Zionism, not to hold impartial hearings . . . Therefore, we oppose the CPCCA as an ideologically biased organisation with an agenda that will harm free speech and human rights activity in Canada. We oppose the CPCCA's Orwellian distortion of anti-Semitism. It is a danger to both Canadian liberties and to the genuine and necessary fight against anti-Semitism.

As part of its suppression of criticism of Israel, Canada — generally regarded as a global human rights beacon — on January 21, 2014, signed a Canada-Israel Strategic Partnership Memorandum of Understanding (MOU), which reaffirmed the close and special friendship that underpinned the bilateral relationship, and laid out a strategic direction for stronger future relations between the two countries with the claim that "the selective targeting of Israel is the new face of anti-Semitism" and declared that Canada will oppose those who support the BDS movement.

Signing of the agreement was instigated by Prime Minister Stephen Harper — who like other western leaders such as Britain's former smarmy war criminal Prime Minister Tony Blair and France's former President Nicolas "weasel" Sarkozy (found guilty of corruption and sentenced to prison on March 1, 2021 — was on behalf of the Canadian People, equally enthusiastic about brown nosing Israel's Apartheid backside.

> *Some civil-society leaders today call for a boy-cott of Israel . . . Most disgracefully of all, some openly call Israel an apartheid state. Think about that. Think about the twisted logic and outright mal-ice behind that. A state, based on freedom, democra-cy and the rule of law, that was founded so Jews can flourish as Jews, and seek shelter from the shadow of the worst racist experiment in history.*
>
> **Stephen Harper addressing the Knesset during a 2014 visit to an irrefutably Apartheid Israel**

The vile hypocrisy this political prostitute was spouting on behalf of the Canadian people, was mind-boggling. Apart from earlier cutting funding to the United Nations Relief and Works Agency (UNRWA) that provided support with cloth-ing, food and health services to approximately 4.7 million registered Palestinian refugees in Jordan, Lebanon, Syria and the occupied Palestinian territories, Harper's minority Conservative government also cut funding to many Canadi-an non-governmental organisations including those who in some way worked on issues related to Israel/Palestine, or had spoken out against ongoing Israeli human rights abuses. By using the conference as an opportunity to reaffirm his dedication to Israel rather than to Canada and its relations with other countries, Harper raised questions about his mental stability with an Israeli-scripted rant designed to counteract the global effort to de-legitimise the Apartheid State of Israel.

> [As] long as I am Prime Minister, whether it is at the United Nations, the Francophonie, or anywhere else, Canada will take that stand whatever the cost. I say this, not just because it is the right thing to do, but because history shows us, and the ideology of the anti-Israeli mob tell us all too well if we listen to it, that those who threaten the existence of the Jewish people are a threat to all of us ... Harnessing disparate anti-American, anti-Semitic and anti-Western ideologies, it targets the Jewish people by targeting the Jewish homeland, Israel ... We must be relentless in exposing this new anti-Semitism for what it is.

Despite the best efforts of Canadian politicians to make Canada a compliant colony of the Apartheid Israeli State and impose censorious policies on the Canadian people, a new survey conducted by EKOS Research Associates revealed in September 2020 that an overwhelming majority of Canadians think the ICC should investigate Israeli officials over alleged war crimes. The poll, which was co-sponsored by Canadians for Justice and Peace in the Middle East (CJPME), Independent Jewish Voices Canada (IJV), and the United Network for Justice and Peace in Palestine-Israel (UNJPPI), found that 84 percent of Canadians think the ICC should investigate alleged war crimes committed by Israeli officials; that 86 percent of Canadians do not believe that the human rights record of Israel should be overlooked because the country is an ally of Canada; and that 82 percent want Canada's current policy toward Jerusalem to be maintained, with the city being shared rather than it being recognised exclusively as Israel's capital

IJV's National Coordinator Corey Balsam stated "this demonstrates that Canada's tendency to apply double standards when it comes to Israel is very unpopular with Canadians . . . Although successive governments have tended to mute their criticism of Israel, Canadians believe that Israel's violations should be treated as seriously as those of any other country."

The decades-old erasure of Palestinian national identity by both the Canadian government and the media resurfaced in January 2021 when it was revealed that an investigation regarding the censorship of the word "Palestine" by the Canadian Broadcasting Corporation (CBC) in August 2020, had — according to the Ombudsman's website — yet to be completed and when a decision was made, the results would be made public.

In February 2021, Canada's House of Commons voted to declare China's treatment of its Uighur minority population a genocide with the motion being passed 266 to 0. And yet this august collection of honourable Canadian politicians dare not raise the subject of the decades-long and far more evident genocide of the Palestinian people. So despite persistent and self-righteous depictions of itself as a champion of democracy and human rights, Canada's "democracy" is controlled by a subversive pro-Apartheid Israel. But then, what is to be expected from a nation which like Israel was established on the back of genocide, land theft, the plunder of natural resources, and war profiteering with arms exports in 2019 amounting to CA\$3,757,057,684.

Nonetheless in April 2021, at the New Democratic Party's convention — The centre-left NDP has existed since 1961 — party members overwhelmingly passed a motion to sanction Israel including a boycott of goods from illegal settlements and an arms embargo. Hopes for a vote on a resolution rebuking the International Holocaust Remembrance Alliance's (IHRA) working definition of antisemitism — which includes criticisms of Israel — were, however, quashed following enormous pressure from pro-Israel groups.

> *The adoption of this policy today firmly positions the NDP as one of the few parties demanding the end of Canada's support for illegal settlements and suspending the flow of weapons to and from Israel until Palestinians are free.*
>
> **Geneviuve Nevin, an organiser of the resolution**
>
> *For the first time, the NDP has endorsed concrete and proactive measures that the Canadian government can take to force Israel's compliance with international law . . . This is a major step forward for*

the NDP, and an encouraging development for all Canadians who want to see our political leaders respond to the call for action coming from Palestinian civil society.
Michael Bueckert, vice president of Canadians for Justice and Peace in the Middle East (CJPME)

The danger for Israel of weaponising anti-Semitism to silence criticism — such as that of its military assaults on Gaza; its unabated settlement building in defiance of international law and UN condemnations; its Nationality Law which enshrined Apartheid and formally sanctioned the discrimination and segregation that already existed; and its murderous suppression of Palestinian protests at the Gaza border — is that it is more likely to stoke, rather than prevent anti-Semitism.

Ever since the Jews invented the libel charge of "anti-Semitism" in the 1880s. It was first published in the Jewish Encyclopaedia (1901 Vol. 1, p. 641), and has been built up with Jewish money, organisations, propaganda and lies (such as the Holocaust — Holohoax), so that now the word is like a snake venom which paralyses one's nervous system. Even the mention of the word "Jew" is shunned unless used in a most favourable and positive context.
Charles A. Weisman, Who Is Esau-Edom?

18

The Remaining Vestiges of American Democracy Undermined by Pro-Israel Lobby Control of Congress and White House

. . . Against the insidious wiles of foreign influence (I conjure you to believe me, fellow-citizens) the jealousy of a free people ought to be constantly awake, since history and experience prove that foreign influence is one of the most baneful foes of republican government. But that jealousy to be useful must be impartial; else it becomes the instrument of the very influence to be avoided, instead of a defence against it. Excessive partiality for one foreign nation and excessive dislike of another cause those whom they actuate to see danger only on one side, and serve to veil and even second the arts of influence on the other. Real patriots who may resist the intrigues of the favourite are liable to become suspected and odious, while its tools and dupes usurp the applause and confidence of the people, to surrender their interests . . .

To announce his decision not to seek a third term as President, George Washington presented his Farewell Address in a newspaper article on September 17, 1796 (complete text available on the internet).

The demise of American democracy — as Helen Thomas the American reporter, author, and longtime front row member of the White House press corps once observed — was confirmed as a reality when Thomas was subsequently obliged to step down from her job as a columnist for Hearst News after a rabbi and independent filmmaker videotaped her outside the White House calling on Israelis to get "out of Palestine."

> *You cannot criticise Israel in this country and survive.*
> **Helen Thomas (1920-2013)**

Helen Thomas' controversial but irrefutable observation would not have come as a surprise to those aware that while the impressive facades on Capitol Hill symbolised the US federal government's three distinct legislative, executive, and judicial branches — with powers having been vested by the US Constitution in the Congress, the president, and the federal courts respectively — it was in fact a far less spectacular building at 251 H Street NW, the headquarters of the American Israel Public Affairs Committee (AIPAC), where much of this "superpower" nation's domestic and foreign policy was determined by influence over compliant, corrupt, and craven Members of Congress. AIPAC always gets whatever it wants with substantial donations or whatever else is necessary to ensure the election of candidates whose first loyalty will be to Israel rather than the American people.

In 1948, when an attempt was made in April — by the Executive Director of the deceptively named American Friends of the Fighters For the Freedom of Israel — to solicit Albert Einstein's help in raising American money for the weapons required to help the creation of a Jewish State by driving out the Palestinians as was confirmed by the infamous April 9 massacre of Palestinians at Deir Yassin. Einstein's reply was "when a real and final catastrophe should befall in Palestine the first responsible for it would be the British and the second responsible for it the terrorist organisations built up from our own ranks. I am not willing to see anybody associated with those misled and criminal people."

Then subsequent to Israel's establishment as a state it became apparent that in order to cope with the influx of some 600,000 Jewish immigrants — room had been made for them by the killing of thousands of Palestinians and the expulsion of some 750,000 others whose homes and land were illegally expropriated — Israel would require much more than the US Jewish money that was raised for Jewish Terrorist groups including the notoriously savage Stern Gang responsible for the murdering of innocent civilians as part of an agenda to expel all Palestinians from the "promised land" which according to the Tanakh (Hebrew Bible) fable, was promised and subsequently given by god to Abraham and his descendants.

Though US Jews had responded with unprecedented generosity by 1950 — the September 2020 results of a survey by an Israeli rightwing think-tank showed that currently up to 1 in 4 US Jews regard Zionism as a racist, colonialist apartheid movement! — it became apparent to US Zionist leaders that much more financial assistance was required and they accordingly devised a four-point strategy that included increasing donations from Jewish individuals; encouraging US corporate investment in Israel; promoting the sale of Israeli bonds; and requesting that Israel become a recipient of assistance from the US aid program for underdeveloped countries. Despite such efforts, the economic demands for increased Jewish settlement in Palestine and the military's requirements could not be met by handouts alone.

Consequently in 1951 the American Zionist Council (AZC) was established to promote a pro-Israel lobbying campaign that would concentrate on influencing Congress. Having, however, been established as a tax-exempt entity, the AZC was not legally permitted to Lobby in the US on Israel's behalf and as a result in 1954 faced a possible investigation for its violations. To avoid the possibility of that occurring, the AZC rebranded itself as the non-tax-exempt American Zionist Committee for Public Affairs. That organisation's subsequent realisation that its "Zionist" tag and objectives may be too harsh for many of the American Jews whose support it required, caused it to shrewdly once again rebrand itself by substituting the word "Israel" for "Zionist" to become the American Israel Public Affairs Committee but with the same modus operandi of blackmailing, bribing, and bullying to implement its agendas including the all-important and incessant instigation of Islamophobia.

We are owned by propagandists against the Arabs. There's no question about that. Congress, the White House, and Hollywood, Wall Street are owned by the Zionists. No question in my opinion. They put their money where their mouth is . . . We're being pushed into a wrong direction in every way . . .

Helen Thomas

Support for Zionist Israel's Apartheid agenda required not only AIPAC's pro-Israel lobbying, but also control of US policy decisions with millions of dollars being spent annually on coercing members of Congress while flaunting the following uncharacteristically honest mission statement on its website:

The mission of AIPAC — the American Israel Public Affairs Committee — is to strengthen and expand the US-Israel relationship in ways that enhance the security of the United States and Israel . . . We engage with and educate decision-makers about the bonds that unite the two countries, and how it is in America's best interest to help ensure that the Jewish State remains safe, strong and secure.

Apart from "engaging with" and "educating" — in reality blackmailing, bribing, and bullying — US decision-makers, AIPAC has also ensured that the US media maintained a pro-Israel bias so that according to an IRmep (Institute for Research: Middle Eastern Policy) simultaneous poll fielded by Google Consumer Surveys in 2016, an astonishing 49.2

percent of gullible Americans had been duped into believing that it was the Palestinians who were illegally occupying Israeli land rather than the other way round; that 51.4 percent of Canadians and 54.6 percent of Mexicans correctly believed that the Israelis were the occupiers rather than the Palestinian; and that 57.7 percent of Britons also knew the Israelis were the occupiers.

> *A free press stands as one of the great interpreters between the government and the people. To allow it to be fettered is to fetter ourselves.*
> **George Sutherland (1862-1942) US Supreme Court Justice, from Grosjean versus American Press Co., 1936**

With some fifteen billionaires owning America's news media companies — according to Forbes — the concept of an unfettered American press is but a delusional fantasy that only benefits media moguls including Michael Bloomberg (Bloomberg LP and Bloomberg Media); Rupert Murdoch (News Corp); Donald and Samuel "Si" Newhouse (Advance Publications); Cox Family (Atlanta Journal-Constitution); Jeff Bezos (The Washington Post); John Henry (The Boston Globe); the now deceased Sheldon Adelson (The Las Vegas Review-Journal); Joe Mansueto (Inc. and Fast Company magazines); Mortimer Zuckerman (US News & World Report, New York Daily News); Barbey Family (Village Voice); Stanley Hubbard (Hubbard Broadcasting); Patrick Soon-Chiong (Tribune Publishing Co.); Carlos Slim Helu (The New York

Times); Warren Buffett (regional daily papers); and Victor Vekselberg (Gawker).

> . . . *In America, we have achieved the Orwellian prediction — enslaved, the people have been programmed to love their bondage and are left to clutch only mirage-like images of freedom, its fables and fictions. The new slaves are linked together by vast electronic chains of television that imprison not their bodies but their minds. Their desires are programmed, their tastes manipulated, their values set for them.*
>
> **Gerry Spence, American lawyer, From Freedom to Slavery: The Rebirth of Tyranny in America**

In 1961 AIPAC and Zionism suffered a setback with the inauguration of President John F. Kennedy (JFK) whose quest for peace included a determination to prevent a nuclear arms race in the Middle East which he reiterated on June 15, 1963, in the last of a series of letters to Israeli Prime Minister David Ben-Gurion who believed that possession of nuclear weapons was essential for Israel's survival.

JFK's letter to Ben-Gurion was hardly friendly and stressed that as a professed ally, Israel should prove "beyond a reasonable doubt" that as the Middle East's Zionist enclave it was not developing nuclear weapons. The letter was cabled to Tel Aviv but before it could be physically delivered by the US ambassador, Ben-Gurion abruptly resigned for undisclosed personal reasons. Bearing in mind the fact that the

Israelis routinely intercepted communications and spied on the US — as in fact they still do — it can be safely assumed that having learnt of the letter's content, Ben-Gurion decided not only to preempt the letter's significance, but also to deprive JFK of an Israeli government with whom to negotiate. JFK had at the time simply sought what Israel has been demanding of Iran: international inspections of its nuclear facilities.

During that same 1962-63 period Senator William J. Fulbright of Arkansas, chairman of the Committee on Foreign Relations, convened hearings on the legal status of the AZC. The Committee uncovered evidence that the Jewish Agency, a predecessor to the state of Israel, operated a massive network of financial "conduits" which funnelled funds to US Israel lobby groups. As a result, Attorney General Robert F. Kennedy (RFK) ordered the AZC to openly register and disclose all of its foreign funded lobbying activity in the US. The attempt was subsequently thwarted first by the Israel lobby itself and then by the death of JFK which led to growing concerns regarding the impact of the increasing Zionist influence on US policy making decisions. On April 15, 1973, Fulbright — who lost his Senate seat the following year when the pro-Israel lobby generously backed his opponent — had no qualms about stating the following on CBS *Face the Nation*:

> *Israel controls the US Senate. The Senate is subservient, much too much; we should be more concerned*

about US interests rather than doing the bidding of Israel. The great majority of the Senate of the US — somewhere around 80% — is completely in support of Israel; anything Israel wants; Israel gets. This has been demonstrated time and again, and this has made [foreign policy] difficult for our Government.

On July 4, 1963, JFK warned Ben-Gurion's successor, Levi Eshkol, that US support for the young country would be "seriously jeopardised" if Israel did not allow the US periodic inspections of its nuclear reactor. On realising that JFK would not budge on the issue, Israel joined forces with Communist China which was also desirous of becoming a nuclear power. Both countries then began secretly developing nuclear capabilities through intermediary "and richest Jew in the world" Shaul Eisenberg who was a close friend of the duplicitous Henry Kissinger, a partner of Mossad gun-runner Tibor Rosenbaum, and pivotal in JFK's subsequent November assassination.

The probability of Mossad's involvement in JFK's assassination was in 1994 clearly substantiated by author Michael Collins Piper who in his incisive book, *Final Judgment: The Missing link in the JFK Assassination Conspiracy*, asserted that Israel's motive for the assassination was JFK's opposition to Israel's nuclear ambitions which outraged Ben-Gurion who commanded the Mossad to become involved. Piper concluded "Israel's Mossad was a primary (and critical) behind the scenes player in the conspiracy that ended the life of JFK.

Through its own vast resources and through its internation-al contacts in the intelligence community and in organised crime, Israel had the means, it had the opportunity, and it had the motive to play a major frontline role in the crime of the century — and it did."

> *"It is interesting — but not surprising — to note that in all the words written and uttered about the Kennedy assassination, Israel's intelligence agency, the Mossad, has never been mentioned. And yet a Mossad motive is obvious. On this question, as on almost all others, American reporters and commen-tators cannot bring themselves to cast Israel in an unfavourable light — despite the obvious fact that Mossad complicity is as plausible as any of the other theories."*
> **Paul Findley, in the Washington Report on Middle East Affairs, March 1992**

Israel's vendetta with the Kennedys resurfaced on June 6, 1968, with the assassination of Senator Robert Kennedy (RFK) after he had won the California primaries making him the most likely Democratic nominee for the forthcoming presidential election and certain to beat Richard Nixon. Just as Lee Harvey Oswald was made the patsy for JFK's assassi-nation, Sirhan Sirhan was made the Patsy for the killing of RFK despite overwhelming evidence to the contrary

Robert F. Kennedy Jr. — 14 years old at the time of his fa-ther's death — who visited Sirhan in prison, believed he was innocent and that there was another gunman. Paul Schrade, an aide to RFK and the first person shot that night, has also stated that Sirhan was not the gunman and is not alone in having credible evidence.

On the evening of July 16, 1999, the son of JFK, John F. Kennedy Jr., his wife Carolyn Bessette, and sister-in-law Lauren Bessette, died when their light aircraft crashed into the Atlantic Ocean off Martha's Vineyard. A subsequent investigation — like those into the deaths of his father and uncle — left many questions unanswered: not least because at age 39, he had decided to launch his political career by seeking an electoral mandate in New York State, and was about to announce it publicly. It would seem that fate and Israel had once again decided against having a Kennedy in a position of influence.

The extent of the powerful influence and control exerted by the AIPAC-led Israel lobby over the US government — which unconditionally provides Israel with grovelling, uncritical, servile, and amoral support — can be best appreciated by visiting journalist Alison Weir's *If Americans Knew* website where a trove of information — including a partial but astonishing list of the estimated 400 to 600 pro-Israel organisations — is available and introduced with the assertion that "the Israel lobby is not one unified organisation, but rather it consists of numerous institutions with various agendas. Some differ in orientation, emphasis, or political views, but all promote a strong and often dangerous and dishonest pro-Israel slant in the American media and government."

Following Israel's 2008-9 Operation Cast Lead's three-week-long onslaught — the Gaza massacre — that killed some 1,400 Palestinians including children, Obama administration officials obligingly met with Israeli generals to counter the "poisonous" Goldstone Report by getting Israel's propaganda out quickly to justify its act of savagery. Judge Richard Goldstone, a South African Jewish jurist whose past judgments in South Africa helped to undermine Apartheid — and who later also worked with the international criminal tribunals for the former Yugoslavia and Rwanda — had agreed to lead a UN fact-finding mission which concluded that the Israeli Defence Forces (IDF) and Palestinian militant groups had committed war crimes and possibly crimes against humanity. The report, however, differentiated between the moral and legal severity of the violations by the IDF compared to those of Palestinian armed groups such as Hamas.

The ensuing and predictable Israeli reaction was Goldstone's vilification as a "self-hating Jew" by pro-Israel groups who likened his report to a blood libel: the false charge against Jews with roots in medieval anti-Semitism. Goldstone was consequently boycotted by Jewish communities around the world and was even not allowed to attend his grandson's bar mitzvah in South Africa. The pressure of such vilification forced Goldstone to recant in a *Washington Post* article in which he questioned his own report's findings by asserting "if I had known then what I know now the Goldstone report would have been a very different document." Yes, indeed! If only he had foreseen how his fellow god chosen people would react to the truth being told.

In February 2021 — Ben Rhodes former deputy national security adviser under President Obama — revealed that he had to meet with Israel lobbyists as often as all other interest groups combined; that those lobbyists were the same 10 to 20 individuals from the American Jewish community who invariably took pro-Israel positions that were in some cases scripted by the Israelis; that White House national security aides were expected to attend AIPAC's annual conference, but could "get in trouble" if they paid attention to Arab-American or peace groups; and that Israel lobby's access was supported by a compliant media and members of Congress who at times warned him about the "acute" financial threat of challenging the lobby.

The Israel lobby's buying of access to, and influence over the US government and media is overwhelmingly financed by Jewish advocates and supporters of the Zionist agenda for a state for Jews only. Furthermore, the majority of these groups are for tax purposes registered with the Internal Revenue Service as being either "educational" or "charitable" foundations, which enables them to solicit tax exempt donations. The American people have apparently been successfully brainwashed into believing that supporting a brutal, illegal occupation involving ethnic cleaning, land theft, and plunder of natural resources was a kosher "educational" and extremely "charitable" enterprise.

Apart from such blatant tax dodging tactics being ignored, there is also the question of whether it is legal under the 1938 Foreign Agents Registration Act (FARA) which requires that agents representing the interests of foreign powers in a "political or quasi-political capacity" disclose their relationship with the foreign government and information about related activities and finances. Originally enacted to identify and observe German agents spreading Nazi propaganda in the US, FARA has since been used against individuals and groups with links to other nations including Russian news agencies RT America and Sputnik.

In September 2020 it was revealed by various sources — including *The Forward* (news that matters to American Jews) — that Israel had been manipulating US policies with the assistance of some US organisations and politicians in what appears to be violation of US laws. But unlike with the constant US claims of "Russian interference," Israel and US pro-Israel groups are never mentioned or censured for failing to disclose grants received from the Israeli government. Meanwhile the mainstream media continually fails to report such news, Congress shows no interest in investigating glaring evidence of Israeli tampering, and a Congressional caucus with 80 members remains connected such groups.

One of the groups, the Israel Allies Foundation (IAF) — a nonprofit established in 2007 to foster cooperation between pro-Israel forces and governments around the world

— helped develop South Carolina's anti-BDS law prohibiting state entities from contracting with groups boycotting Israel. The IAF, which failed to disclose the more than $100,000 it was given in 2019, went on to lobby 25 additional states to adopt anti-BDS laws similar to those approved by South Carolina. The IAF, however, was not the only such organisation to receive money from Israel. Eleven other pro-Israel groups have received a total of $6.6 million from Israel since 2018. The irony of it all, is that this subversion of American "democracy" is actually being financed by American taxpayers with Israel receiving over $10.41 million of US aid per day.

As well as lobby groups acting on its behalf, Israel is also aided by the nefarious activities of various private intelligence agencies run by former Israeli intelligence personnel — including a deputy director of Mossad and a former national security adviser to Prime Minister Netanyahu — who apart from courting Trump's 2016 campaign, also tried to influence US local elections in favour of private clients with smear campaigns, fake websites, and online avatars to change election outcomes. The owner of one such private agency, who was regarded as being a "social media expert" specialising in "social media manipulation," was known to have also founded a company offering "honey traps" and "deep web" capabilities.

In addition to its numerous groups, the pro-Israel lobby also has the support of many wealthy Jewish individuals as illustrated by publicly available campaign finance data showing that the late conservative Zionist casino billionaire, Sheldon Adelson — a staunchly pro-Israel conservative— was the biggest spender on US elections. Adelson, who was also the biggest donor to Trump's presidential campaign and the Republicans, had by the end 2020 donated a whopping amount to Trump and the Republicans. In the meantime he managed to stock the Trump administration with his own confidantes and politicians whom he had long supported including Nikki Haley — the former US Ambassador to the UN who as a less than reputable politician was unashamedly biased towards Israel — was given $250,000 donation three weeks before the June primaries in 2012.

We have the best government that money can buy.
Mark Twain (1835-1910), American writer, humorist, entrepreneur.

Giving $82 million to Trump's campaign in 2016 may have seemed like a gamble for Adelson and his wife Miriam, but in December 2016 his comprador and bigoted "war hawk" John Bolton — who consistently called for regime changes in Iran and North Korea — promised members of the American Friends of Beit El that Trump would not only move the US Embassy to Jerusalem with the declaration that it the true capital of Israel, but that he would also not oppose any Jewish settlement expansion in the West Bank. In return Adelson facilitated Bolton's appointment as the US National Security Adviser whom Trump subsequently ousted over differences of opinion on policy issues.

As an accomplished subverter of US democracy, billionaire Adelson — who had neither respect for the human rights of others, nor the democracy of the country of his birth which enabled him to become extremely wealthy — had also expressed delight with the threats made by key foreign and national security policy officials regarding Iran and would have liked to see the US launch a war against the Iranians; destroy their government to effect regime change; and to pursue policies that would favour Israel irrespective of any catastrophic consequences for the region or the rest of the world.

Adelson's success in US policy meddling including the election of Trump, and resulted in regular private phone calls and meetings with Trump to whom he gave instructions regarding pro-Israel policies. This included removing the US from the Joint Comprehensive Plan of Action (JCPOA), more commonly known as the Iran nuclear deal; the withdrawal of US funding for UNRWA; the closing of the Palestine Liberation Organisation's diplomatic office in Washington; the appointment of a Special Envoy to serve as the primary advisor to the US government on the monitoring and combating of anti-Semitism and anti-Semitic incitement which included criticism of Israel; the moving of the US Embassy from Tel Aviv to Jerusalem; US recognition of Israel's sovereignty over the occupied West Bank and Syria's Golan Heights — with its oil reserves — which has been occupied since 1967; and the all-important passing of an anti-BDS bill — under the guise of preventing "anti-Semitism" — with its Orwellian intrusion into the private lives of Americans and their constitutional right to make politically motivated decisions.

Adelson was not the only wealthy and zealous supporter of Zionist Israel, and many others including Adam Milstein — a real estate millionaire — who sat on AIPAC's national council, and who through his family foundation, generously donates to the American Israel Education Foundation, AIPAC's nonprofit arm. His support for AIPAC is just one part of his portfolio for pro-Israel "philanthropy," which is also bankrolling attempts to end American support for the BDS movement.

Two bills cosponsored by Republican Senator Marco Rubio — a man without any moral principles and recipient of pro-Israel lobby donations — are an example of the "best that money can buy." The first, "Strengthening America's Security in the Middle East Act of 2019," passed on May 2, 2019, will increase the scope of the witch-hunt already affecting numerous intellectuals and human rights activists in US society to include ordinary citizens — who will become subject to Israel's unchecked power in that sadly laughable entity known as American democracy — allows state and local governments to withhold contracts from any individual or business entity that boycotts Israel. More than half of the 50 states have already passed legislation or some form of condemnation regarding the civil act of boycott, as championed by the BDS movement.

The second (United States-Israel Security Assistance Authorisation Act) passed on January 9, 2020 — providing Israel with $3.3 billion in annual aid — was intended as an assurance to the Zionist Apartheid State, that the US is committed to its security and military superiority in the Middle East and confirmed the fact that the US will continue wallowing in the quagmire of Middle East conflicts because it is either reluctant or fearful of shedding the beneficent yoke of the pro-Israel lobby with its subversive monetary influence over every aspect of the American government

Though Israel from the day of its inception had covetous intent for East Jerusalem — part of the Palestinian territory it occupied in 1967 and then annexed as a means of preventing the emergence of an independent Palestinian State — it had so far proceeded with caution and stealth so as not to either provoke serious condemnation from otherwise wimpish western governments, or risk goading Arab nations into forming an effective and united front. Having the US move its embassy to Jerusalem, however, emboldened Israel's disregard for, and persecution of the Palestinian people; helped create a perception of legitimacy for its desire to have all of Jerusalem as the "undivided capital" of a Jewish State; and even encouraged some politically unprincipled banana republics such as Guatemala to follow the US example by also moving its embassy to Jerusalem.

Further evidence of the insidious relationship between Adelson and an undeniably corrupt to the core Donald

Trump came from a report revealing that the President informed the Japanese Prime Minister that he should strongly consider allowing his benefactor — who apart from spending tens of millions to get Trump elected, also donated a further $5 million to Trump's 2017 corruption-ridden inaugural committee — to open a casino in Japan. This beneficent god-chosen billionaire, incidentally, was also infamously known for having stated "there's no such thing as a Palestinian," thereby echoing the equally bigoted view of former Israeli Prime Minister Golda Meir who asserted " . . . it was not as though there was a Palestinian people in Palestine considering itself as a Palestinian people and we came and threw them out and took their country away from them. They did not exist."

As major benefactor of Republican causes, the Adelsons had since 2015 donated over $250 million to GOP candidates and super PACs; had according to federal campaign finance data, given Republican candidates and committees some $176 million for the 2020 election cycle; and in mid October 2020, poured $75 million into a new super PAC backing Trump's struggling reelection campaign. While media outlets did report that last donation — with the obligatory neutral if not grovelling characterisation of the Adelsons — they nonetheless failed to mention that the Adelsons' prime priority was unconditional support for Israel, and that in return for their donations, the transactional Donald Trump provided Israel with virtually everything it wanted. Media coverage had instead focused on the "Russian influence" story.

Meanwhile, Israeli citizen Mrs Miriam Adelson, was in 2018 presented with the Presidential Medal of Freedom — the nation's highest civilian honour — and in 2019 became Israel's wealthiest individual with some $22 billion following the transfer of assets from her husband. In February 2020, the Israeli American Council (IAC), circulated a blogpost written in January by Miriam that lamented the assimilation of Jews — with the all too familiar assertion among "victimised" Israel supporters — that Jews who support Palestinian rights have either a weak connection to their Jewish heritage, or are self-hating Jews. The following excerpt from Miriam's diatribe illustrates the pernicious mentality that exploits victimhood.

> . . . *We Jews cannot afford division. There are too few us, and too many others who want us to fail, falter, disperse or perish. Scholars believe that, in King David's time, three millennia ago, the Jewish population numbered around 5 million. Today, we are 14 million — barely a threefold increase. Consider that the Chinese population is believed to have increased about a hundred-fold over the same period. By rights, we Jews should number at least a half-billion today.*

> *But, all too often, anti-Semitism has had its way: from the Inquisition to the pogroms to the Holocaust. In the words of the Passover Haggadah: "In each and every generation, they rise up against us to destroy us."*

And hatred for us from the outside has engendered drift and doubt among us: All too many Jews assimilate and are lost to the community because they see no good reason to stay. And all too many of these Jews see anti-Israel activism as an express-ticket to successful assimilation . . .

Apart from using their wealth to undermine the tattered remnants of American democracy, the Adelsons — and others with the same selfish supremacist god chosen mindset — are contributing to serious violations of human rights in Palestine that are driven by a desire to obliterate the incontestable reality of a Palestinian people and replace it with an illegal Apartheid State surrounded by an "Iron Wall" where "victimised" Jews can take refuge from anti-Semitism, revel in their own exclusive "chosenness," and avoid assimilation with those dreadful goyim.

Establishing the premise of Palestinian "non-existence" required coordination, coercion, and cunning such as was used by a relatively unknown pro-Israel lobby organisation — the Alliance for Israel Advocacy (AIA) — with close ties to "Christian supremacist" and now former US Vice President Mike Pence which began lobbying high-ranking members of Congress and the White House to support a proposal that could be described as a "US-funded ethnic cleansing plan of Palestinians."

The AIA's proposal was to redirect US funding intended for UNRWA in Palestine to an alternative fund managed by the Israeli government that would offer West Bank Palestinian families "vouchers" that could be exchanged for cash to finance resettlement abroad: a ploy that would reshape the ethnic and religious populations of territories illegally annexed by Israel and made available for the settlement of the more than 250,000 Jewish immigrants — from 150 different countries with the main countries of origin being Russia, Ukraine, France, United States, and Ethiopia — who moved to Israel in the past decade.

As a consequence of such persistent lobbying by pro-Israel groups and very wealthy Jews including that included Adelson — who transformed the Republican Party into an Israeli Apartheid party — that principled genius and "least racist" President Trump cut all aid to UNRWA — which provided assistance to five million Palestinian refugees not only in the occupied territories but also in Jordan, Lebanon, and Syria — and thereby denied much needed support for schools, healthcare, and social services.

On January 11, 2021, Sheldon Adelson died at his home in Malibu, California, at age 87 from complications related to treatment for non-Hodgkin's lymphoma — a type of blood cancer — no doubt with the knowledge that his 75 year-old wife, Miriam will continue using Adelson wealth to subvert American democracy as means of assisting Israel in its quest for elimination of the Palestinian people and complete domination of the Middle East. As a typical blinkered and Israeli stooge, former US president George W. Bush said of Adelson that "he was an American patriot, a generous benefactor of charitable causes, and a strong supporter of Israel . . . He will be missed by many — none more than his beloved family."

Apart from its general lobbying and subversive activities, one of AIPACh 's prioritised targets is the non-violent BDS movement which has transformed the Israeli-Palestinian debate to the extent of being regarded by Israel as an existential threat to the Jewish State, and by the Palestinians as their last hope of global support for their very existence as a people. At a time when corporate social responsibility is emerging as a business model, BDS has given adverse publicity to major companies involved with Israel's illegal occupation; disrupted concerts, exhibitions, and film festivals worldwide; and infuriated academic and sports organisations by politicising them.

While pro-Israel lobbying has managed to coerce the UK and other European governments into banning public bodies from supporting BDS by claiming that BDS has fuelled a rise in anti-Semitism, it is in the US that such lobbying has been inevitably most successful with Texas for example having sweeping legislation — to ensure that no public funds ever go to anyone who supports a boycott of Israel — so that for example victims of the August 2017 Hurricane Harvey, which devastated Southwest Texas, were told they could only receive state disaster relief if they first signed a pledge to never boycott Israel, thereby providing further confirmation that "the land of the free and the home of the brave" is nothing more than a fraudulent fantasy.

Such repressive legislation has had the effect of pitting pro-Israel activists against free speech advocates such as the American Civil Liberties Union; igniting debates in Protestant churches of which some of the largest have divested from companies profiting from Israel's occupation; forcing college administrators to adjudicate complaints from BDS-supporting professors and students who were having their free speech stifled; and attracting greater support for the Palestinian cause.

US legislation that restricts the right to boycott goes against a landmark decision from 1982 when the US Supreme Court ruled (8-0) that a National Association for the Advancement of Coloured People (NAACP) boycott of white-owned businesses in Mississippi to protest against segregation and racial injustice, was a protected form of free association and free expression. The court recognised that political boycotts empowered individuals to collectively express their dissatisfaction with the status quo and enabled them to advocate for political, social, and economic change: the freedoms that the Constitution was precisely intended to protect. Despite the fact that the First Amendment clearly protects the right to boycott, US federal and state legislation was stifling the rights of the American people in order to support an Apartheid State which with habitual supremacist and racially arrogant impunity violates international law.

The ending of Trump's presidency in the November

2020 election will, however, do little if anything to reverse the decline of American democracy because the malignancy afflicting the country's fundamental nature will defy attempts at finding an effective remedy. While the curse of a Trump presidency may have been removed, the more than 74,196,000 like-minded Americans who voted for him — despite his being a semi-illiterate and repugnant reprobate with undeniably deplorable sexist, racist, and xenophobic tendencies and whom hundreds of mental heath professionals have described as suffering from a mental pervasive disorder characterised by aggression, egomania, cheating, grandiosity, instability, lying, narcissism, self-interest, and stealing — will still be around to scupper any hope of recovery because of a national failure to recognise and accept some basic realities that were mentioned by Senator Fulbright in his book *The Arrogance of Power.*

> *There are many respects in which America, if it can bring itself to act with the magnanimity and the empathy appropriate to its size and power, can be an intelligent example to the world. We have the opportunity to set an example of generous understanding in our relations with China, of practical cooperation for peace in our relations with Russia, of reliable and respectful partnership in our relations with Western Europe, of material helpfulness without moral presumption in our relations with the developing nations, of abstention from the temptations of hegemony in our relations with Latin America, and*

of the all-around advantages of minding one's own business in our relations with everybody. Most of all, we have the opportunity to serve as an example of democracy to the world by the way in which we run our own society; America, in the words of John Quincy Adams, should be "the well-wisher to the freedom and independence of all" but "the champion and vindicator only of her own" . . . If we can bring ourselves so to act, we will have overcome the dangers of the arrogance of power. It will involve, no doubt, the loss of certain glories, but that seems a price worth paying for the probable rewards, which are the happiness of America and the peace of the world.

Though Trump's removal from the White House — despite his megalomanic reluctance to accept it was time to go — may provide Americans with a veneer of apparent sanity and elicit a huge sigh of relief from the majority of reasonable people in the world, the thrust of America's desire for global domination and morally degenerate conduct will continue with some 800 military bases in more than 70 countries and territories overseas (Britain, France, and Russia combined do not even have even a quarter of that amount); will continue adding to the more than 20 million people it has already killed in some 40 "victim nations" since World War Two; will with its flawed concept of "American exceptionalism" presume to interfere in the affairs of other nations either politically or with military interventions as was the case in the 2003 Iraq War; will accommodate the military industrial complex's desire for endless wars with a Department of Defence budgets in the region of $636 billion or more; will in the meantime spend only $66.6 billion on education so that half of the nation's adults double remain incapable of reading a book written at the 8th-grade level; will continue trading in death and destruction with conventional weapons sales to some 170 countries which between 2002 and 2018 amounted to more than $200 billion; and will continue to be governed by unprincipled politicians whose subservience to Israel takes precedence over their "Oath of Office. Consequently the government's gratuitous grovelling to an Apartheid State; the mainstream media's duplicitous double standard mendacity; and the average citizen's parochial mindset, will ensure the continued decline of an America that can never be made "Great Again."

Every ambitious would-be empire clarions it abroad that she is conquering the world to bring it peace, security and freedom, and is sacrificing her sons only for the most noble and humanitarian purposes. That is a lie, and it is an ancient lie, yet generations still rise and believe it! . . .

If America ever does seek Empire, and most nations do, then planned reforms in our domestic life will be abandoned, States Rights will be abolished — in order to impose a centralised government upon us for the purpose of internal repudiation of freedom, and adventures abroad.

The American Dream will then die — on battlefields all over the world — and a nation conceived in liberty will destroy liberty for Americans and impose tyranny on subject nations.

George S. Boutwell (1818-1905), American statesman, Secretary of the Treasury under President Ulysses S. Grant, Governor of Massachusetts, Senator and Representative from Massachusetts

19

The American Nightmare

And when I speak, I don't speak as a Democrat. Or a Republican. Nor an American. I speak as a victim of America's so-called democracy. You and I have never seen democracy — all we've seen is hypocrisy. When we open our eyes today and look around America, we see America not through the eyes of someone who has enjoyed the fruits of Americanism. We see America through the eyes of someone who has been the victim of Americanism. We don't see any American dream. We've experienced only the American nightmare.
Malcolm X (1925-1965), American minister and activist who was assassinated.

The reality of an American nightmare was emphatically confirmed when on Tuesday, November 8, 2016, in the US presidential election, 62,984,828 Americans voted for Donald Trump who during his term in office managed to tell some 30,000 blatant lies; to pursue self-enriching policies and unabashed nepotism; to corrupt government institutions such as the Department of Justice and in the process destroy the concept of a just democracy; to withdraw from the Trans-Pacific Partnership trade deal, the Paris climate accord, the Iran nuclear pact, and terminated DACA — Deferred Action for Childhood Arrivals — which protected some 800,000 young unauthorised immigrants from deportation; to abandon many other treaties and agreements including defence pacts with Western allies and thereby undermine the credibility of the US; to audaciously belittle other nations and refer to Haiti, El Salvador, and an assortment of African nations as "shithole countries"; to make the US the laughingstock of a world in urgent need of the critical thinking and moral leadership to combat urgent problems including the COVID-19 pandemic; and to confirm he is a populist demagogue preying on voter disaffection by stoking racist rage and vicious violence to fan the flames of class divisions and political polarisation — such as was evident during the storming of the Capitol on January 6, 2021— that altogether have increased the horror of America's Nightmare.

Other aspects of that nightmare include the seditious control of the US Congress by pro-Israel organisations — led by a subversive AIPAC — and their occupation of the American psyche; the debunking of the American Dream's delusional belief that anyone, regardless of where they were born or what class they were born into, could attain their own version of success in a society where upward mobility was possible for everyone, and achievable through sacrifice, risk-taking, and hard work instead of by chance or some other endeavour; the reality that 50 million Americans live below the poverty line and were receiving food stamps which President Trump cut back to thereby cause more of them to go hungry; and the poverty rates of 9% for Whites, 21.2% for Blacks, 17.2% for Hispanics, 9.7% for Asian/Native Hawaiian and Pacific Islanders, and 24.2% for American Indian/Alaskan Natives.

America is also now a nation where 21% of all children — with about 46% of black children and 40% of Latino children — live in poverty and are on food stamps; where the poverty rate is 9.9% for black married couples, and only 30% of black children are born to married couples; and where — according to data from the Centres for Disease Control and Prevention — drug, alcohol, and suicide deaths have reached the highest level since record-keeping began. This American nightmare was further exacerbated by Trump's irresponsible lies and complete failure to address the seriousness of the coronavirus pandemic which he insisted would "go away."

The US is also where 15% of senior citizens live in poverty; where being Black lowers one's credit score by 71 points; where big company CEOs earn — an average $12,400,000 — 335 times more than the average employee at $36,875; and where poverty is criminalised, wealth immunised, and corporate wrongdoing with impunity rewarded with a tax rate reductions subsidised by spending cuts on education, healthcare, and social welfare. The current median family wealth by race and ethnicity is $188,200 for Whites, $142,500 for Hispanics, and $24,100 for Blacks. Another ethnic disparity according to FBI data, is that a disproportionately high proportion of police shootings in the US involve black people.

And to make the situation even worse — according to the US Department of Education and the National Institute of Literacy — some 32 million adults (14 percent of the population) can't read; between 40 and 44 million (approximately 20 to 23%) of adults are limited to reading at the basic or below basic proficiency levels; some 30 million adults aren't able to comprehend texts that are appropriate for 10-year-olds; an estimated 63 million adults read between a sixth and eighth grade level with just 11% of men and 12% of women making the grade as proficient readers; 50 percent can't read a book written at an eighth-grade level; one-third of adults who struggle with illiteracy are aged 65 or older; 19 percent of high school graduates can't read at all; every year, one in six young adults — more than 1.2 million — drop out of high school; 43 percent of the adults with the lowest literacy levels, live in poverty; and 70% of adult welfare recipients have low literacy levels. This clearly indicates a correlation between more education and higher earnings, and between higher educational scores and higher earnings.

Illiteracy results in people being excluded from participation in those things that enable them to become fully functional citizens capable of making choices; deprives them of access to information, excludes them from making choices about their rights or who governs them through voting, and lessens their opportunities for employment; and keeps them trapped in a cycle of poverty and subjugation that limits life choices and makes it difficult to achieve social mobility. Literacy — and knowledge — means having power over one's own life: a power which most Americans don't have, and are unlikely to ever have because government spending on post-9/11 wars and military action in the Middle East and Asia is due to exceed $6 trillion — which would be better spent on the urgent need to provide education, healthcare, and social justice for all American people — instead of denying them the knowledge necessary for social satisfaction and informed participation in the democratic process.

Human history becomes more and more a race between education and catastrophe.
H. G. Wells, The Outline of History

Despite the critical necessity for seriously addressing the deplorable rate of illiteracy, the US Federal Outlay on education is only some 6 percent ($72.6 billion) compared to 54 percent ($622.6 billion) on defence which enables the US to pursue a global domination agenda whose negative impact on humanity is beyond the comprehension of the average ill-informed American. The ongoing bogus "War on Terror" with its crimes against humanity merely confirms Martin Luther King's past assertion of the US being "the greatest purveyor of violence in the world today."

That there are men in all countries who get their living by war, and by keeping up the quarrels of Nations is as shocking as it is true . . .
Thomas Paine (1737-1809), English-born American political activist, philosopher, political theorist, and revolutionary

In addition to its military coups and regime change endeavours following the election of foreign leaders of which it disapproved — as was for example the case in Iran, Guatemala, and Chile — the US also has a long history of meddling in presidential elections of some 81 countries between 1946 and 2000. The scope of that meddling has included funding the election campaigns of specific political parties; spreading misinformation or propaganda; providing training for the favoured party in campaigning or get-out-the-vote techniques; assisting the favoured party with the design of campaign materials; publicly declaring or threatening in favour of or against a particular candidate; and either providing or withholding foreign aid.

Most terrorists are people deeply concerned by what they see as social, political, or religious injustice and hypocrisy, and the immediate grounds for their terrorism is often retaliation for an action of the United States.
William Blum, American author, historian, and critic of US foreign policy

The daily perpetration of crimes on a global scale has become a regular feature of an American foreign policy shaped by the major defence contractors — not to mention Israeli instigation — who in 2019 with some 681 lobbyists descending on Capitol Hill, spent some $112,305,596 on lobbying to influence the government. The heavy spending is invariably led by five US companies — Lockheed Martin, Northrop Grumman, General Dynamics, Boeing, and Raytheon — who have dominated the global arms business with the US exporting $55.4 billion in fiscal 2019, which ended on September 30, and $55.6 billion in 2018. Weapons produced by those five companies were sold to countries such as Saudi Arabia, Israel, and Egypt who have systematically massacred civilians, destroyed civilian infrastructures, and committed numerous other violations against humanity.

US defence contractors — against whom President Eisenhower warned in his January 1961 Farewell Address to the Nation — continue to profit from the death and destruction being perpetrated through the Pentagon without any moral justification on some of the poorest and most vulnerable people in the world. Like a pack of insatiable scavenging hyaenas they gorge themselves on cadavers resulting from the endless conflicts instigated by manic neoconservatives exploiting the bigotry, ignorance, and fear of a people infantilised and deliberately kept misinformed by the government and the media.

In the councils of government, we must guard against the acquisition of unwarranted influence, whether sought or unsought, by the military-industrial complex. The potential for the disastrous rise

> *of misplaced power exists and will persist . . . We must never let the weight of this combination endanger our liberties or democratic processes. We should take nothing for granted. Only an alert and knowledgeable citizenry can compel the proper meshing of the huge industrial and military machinery of defence with our peaceful methods and goals, so that security and liberty may prosper together.*

President Dwight D. Eisenhower

The victims of such conflicts have also included US casualties with even those who survived and returned to civilian life often suffering from PTSD, substance abuse, depression, and thoughts of suicide with an estimated 50,000 of them being currently homeless. The Pentagon meanwhile has "mislaid" some $21 Trillion — that Is $65,000 for every person in the US — which would not have been possible without the Federal Reserve — the central banking system of the US — with its member banks being complicit in such illegal laundering and misplacement of the taxpayers' money. Major private accounting firms hired to carry out and audit the Pentagon concluded they that a reliable audit was simply impossible because the DoD's financial records were so riddled with numerous bookkeeping deficiencies, irregularities, and errors. U.S taxpayers are consequently left in the dark as to the true identity of the individuals, corporations, or nations such as Israel that are the beneficiaries of such "misplaced" funds.

No money shall be drawn from the treasury, but in consequence of appropriations made by law; and a regular statement and account of receipts and expenditures of all public money shall be published from time to time.

Article I, Section 9, Clause 7, U.S. Constitution.

Apart from its immoral "War on Terror," the US has continued its historic violation of international laws and treaties with no repercussions from international organisations including the ICC and the UN which it bullies into tolerating and rubber stamping its illegal interventions and wars which have undermined democracy and destroyed numerous countries refusing to capitulate to its demands.

Other imperious US violations have included rendition — the practice of covertly sending foreign criminal or terrorist suspects to be interrogated and tortured in countries with less rigorous regulations for the humane treatment of prisoners. CIA interrogation techniques were enhanced by projects that experimented on humans to identify and develop drugs and procedures to weaken individuals and force confessions through mind control. One such project — known as MKUltra — was organised through the Office of Scientific Intelligence of the CIA and coordinated with the US Army Biological Warfare Laboratories.

The unmitigated arrogance of the US has led it to believe that it has the paramount authority to decide which kind of government other countries should have and the manner in which they should conduct their affairs. In Latin America alone the US has intervened more than 50 times while often overthrowing democratically elected leaders as was the case in Guatemala in 1954 when U.S.-backed dictators and death squads killed 200,000 Guatemalans; in the Dominican Republic in the early 1960s; and in Chile in 1973 to overthrow democratically elected President Salvador Allende.

Recent US interference included undermining Nicaragua to prevent it posing the threat of becoming an example to the rest of Latin America, and endeavouring to topple the Venezuelan government led by President Nicolás Maduro who like his predecessor President Hugo Chavez — reviled for recognising the State of Palestine and establishing diplomatic relations with the Palestinian Authority in April 2009 — and who also supported Palestinian rights during the 2014 Israel-Gaza conflict and said that the government "vigorously condemns the unfair and disproportionate military response by the illegal state of Israel against the heroic Palestinian people." Countries who criticise Israel invariably and coincidentally end up becoming targets for neoconservative instigated American interference ranging from economic sanctions to regime change.

In Venezuela's case for example, fomenting acceptance of regime change is concocted by a mainstream corporate media that is hardly ever concerned with the truth but is instead simply intent on spewing out the propaganda of Western imperialism. This now well established approach to journalism is achieved through diligent selection of "right-think-ing" editors and journalists who have been conditioned to disseminate information — self-censored if necessary — in a manner that safeguards and promotes the agendas of bil-lionaire media company owners, the goals of major corpo-rate advertisers, and the need for endless "Wars on Terror" to satisfy the egos of self-serving narcissistic politicians and the amoral profiteering of military industrial complexes.

US interference in Venezuela is also driven by a covet-ous interest in Venezuela's Orinoco Belt — a territory in the southern strip of the eastern Orinoco River Basin which has the world's largest petroleum deposits — with an estimated 1.4 trillion barrels. On the basis of the current global oil con-sumption being 35 billion barrels a year, the Orinoco Belt alone could fulfil 100% of the world's demand for almost 30 years.

An important contributory factor to the "success" of US exploitation and interference in Latin America is the unpub-licised US Army "School of the Americas" located in Fort Benning, Georgia, where Latin American military officers and soldiers are trained to subvert governments and deny the human rights of people in their own countries. Also known as the "School of Dictators," this so-called university has training manuals that advocate assassination, blackmail, ex-tortion, torture, and the targeting and repression of civilian populations. It has produced thousands of villainous grad-uates subsequently linked to terror, torture, massacres, and military death squads.

As well as targeting Latin America, high-handed US interventions and adventurism — frequently encouraged by the pro-Israel lobby — also included a unilateral decision to "take out" seven predominantly Muslim countries in five years, a decision which incidentally happened to be in line with Israel's "Yinon Plan" of causing adjoining Arab countries to "fall apart along sectarian and ethnic lines" — as in the Saudi Arabian-led war on Yemen — with the resulting fragmentation compelling each state to be hostile to its neighbours. The war in Iraq and subsequent interventions in other countries for example, were conceived by some 25 neo-conservative intellectuals, most of them crypto-Israeli Jews — including Eliot Abrams, Douglas Feith, Robert Kagan and his wife Victoria Nuland, Charles Krauthammer, William Kristol, Richard Perle, Paul Wolfowitz, Tony Blinken, and Wendy Sherman amongst others — who prevailed on President Bush to invade Iraq in 2003, and influenced Obama's foreign policy so as to help Israel.

Some of these players are still around including Sherman and Nuland whom Joe Biden has chosen for the number two and three senior positions at the State Department as support for Secretary of State Tony Blinken who has questionable lobbying connections. Nuland was the Obama Administration's regime change fiend when she served as Assistant Secretary of State and was instrumental in the intervention in Ukraine where she strolled around Kiev's Maidan Square handing out cookies to demonstrators while expressing support for their cause which resulted in thousands dying during the turmoil over a contested election which ended up with a coup. That regime change was funded by $5 billion courtesy of US taxpayers.

Evolutionary psychologist Kevin MacDonald — an alleged American anti-Semitic conspiracy theorist and white supremacist — best described neoconservatism as "a complex interlocking professional and family network centred around Jewish publicists and organisers flexibly deployed to recruit the sympathies of both Jews and non-Jews in harnessing the wealth and power of the United States in the service of Israel." He also asserted that proof of the neocons' being crypto-Israelis, was in their US foreign policy.

> *The confluence of their interests as Jews in promoting the policies of the Israeli right wing and their construction of American interests allows them to submerge or even deny the relevance of their Jewish identity while posing as American patriots. [. . .] Indeed, since neoconservative Zionism of the Likud Party variety is well known for promoting a confrontation between the United States and the entire Muslim world, their policy recommendations best fit a pattern of loyalty to their ethnic group, not to America.*
>
> **Kevin B. MacDonald, Cultural Insurrections: Essays on Western Civilisation, Jewish Influence, and Anti-Semitism, 2007**

In 1997 William Kristol and Robert Kagan founded a neoconservative think tank, the Project for the New American Century (PNAC) which held "American leadership is good both for America and for the world," and played a key role in building support for the "taking out" of oil-rich Iraq that resulted in millions of civilians being dehumanised or killed. According to a report from Physicians For Social Responsibility (PSR), a US-based medical and public health organisation, the US military did between 1991 and 2003 kill 1.9 million Iraqis with over one million more being killed since 2003.

With the main reason for the US invasion of Iraq allegedly being Saddam Hussein's possession of a weapons of mass destruction (WMDs) program, the non-existence of any such program subsequently required some mitigation which variously included the assertion that the mistake about Hussein's WMDs was sincere; that the covert nature of intelligence gathered — some of it obligingly provided by Israel — is complicated; and that in the light of September 11, 2001 attacks against the US, the government genuinely misconstrued the extent of the danger posed by Hussein's Iraq.

Expert observers who have challenged such explanations, have also debunked claims that the US was trying to "spread democracy"; to support the oil industry; and to comply with Israeli lobby demands. Instead they argue that the main objective of the invasion and a decisive victory was to flaunt US power to the world — particularly the perceived

rogue regimes of Libya, Iran, Syria, and North Korea —
and to reaffirm US military dominance and standing as the
world's leading power

The US destruction of Iraq — which along with Kuwait,
parts of Northern Saudi Arabia, and the eastern parts of Syria — once formed Mesopotamia where glorious, rich, and
powerful civilisations were born along the banks of the Ti-
gris and Euphrates rivers. It was a Fertile Crescent serving
as a cradle for new forms of society that rose, flourished,
and fell over thousands of years. Sumerians, Assyrians, Ak-
kadians, and Babylonians built incredible structures, established legal codes, developed writing systems and literature,
inspired early mathematics and astronomy, and created vast
city-states, forming centres of culture and societies so influential that today that land of plenty is spoken of as a "Garden
of Eden," a place sacred to both gods and humans. It was the
genesis of Gilgamesh; the era of Ziggurats; the splendour of
the Hanging Gardens; the age of Sargon of Akkad and Cyrus
the Great; and the realm of Tiamat and Marduk.

The PSR study also found that four million Muslims
have been killed in countries ranging from Iraq to Pakistan.
Though the situation in Iraq had alone mobilised some token anti-war activism in the US, not enough people had been
spurred into action because of the alleged global "War on
Terror" which had the Bush administration, the British government, and other Western allies describing Muslim civilian casualties as "collateral damage" ⊠ and all armed factions

resisting the US-led interventions as barbarians ⊠ thereby denying their "enemy" victims any semblance of humanity. This is not "collateral damage," but deliberate, coldblooded murder that in a world with impartial justice would be punishable as a crime against humanity.

Those same neoconservatives who successfully prevailed on the US to attack Iraq — which had neither threatened the US nor possessed the WMDs that the Bush administration cited as a pretext for war, are once again actively promoting war against Iran to ostensibly prevent it acquiring nuclear weapons: a war that would serve the agenda of Israel with its stockpile of nuclear weapons, and not the interests of the American people whose elected representatives are mostly puppets being manipulated by AIPAC.

> *"When a nation has reached this point, it must either change its laws and mores or perish, for the well of public virtue has run dry: in such a place one no longer finds citizens but only subjects."*
> **Alexis de Tocqueville (1805-1859), French diplomat, political scientist, and historian in his Democracy in America**

But while America's military might has been gratuitously killing millions and destroying cultures overseas, the American people — at least some of those who are literate — have themselves begun to sense that something is very wrong with their own society and are concerned about rising socio-economic inequality, the erosion of national identity and purpose, increasing social polarisation, and a growing contempt around the world for their country which during the 1950s and 1960s was the richest and most envied nation. Since then, America, once the world's premier creditor nation, has become the number one debtor nation — and on track for a $4 trillion deficit by 2020 — whose ideology of denial, falsehoods, wishful thinking, and self-deception has decayed its moral fibre to the extent that 48 percent of American children are born to an unmarried mother while 43 percent of American children live in a home without a father. The US obsession of having unchallenged global hegemony has become a terrifying nightmare from which the majority of American people would like to escape by waking up to a new dawn with meaning and purpose.

The rising of that new dawn, however, will not miraculously appear over the horizon with the election of a Joe Biden well beyond his "use by date," or some other pandering politician. Following his inauguration, Biden wasted no time in confirming it would be "business as usual" by reneging on his campaign promise to punish Saudi Arabia's crown prince Mohammad bin Salman (MBS) for ordering the murder of *The Washington Post* correspondent Jamal Khashoggi despite US intelligence reports confirming MBS complicity; in his first publicly acknowledged military act as commander-in-chief, ordered an assault on Syria; retained the mandatory tradition of recent US presidents of brown-nosing Israel by comparing the Passover holiday — which marks the mythic Jewish Exodus from bondage in Egypt — to the recovery from the COVID-19 pandemic; and despite vowing to make human rights and multilateralism cornerstones of his approach to global affairs, Biden's State Department criticised the ICC's decision to investigate possible war crimes and crimes against humanity perpetrated in the West Bank and Gaza Strip.

Any improvement in the current political climate can only come from the will of the people, and the soul of the nation: a nation where the traditional "right of the people to keep and bear Arms" has been integrated in the fabric of American society. While Americans make up only 4 percent of the world's population, American civilians nonetheless own almost 50 percent (over 400 million) of the entire global stock of 857 million civilian firearms.

> *Americans have bought nearly 17 million guns so far in 2020, more than in any other single year, according to estimates from a firearms analytics company . . . Gun sales across the United States first jumped in the spring, driven by fears about the coronavirus pandemic, and spiked even higher in the summer, during massive racial justice protests across the country, prompted by police killings of black Americans.*
> **The Guardian, October 30, 2020**

Gun possession has consequently come to be regarded by many Americans as a symbol of their "freedom" and they use guns to vent hate, commit violence, and express racist sentiments as was the case with their European colonist forefathers whose racist and xenophobic obsessions were frequently expressed openly and acted upon by Christian leaders invoking god's name.

> *Damn any man who sympathises with Indians. I have come to kill Indians, and believe it is right and honourable to use any means under God's heaven to kill Indians . . . Kill and scalp all, big and little; nits make lice.*
> **John Milton Chivington (1882–1894), a former Methodist Pastor who served as a Colonel in the US army**

In the November 1864 Sand Creek Massacre — also known as the Chivington Massacre — a 675-man force of Colorado US Volunteer Cavalry under Chivington's command, destroyed a village of Cheyenne and Arapaho Native Americans in southeastern Colorado Territory, killed and mutilated an estimated 500 of whom about two-thirds were women and children.The panel of a subsequent Joint Committee on the Conduct of the War declared the following:

> *As to Colonel Chivington, your committee can hardly find fitting terms to describe his conduct. Wearing the uniform of the United States, which should be the emblem of justice and humanity; holding the important position of commander of a military district, and therefore having the honour of the government to that extent in his keeping, he deliberately planned*

and executed a foul and dastardly massacre which
would have disgraced the verist [sic] savage among
those who were the victims of his cruelty . . .

Anyone believing that attempts to eliminate racist bar-barity by "civilised" Americans have been successful, should google "Category: United States war crimes" and revisit the history of racist US military crimes against humanity includ-ing the violations against detainees in the Abu Ghraib prison in Iraq: violations that included physical and sexual abuse, rape, sodomy, torture, and murder. Colonel Chivington — if he were alive today — would have been extremely proud of how his fellow Americans are spreading the "democracy" en-visioned in that disastrous delusion known as the "American Dream."

In reality that dream has become a nightmare where for example, African Americans are systematically hampered by a dysfunctional educational system; face obstacles to voter registration (witness the recent racist legislation in Georgia); are denied equal economic opportunities; are paid $6-7 per hour less than white workers even though race should not be a skill or characteristic with a market value in relation to wages; are denied basic civil and human rights; and are dis-proportionately incarcerated in brutal for-profit prison-in-dustrial-complexes operated by out of control racists, aided by militarised, and often murderous police forces backed by an unjust and jaundiced judicial system, and corrupt, hypo-critical politicians.

Oh! Had I the ability, and could I reach the nation's ear, I would today pour out a fiery stream of biting ridicule, blasting reproach, withering sarcasm, and stern rebuke. For it is not light that is needed, but fire; it is not the gentle shower, but thunder. We need the storm, the whirlwind, and the earthquake. The feeling of the nation must be quickened; the conscience of the nation must be roused; the propriety of the nation must be startled; the hypocrisy of the nation must be exposed; and its crimes against God and man must be proclaimed and denounced . . .

Frederick Douglass (1818-1895), American social reformer, abolitionist, orator, writer, and statesman who after escaping from slavery in Maryland, became a national leader of the abolitionist movement in Massachusetts and New York, gaining renown for his oratory and incisive writings on antislavery

A report by FWD.us — a lobbying group for prison reform — and Cornell University published in December 2018 revealed that approximately half of all adults in the US — some 113 million people — have an immediate family member who either has been, or is currently being incarcerated. While such incarceration apparently impacts people from all walks of life — with rates of family incarceration being similar for Republicans and Democrats — the impact is, however, unevenly borne by communities of colour and low-income families. Black people are 50 percent more likely than white adults to have a family member who either has been, or is currently incarcerated, and a shocking three times more likely to have a family member who has spent at least ten years in prison.

> *All I ask is a square deal for every man. Give him a fair chance. Do not let him wrong any one, and do not let him be wronged.*
>
> **Theodore Roosevelt, US President from 1901-1909**

Roosevelt's proposal for a "Square Deal" for all Americans did not bargain on either the US Congress in the future being controlled by powerful pro-Israel groups, or that the White House would be occupied by a president like Donald Trump who more than any other in American history, personifies the psyche of a seriously sick nation: a tragedy which Mencken — the American journalist, essayist, satirist, cultural critic, and scholar of American English — uncannily predicted.

> *As democracy is perfected, the office of president represents, more and more closely, the inner soul of the people. On some great and glorious day the plain folks of the land will reach their heart's desire at last and the White House will be adorned by a downright moron.*
>
> **H.L. Mencken (1880-1956), On Politics: A Carnival of Buncombe**

Apart from their stranglehold on freedom of speech and restrictions on freedom of choice — the opportunity and autonomy to perform an action selected from at least two available options, unconstrained by external parties — pro-Israel lobby groups in the US have also usurped the power of Congress and exploited the harsh reality of a country founded as a republic, rather than a democracy.

As Alexander Hamilton and James Madison emphasised in the Federalist Papers, the essence of this republic would consist "IN THE TOTAL EXCLUSION OF THE PEOPLE, IN THEIR COLLECTIVE CAPACITY, from any share" in the government. Instead, popular views would be translated into public policy through the election of representatives "whose wisdom may," in Madison's words, "best discern the true interest of their country." The fact that this radically curtailed the degree to which the people could directly influence the government was by no means an accident.

During the course of the nineteenth century, however, entrepreneurial thinkers began giving the ideologically self-conscious republic a more democratic image. Concurrently, the old social hierarchies were being upended by rapid industrialisation, mass immigration, westward expansion, and a civil war. Egalitarian sentiment gained ground and the idea of the people's involvement in governance became popular. Furthermore, the institutions that were initially intended to exclude the people from governance, began promoting the concept of a government "of the people, by the people, for the people."

Subsequent reforms of importance began in 1913 when the Seventeenth Amendment stipulated that senators had to be elected directly by the people, not by state legislatures; in 1920 the Nineteenth Amendment gave women the right to vote; and in 1965, the Voting Rights Act, drawing on the Fifteenth Amendment, set out to protect the vote of black Americans. So while the once-elusive claim that the United States was a democracy was given some credibility, the Voting Rights Act was subsequently gutted in 2013 when the Supreme Court declared that racism was essentially a thing of the past.

That calamitous Supreme Court decision had the effect of prompting more than half the states to pass a series of voter suppression laws that targeted minority voters, breached a vital firewall that protected American democracy, and influenced the 2016 presidential election in favour of Donald Trump: a man whose well known greed, racism, sexism, and contemptuous disregard for the law, the Constitution, and democratic principles made him unfit for office.

The gradual demise of America's "Dream" and "Democracy" — regardless of Donald Trump's contribution — actually began in November 1947 with Israel exploiting US influence to get the UN General Assembly to pass Resolution 181 — a resolution which Israel has since consistently and arrogantly ignored — calling for partition of Palestine into Arab and Jewish states. The real subversion of US democracy, however, began following the 1948 establishment of Israel when Jewish lobby groups — led by one that was eventually to become the American Israel Public Affairs Committee

(AIPAC) — began seriously influencing Congress.

The process of AIPAC's creation occurred soon after Israel's 1948 establishment when it became apparent that in order to cope with the influx of some 600,000 Jewish immigrants — room was made for them by expelling and killing Palestinians and expropriating their land and homes — Israel would require the assistance of US Jews. But even before then, US Jewish money was already being raised under the deceitful name of American Friends of the Fighters for Freedom of Israel. The money was for two brutal Jewish Terrorist groups — including the savage Lohamei Herut Yisrael also known as the LEHI or Stern Gang after its founder Avraham Stern — who were murdering innocent civilians as a matter of course to cleanse Palestine of its British occupiers and its indigenous inhabitants. Albert Einstein was asked to help the Stern Gang raise American money for arms to drive out the Arabs and help create a Jewish State. On April 10, 1948, the day after the infamous massacre of Arabs at Deir Yassin, Einstein replied as follows:

"Dear Sir: When a real and final catastrophe should befall in Palestine the first responsible for it would be the British and the second responsible for it the terrorist organisations build up from our own ranks. I am not willing to see anybody associated with those misled and criminal people. Sincerely yours, Albert Einstein"

Following Israel's establishment in may 1948, Einstein on December 4, 1948 sent a letter to the Editors of *The New York Times* — that was also signed by Hannah Arendt and twenty-six other Jewish scholars and teachers — warning of Zionist Fascism in Israel and the current visit of Menachem Begin which was intended to give the impression of American support for his party in the coming Israeli elections. The letter began as follows:

> *Among the most disturbing political phenomena of our times is the emergence in the newly created state of Israel of the "Freedom Party" (Tnuat Haherut), a political party closely akin in its organisation, methods, political philosophy and social appeal to the Nazi and Fascist parties. It was formed out of the membership and following of the former Irgun Zvai Leumi, a terrorist, right-wing, chauvinist organisation in Palestine . . .*

Though US Jews subsequently responded with unprecedented generosity, by 1950 however, it became apparent to US Jewish leaders that much more financial aid was required and accordingly they devised a four-point strategy to increase donations from Jewish individuals; encourage corporate investment in Israel; promote the sale of Israeli bonds; and request that Israel becomes a recipient of assistance from the US aid program for underdeveloped countries. Despite such efforts, the demand of Israel's economic and military requirements could not be met by handouts alone. Consequently in 1951 the American Zionist Council (AZC) was established to promote a pro-Israel lobbying campaign that would concentrate on influencing the US Congress to provide very substantial aid.

Having established itself as a tax-exempt entity, the AZC was not legally permitted to Lobby in the US on Israel's behalf and as a result in 1954 faced a possible investigation for its violations. To avoid that possibility, the AZC rebranded itself as the non-tax-exempt American Zionist Committee for Public Affairs. Another rebranding became necessary when it was subsequently realised that its Zionist objectives may trouble some American Jews whose support was required. The Committee consequently yet again shrewdly rebranded itself by substituting the word "Israel" for "Zionist" to become the American Israel Public Affairs Committee in 1963.

Creating a favourable image of Israel amongst a mostly apathetic American public had, however, begun some years earlier in the mid-1950s when the eminent public relations consultant Edward Gottlieb was asked "to create a more sympathetic attitude" toward the newly established Jewish State. Gottlieb then persuaded Leon Uris — a Jewish American author who admitted to being biased towards Israel — to write a novel about the founding of Israel which was subsequently published in 1958 and became an international bestseller that was translated into over fifty languages. In 1960, Otto Preminger produced and directed *Exodus* — with help from Israel — an epic film starring Paul Newman which served to pervert and dominate American public opinion. Bradley Burston in a 2012 *Haaretz* article — headlined The 'Exodus' Effect: The Monumentally Fictional Israel That Remade American Jewry — began by stating "It's hard to underestimate the impact of this book — along with the Paul Newman film — on a generation of Americans and beyond."

> *As a piece of propaganda, it's the greatest thing ever written about Israel.*
> **David Ben-Gurion**

AIPAC is currently headquartered a few blocks from Capitol Hill in a nondescript but secure and heavily guarded building where staff work closely with the office in Jerusalem and coordinates the activities of a further 17 regional offices. By working closely with their Washington Headquarters, each regional office maintains a year-round hands-on involvement with the more than 100,000 AIPAC members — including a vast pool of donors — who are kept informed with seminars on Israeli issues and encouraged to become effectively involved on Israel's behalf in both local and national politics.

> *"The Israel lobby is one of the most powerful and pervasive special interest groups in the United States. It consists of a multitude of powerful institutions and individuals that work to influence Congress, the president, academia, the media, religious institutions, and American public opinion on behalf of Israel."*

Alison Weir, the President of the Council for the National Interest and founder of the If Americans knew. com site with its vast amount of information including a partial list of some 70 Israel; lobby organisations

In the bicameral Congress AIPAC enforces an allegiance to Israel — that far surpasses any congressional loyalty to the US or its people — by requiring from every candidate a "signed pledge" to support Israel which if refused results in a cutoff from AIPAC's financial support and a campaign of demonisation. Candidates who comply — sellout the US — will then join the AIPAC gravy train with constituency rewards and free junkets to Israel. AIPAC's organisational skills through its regional offices also ensures that while there are only some 7.5 million Jews in the US — less that 2.5 percent of the population — they will nonetheless be the highest ethnic group percentage of actual voters estimated to be around 90 percent of whom 89 percent live in the twelve key electoral college states.

A total of 41 Democrats and 31 Republicans are in Israel on overlapping party tours to get a firsthand view of the complex security challenges Israel faces and to express their unconditional, bipartisan support for the Jewish state.

. . . The concurrent trips (the Democrats arrived on Aug. 5 and were scheduled to leave on Aug. 11, and the Republicans arrived on Aug. 9 and are staying until Aug. 15) come among growing political discord

between the parties in the United States, as well as sharp criticism of Israel from the progressive wing of the Democratic Party. Most notably, rhetoric has sounded from three members of the four-person "Squad" of new congresswomen — Reps. Rashida Tlaib (D-Mich.), Ilhan Omar (D-Minn.) and Alexandria Ocasio-Cortez (D-N.Y.) — calling into question America's (and Congress's) relationship with Israel while promoting calls for the boycott of Israeli products.

Tlaib, Omar and Ocasio-Cortez refused to participate on the trip specifically designed for fellow freshmen members of Congress by the American Israeli Education Foundation (AIEF), a division of the American Israeli Public Affairs Committee (AIPAC).
Jewish News Syndicate, August 11, 2019

Approximately one-third of AIPAC's Washington staff are administrative and clerical with the remainder being specialists in areas of strategic importance including communications and leading-edge weapons technology. AIPAC is structured to effectively maximise efforts by concentrating on the Executive Branch, Legislation, Research, and political development. Influencing the Executive Branch that is not elected but appointed and accountable only to the President is of vital importance when dealing with issues — such as the ongoing charade of the Middle East peace process — that are initiated in the Oval Office rather than by the bicameral Congress. By ensuring the presence of Jews within the ranks of the Executive Branch, AIPAC, rather than having to react to US Middle East policy decisions, is instead able to exert influence during their formulation.

AIPAC also helps track House and Senate races; assists with planning and executing local Congressional Club events and Congressional Club components in local events; attends and assists in regional events; establishes and maintains contact with House and Senate campaigns to assist in the scheduling of candidate meetings and facilitate the submission of position papers; solicits financial support for AIPAC's Annual Campaign; conducts candidate meetings; researches, tracks and records FEC and polling data; works with colleagues to increase pro-Israel political participation in the region by soliciting Congressional Club commitments; assists with AIPAC legislative grassroots mobilisations; assists with scheduling and organising of caucuses in the regions and lobbying appointments during the AIPAC Policy Conference; assists with the integration of AIPAC's activist bases in the Jewish and Outreach communities; promotes participation at local and national AIPAC events including regional events and national political training conferences; researches, gathers, and delivers information requested by pro-Israel political activists; and oversees AIEF's congressional lobbying junkets — blatant bribes — to Israel which are actually illegal.

Another example of AIPAC's influence on Congress became evident measly $600 payment to help struggling American families was subject to several months of intense debate, while there was little congressional discussion over the large funds handed out to Israel without returns. Support for Israel is considered a bipartisan priority that has, for decades, been regarded as an essential part of US foreign policy. The question how Israel uses the funds — whether it is for sustaining the illegal occupation; for financing Jewish settlements; for funding West Bank annexation; or for violating Palestinian human rights — is strictly forbidden.

For the last 30 years, I have witnessed and experienced the severe restraints on any free and balanced discussion of the facts. This reluctance to criticise any policies of the Israeli government is because of the extraordinary lobbying efforts of the American-Israel Political Action Committee and the absence of any significant contrary voices. It would be almost politically suicidal for members of Congress to espouse a balanced position between Israel and Palestine, to suggest that Israel comply with international law or to speak in defence of justice or human rights for Palestinians.

Former President Jimmy Carter in the Los Angeles Times, 2006

20

Western Democracies
Blackmailed, Bribed, and Bullied

We shall not flag or fail. We shall go on to the end. We shall fight in France, we shall fight on the seas and oceans, we shall fight with growing confidence and growing strength in the air. We shall defend our island, whatever the cost may be. We shall fight on the beaches, we shall fight on the landing-grounds, we shall fight in the fields and in the streets, we shall fight in the hills. We shall never surrender.
Sir Winston Churchill (1874-1965), June 4, 1940, following the evacuation of British and French armies from Dunkirk as the German tide swept through France.

Having made enormous sacrifices in both human and material terms to overcome the threat of Hitler's Nazism and Mussolini's Fascism during World War Two, Western nations understandably paused — but only briefly — to contemplate the cost of preserving their precious freedoms before proceeding to surrender them to an Israeli State where Fascism would flourish within an Apartheid regime. Validating the legitimacy of that state while denying its Apartheid reality, required the creation of a dedicated, determined, and diabolic "Holocaust Industry" that masqueraded as the watchdog against anti-Semitism and a defence against another Holocaust. It was a Zionist ploy that also coerced the world into accepting the callous ethnic cleansing of the Palestinian people, the eradication of their history and existence, and the theft of their land and natural resources.

It was at the behest of the Israeli government with a $72 million war chest to fight BDS, that an October 2018 conference was convened in Brussels to push for all European political parties signing up to "red lines" that declared BDS tactics to be "fundamentally anti-Semitic." The text urged EU member states to sign up to the International Holocaust Remembrance Alliance's working definition of anti-Semitism and to exclude from government any politicians or parties that breach it. One of those red lines — based on a resolution adopted by Angela Merkel's Christian Democratic Union in Germany in 2016 — called on all political parties to pass a binding resolutions rejecting BDS activities. The legislation represented yet another assault on the fundamental rights of freedom of expression and choice and undermined the principles of democracy as had happened in Germany under Nazi rule.

Every person shall have the right freely to express and disseminate his opinions in speech, writing, and pictures and to inform himself without hindrance from generally accessible sources. Freedom of the press and freedom of reporting by means of broadcasts and films shall be guaranteed. There shall be no censorship.

Basic law of the German Constitution, Article 5 (1)

Germany's disregard for its own Constitution and compliant adoption of Israeli instigated resolutions no doubt stems from the country's still lingering feelings of guilt over the Holocaust. Though some uncertainty may still exist as to just how much the German people back in Hitler's time actually knew about the atrocities being perpetrated by the Nazi regime, there can be no doubt that today's German subjects along with their political and religious leaders have been fully aware — for more than 70 years — of the documented and irrefutable evidence of Israel's inhumane crimes against the Palestinian people. Even if the majority of Germans had in fact knowingly tolerated the atrocities perpetrated by the Nazis against Jews, that does not mean they must now with full knowledge make amends by tolerating the atrocities being committed by Jews against the Palestinians.

Palestinian children in particular, are deliberately targeted — to break the spirit of future generations — with callous disregard for the United Nations Convention on the Rights of the Child (UNCRC) which Israel hypocritically signed in July 1990, ratified in October 1991, and is responsible for enforcing in Israel as well as in the Occupied Palestinian Territories. Furthermore, according to the International Court of

Justice, Israel — as the occupying power — is also responsible for the human rights situation in Palestine. Germany, however, like most other Western nations, has unashamedly failed to challenge Israel's criminal arrogance in refusing to recognise its obligation to respect international law by unscrupulously exploiting repeated memories of the Holocaust as a deterrence against criticism.

The reality of Zionism's true nature was established by leaders such as Yehuda Bibas, Zvi Hirsch Kalischer, Judah Alkalai, and Theodor Herzl who promoted Zionist ideas and proposed that the eradication of anti-Semitism required both the active encouragement and promotion of anti-Semitism as a way of gaining sympathy for the creation of a "Jewish State."

> *It is essential that the sufferings of Jews . . . become worse . . . this will assist in realisation of our plans . . . I have an excellent idea . . . I shall induce anti-Semites to liquidate Jewish wealth . . . The anti-Semites will assist us thereby in that they will strengthen the persecution and oppression of Jews. The anti-Semites shall be our best friends*
> **Theodor Herzl**

Herzl's assertion thereby established the importance of having anti-semitism — whether real, imagined, or deliberately concocted — play a vital role in realising the objectives of Zionism which deceptively presented itself as being "the national revival movement of the Jewish people," while asserting that Jewish people had the right to self-determination in their own national home with the right to develop their national culture: a right that the Palestinian people are not allowed to enjoy even on their own land which is slowly but surely being illegally expropriated to satisfy the aspirations of a Zionist ideology that purports to represent all Jewish people.

So even before the guilt-ridden toleration by the West of Israel's destruction of some 560 Palestinian villages and the ruthless expulsion of over 750,000 Palestinian civilians which became known as the Naqba, or "Catastrophe" on whose commemoration Israel has imposed fines, the Zionists were already laying the foundations for the instigation of what would turn out to be a British-sanctioned ethnic cleansing of Palestine. The extent to which Zionism influenced the Balfour Declaration was further confirmed by a recent study — authored by Efraim Halevy, a former head of Mossad which alleges that the Jewish espionage network Nili — an acronym for a phrase from the First Book of Samuel — played a vital role in the formation of the Balfour Declaration that helped pave the way for the establishment of Israel.

Zionism's clandestine subversion of Western democracies with untold influence over their governments was reconfirmed early in 2017 — by that exceptional superpower champion of democracy and human rights — when according to *The Washington Post* "all 100 US Senators signed a letter asking UN Secretary General António Guterres to address what the lawmakers called entrenched bias against Israel at the world body." This was in line with decades of US pro-Israel policy that obligingly vilified and vetoed UN resolutions against Israel's criminality.

If the German people want to atone for their Nazi past, then they should do so with dignity, integrity, and moral purpose by ensuring all 30 Articles outlined in the Universal Declaration of Human Rights (UDHR) are applicable to everyone, everywhere. If the concept of justice is to prevail with impartiality for all humanity, it cannot be conditional, discriminatory, or selective. All people without exception must be judged, treated, and cared for in accordance with the same ethical and moral standards. German people must not surrender the virtue of their nation's soul by ignoring the brutal crimes committed against the Palestinian people just because the perpetrators happen to be Jewish and former victims of the Nazis. If the Jewish vow of "Never Again" is to have any relevance, then it must also be applicable to the ethnic cleansing of all peoples including Palestinians with those responsible for such genocidal policies being tried and punished as were the Nazis at the Nuremberg trials.

While there is no question of Judaism being an ancient religion with established ethical principles, Zionism is a relatively recent phenomenon that can be justifiably described as an ideology whose unprincipled objective was to change the Jewish people's disposition from that of a religious entity into a powerful political movement for the establishment of a state for the "benefit" of the Jewish people. Though that objective was staunchly opposed from the very start by the Jewish people's spiritual leaders, Zionists nonetheless prevailed — with the help of a universally subservient media — by deceiving well-intentioned Jewish people and a very gullible world with fraudulent propaganda, false flag operations, and flagrant acts of terror even against Jews. The chasm between Judaism as a religion and Zionism as the usurper of that religion to front its Fascist mentality and agenda, was confessed to in a quote attributed to one of Israel's former prime ministers:

> *Even today I am willing to volunteer to do the dirty work for Israel, to kill as many Arabs as necessary, to deport them, to expel and burn them, to have everyone hate us, to pull the rug from underneath the feet of the Diaspora Jews, so that they will be forced to run to us crying. Even if it means blowing up one or two synagogues here and there, I don't care. And I don't mind if after the job is done you put me in front of a Nuremberg Trial and then jail me for life. Hang me if you want, as a war criminal. Then you can spruce up your Jewish conscience and enter the respectable club of civilised nations, nations that are large and healthy. What you lot don't understand is that the dirty work of Zionism is not finished yet, far from it.*

Former Israeli Prime Minister Ariel Sharon, in 1983

In February 2019, French President Emmanuel Macron — while subserviently failing to mention Zionist Israel's crimes against the Palestine people — announced measures to combat the rise of anti-Semitism at the annual dinner of the Council of Jewish Institutions in France. Macron added that France would also take steps to define "anti-Zionism as a modern-day form of anti-Semitism" in line with that advocated by the International Holocaust Remembrance Alliance's non-legally binding working definition of antisemitism:

> *Antisemitism is a certain perception of Jews, which may be expressed as hatred toward Jews. Rhetorical and physical manifestations of antisemitism are directed toward Jewish or non-Jewish individuals and/or their property, toward Jewish community institutions and religious facilities.*

As a result of Macron's announcement, France joined Germany, Britain, and some 30 other governments including the US — with the Biden administration enthusiastically embracing the IHRA antisemitism definition — in promoting the false assertion that Anti-Zionism is the "new" anti-Semitism. Zionism's hijacking of Judaism has facilitated having criticism of its crimes against humanity conflated with anti-Semitism. Western leaders who grovel at, and sup from an Israeli "fountain of plenty" overflowing with shekels and Palestinian blood, should understand that condemnation of an Apartheid ideology seeking to destroy the essential foundations for life of a national group, namely the Palestinians — with the aim of completely annihilating them — is not anti-Semitism, but respect and support for human rights: rights including the self-determination which Israeli Jews and their supporters insist on having for themselves while brutally denying them to the Palestinian people. When it comes to kosher moral hypocrisy, god's chosen are second to none.

The gradual but incessant and successful criminalisation of criticism of, or opposition to Apartheid Israel — initiated by Jewish lobby groups that operate throughout the world but more so in the West — has without doubt not only infringed on the basic right to free speech, but has also Zionised the government perceptions of most Western "democracies" where the fear of being accused of anti-Semitism has become Zionism's ultimate weapon for coercing most people and institutions into becoming muzzled accomplices in the criminal oppression of the Palestinian people.

It has to be recognised that Israel will not be satisfied until every drop of drinkable water which it has not already stolen, becomes too contaminated for Palestinians to drink; will not be satisfied until its air, land and sea blockade of the Gaza Strip — that prevents the import of vital food and medical supplies — has induced malnutrition, disease and death amongst the imprisoned and persecuted population; will not be satisfied until all Palestinian children have been traumatised by the experience of seeing their parents being hounded, humiliated, imprisoned without due process, and in many cases simply murdered; will not be satisfied until those same children are further traumatised by being arbitrarily arrested, interrogated without adult or legal council support, beaten, terrorised, and forced into signing confessions — written in a language they do not understand — that incriminate parents and relatives who are then held indefinitely under the misused Administrative Detention Order; will not be satisfied until every Palestinian home, hospital and school has been reduced to rubble with bombs supplied by courtesy of US taxpayers; and Israel will not be satisfied until every drop of Palestinian blood has soaked into the stolen Palestinian lands on which more illegal Jewish settlements will be built. Welcome to the land that god gave to his chosen people.

> *Throughout history, it has been the inaction of those who could have acted, the indifference of those who should have known better, the silence of the voice of justice when it mattered most, that has made it possible for evil to triumph.*
> **Haile Selassie I (1892-1975), Emperor of Ethiopia from 1930 to 1974**

With Germany being one of the acknowledged leaders of the European Union, the German people — though still haunted by the spectre of a Nazi past while being blackmailed by a pernicious "Holocaust Industry" — nonetheless have a responsibility to themselves and the rest of humanity to unconditionally condemn and oppose any racial ideology that asserts its own people are "superior" and/or "god cho-sen." This onerous responsibility has recently become even more pressing as a consequence of the world leadership vacuum created by the US — an already morally decrepit superpower subservient to the dictates of an Apartheid Jewish State — which further diminished its world standing and relinquished any semblance of national character and fortitude with the 2016 election of a deranged racist buffoon for president.

The German debt to the Jewish people can never end, not in this generation and not in any other.
Menachem Begin

In fairness, however, the reality of the US now resembling George Orwell's 1984 — with a government persecuting individualism and independent thinking as a "thoughtcrime" to be enforced by a "Thought Police" (AIPAC} — cannot be blamed entirely on the unstatesmanlike buffoonery of a Donald Trump. This is because subservience to the pro-Israel lobby has over a period of many decades become the hallmark of successive US governments as occurred with the condemnation in the House of a July 2017 State Department report blaming Israel of terrorism and claiming that Palestinians rarely incite attacks.

Such US subservience was also confirmed by a group of US Senators who co-sponsored S.720 — also known as the Israel Anti-Boycott Act — that would make it a felony for Americans to support the boycott of Israel. This outrageous assault on civil liberties prompted the American Civil Liberties Union (ACLU) to publish a letter from which the following is an excerpt:

> *The bill seeks to expand the Export Administration Act of 1979 and the Export Import Bank Act of 1945 which, among other things, prohibit US persons from complying with a foreign government's request to boycott a country friendly to the US. The bill would amend those laws to bar US persons from supporting boycotts against Israel, including its settlements in the Palestinian Occupied Territories, conducted by international governmental organisations, such as the United Nations and the European Union. It would also broaden the law to include penalties for simply requesting information about such boycotts. Violations would be subject to a minimum civil penalty of $250,000 and a maximum criminal penalty of $1 million and 20 years in prison. We take no position for or against the effort to boycott Israel or any foreign country, for that matter. However, we do assert that the government cannot, consistent with the First Amendment, punish US persons based solely on their expressed political beliefs.*

The German people — along with other Europeans including the not-so-independent Brexit British — have also continued to permit their respective governments and corporate media outlets to snuff out any criticism of Israel with even President Macron asserting that France would "not surrender" to anti-Israel rhetoric and that anti-Zionism is a new type of anti-Semitism. So now in our Brave New World condemning the ethnic cleansing of Palestinians by Israeli Jews is anti-Semitic. Whatever happened to France's national motto of *Liberté, égalité, fraternité, ou la Mort* (Liberty, Equality, Fraternity, or death).

Despite the glaring reality of such evidence, recent German generations — still very much guilt-ridden from endless reminders of the Holocaust — continue apologising for the sins of their forefathers; continue paying vast sums in compensation; continue flagellating themselves with obligatory acts and pronouncements of contrition; continue supporting an Apartheid and virtually rogue Jewish State hell-bent on ethnically cleansing the Palestinian people and stealing their land; and continue to supply Israel with substantially discounted military equipment including three nuclear-capable submarines whose acquisition involved the usual Israeli propensity for subterfuge and corrupt shenanigans.

Germany's customary adoration, benevolence, and subservience — due to a fundamental German foreign policy conviction that, given the atrocities committed by the Nazis during World War Two, the country should refrain from criticising Israel — is, however, no longer an inevitable certainty because Germans are beginning to realise the importance of not allowing their historical guilt to lead them to accept Israeli government policies that are widely divergent from the aims and values which both countries hypocritically profess to wholeheartedly embrace and live up to.

Yet in spite of an expression of alleged "great concern" by the German Foreign Ministry over Israeli settlement plans — including Israeli decisions to build settlements inside Palestinian neighbourhoods, in East Jerusalem and around it — the German government like most others in the West has again timidly failed to back such concern with any positive or punitive action. Germany's continuing failure to condemn and take action against blatant Israeli violations constitutes contemptible complicity tantamount to the criminality for which Nazis were made accountable at the Nuremberg Trials.

The German people must therefore by their own example take the lead in helping to disengage Europe from US-led blinkered and cowardly subservience to a Zionist Apartheid State because it is the height of amoral hypocrisy to wring their hands over past Nazi atrocities while simultaneously tolerating the ethnic cleansing of the Palestinian people as has been, and is still occurring right before their very eyes. Furthermore, Europeans must seriously endeavour to regain some degree of self-respect and genuine independence by unconditionally refusing to be blackmailed into silent toleration of Israeli crimes against humanity. They can do that by starting to recognise the spiteful contempt with which Israel regards them as was recently made very apparent with a withering attack by Prime Minister Netanyahu who during closed-door meeting of eastern European leaders in Budapest, arrogantly boasted that the EU would wither and die if it did not change its policy towards Israel: which presumably means not criticising Israel.

There are two life-forces in the world I know: Jewish and Gentile, ours and yours . . . I do not believe that the primal difference between gentile and Jew is reconcilable. You and we may come to an understanding, never to a reconciliation. There will be irritation between us as long as we are in intimate contact. For nature and constitution and vision divide us from all of you forever — not a mere conviction, not a mere language, not a mere difference of national or religious allegiance.

Maurice Samuel, (1895-1972), avowedly Zionist author in his shocking work of Jewish Supremacism, You Gentiles, 1924

21

Israel's Temple Mount Obsession

The Temple Institute is dedicated to all aspects of the Divine commandment for Israel to build a house for G-d's presence, the Holy Temple, on Mount Moriah in Jerusalem. The range of the Institute's involvement with this concept includes education, research, activism, and actual preparation. Our goal is firstly, to restore Temple consciousness and reactivate these "forgotten" commandments. We hope that by doing our part, we can participate in the process that will lead to the Holy Temple becoming a reality once more.

The Temple Institute's statement of principles

Founded in 1987, the Temple Institute — the most prominent of some 30 ultra-Orthodox/Zionist organisations vociferously calling for the rebuilding of the Temple and the reinstatement of ritual sacrifice — is categoric and uncompromising in stating that its ultimate goal is to rebuild a "Third Jewish Temple" on Temple Mount. Such dedication may have been influenced by the assertion by rabbinic sages

— whose debates produced the Talmud — that it was from here that the world expanded into its present form and from where the Abrahamic god gathered the dust used to create Adam, the first man: an assertion already disproven by the already established fact that the evolution of human beings first began definitely in either East or South Africa where archaeological evidence of our ancestral Y chromosome and mtDNA (mitochondrial DNA) was discovered.

In pursuit of that objective, the Temple Institute's international director believes that a pure red heifer could be used as part of a ritual to bring about the Biblical prophecy of a new Jewish temple on the site of the Al-Aqsa Mosque. The director appears to be obsessed with a combination of a 2,000-year-old Judaic tradition and the latest in American cattle-breeding technology. His holy grail is to genetically engineer the perfect red heifer which if successful, he believes would pave the way for the destruction of the Al-Aqsa Mosque and in turn facilitate its replacement by a Jewish temple. In his promotional video, he describes efforts to raise a herd of red cows as an "unprecedented historical project . . . For 2,000 years, we've been mourning the destruction of the holy temple, but the future is in our hands . . . The challenge is to raise a perfect red heifer according to the exact Biblical requirements here in the land of Israel. It's time to stop waiting and start doing." A crowdfunding appeal was launched in order to help fulfil this biblical temple building prophesy.

The idea therefore is to implant red-cow embryos in the

wombs of surrogate mother cows who will be meticulously monitored and cared for during nine months of gestation prior to giving birth. In the eventuality of one of the calfs being a totally red heifer, it would be declared the first authentic red heifer since the days of the Second Temple. Then after becoming two years old, the heifer would be slaughtered, burned, and its ashes mixed with water so that finally, after 2,000 years, Jewish believers could be purified from the ritual impurities associated with coming into contact with the dead, and will then be free to ascend to all parts of the Haram al-Sharif/Temple Mount. Obtaining a truly kosher red heifer is of vital importance because the lack of red heifer ashes is one of the most serious halakhic — the collective body of Jewish religious laws — obstacles to building the third Temple on the Mount. Jewish law asserts every Jew is currently ritually impure from having been near a dead body or gravesite. Such impurity can only be overcome by water mixed with the ashes of a truly red heifer. You can get red heifer video update on YouTube.

Consequently Jews subscribing to this belief have for decades been searching for the miraculous red cow, known in Hebrew as the para aduma. It was not until some years ago, that Temple Institute researchers discovered a farm in Texas with a breed of red cows called Red Angus with reputedly very high-quality meat. A delegation from the Institute flew to Texas and purchased some frozen Red Angus embryos that met the criteria set by Jewish law. A farm was subsequently found in the south of Israel that specialised in raising cows to host the surrogacy process. The surrogate mothers and their offspring at this farm are now subject to closed-circuit television monitoring while receiving extra special treatment and protection to ensure that all halakhic criteria are met.

Though initially regarded as an extremist group on the fringe of lunacy, the Institute has since gained increasing support not only from Jewish settlers and American Christian Zionists, but also from Israeli politicians — with government ministers parroting its call for a third temple — and education ministry funding annually helping to indoctrinate tens of thousands of pupils in its dangerously provocative agenda. The project's eventual success is entirely dependent on breeding a totally red heifer without any white or black hairs because according to the Book of Numbers, God instructed Moses to "speak unto the children of Israel, that they bring thee a red heifer without spot, wherein is no blemish, and upon which never came yoke." The animal was to be ritually sacrificed and its ashes mixed with cedar wood and hyssop so that the high priest could then bathe in the mixture for the "purification of sin."

Jewish scholars subsequently extended this cleansing ritual to the priestly caste that served in both the legendary temple built by King Solomon who probably never existed, and in the Second Temple where a pure red heifer was last seen. Jewish religious teaching maintains that from the time of Moses until the destruction of the Second Temple, only nine perfect red heifers were discovered. According to the Jewish philosopher Maimonides, the tenth will herald the coming of the messiah. One may well wonder what the messiah will have to say about the ethnic cleansing of the Palestinian people.

Apart from the Temple Institute there are other fringe organisations such as the religious group known as the "Women for the Temple" whose members are hard at work preparing themselves for the temple's numerous requirements when it becomes a reality. They spend their time poring over Sacred Texts that provide instructions for the preparation of sacrificial offerings. They learn how to bake the sourdough bread required for the rites; how to cultivate the so-called crimson worm with which the priests' vestments are dyed; and possibly most important of all, they are studying how to make the parochet — the great curtain in ancient times that separated the Temple's main hall from the Holy of Holies which supposedly contained the Ark of the Covenant — nowadays the parochet covers the Torah ark in synagogues.

Groups such as the "Women of the Temple" are supportive of The Temple Institute's tagline of "It's time to build," and for its controversial mission to rally Jews for the construction of a "Third Temple" by using all available means including internet tools such as Facebook to spread its message among the masses.

Everyone has the right to freedom of thought, conscience and religion; this right includes freedom to

*change his religion or belief, and freedom, either
alone or in community with others and in public or
private, to manifest his religion or belief in teaching,
practice, worship and observance.*
**Article 18, The Universal Declaration of Human
Rights**

While all individuals do have — and rightly so — the
right to pursue the religious beliefs of their choice, they have
no right whatsoever to either impose those beliefs on others,
or to use such beliefs as justification for committing crimes
against humanity as for example ethnically cleansing Palestine of its indigenous population because some nonexistent
god "promised" the land to the Jewish people. Any suggestion by some Jews that Judaism is not represented by Israel
and therefore Israeli crimes have nothing to do with Judaism
is without doubt disingenuous because Judaism cannot have
it both ways: Israel is either a Jewish State for Jews, or it is
not!

There is no escaping the fact that in the May 14, 1948,
Declaration of the Establishment of the State of Israel, the
document categorically defines Israel as a Jewish State. It
stresses that the sovereign authority in Israel is the Jewish
people: "This right is the natural right of the Jewish people
to be masters of their own fate, like all other nations, in their
own sovereign state." It repeatedly uses phrases to emphasise
the point of "Jewish people . . . in its own country"; "Jewish
people to rebuild its national home"; "Jewish State"; "right of

the Jewish people to establish their State"; "Jewish people in the upbuilding of its State"; and "sovereign Jewish people." It should be noted that in their infinite holy wisdom, the Jewish people have decided that the document's reference to " . . . people to be masters of their own fate, like all other nations, in their own sovereign state," is not applicable to the Palestinian people who after all do not actually "exist," and if they do, then they are no better than "beasts."

> *To me, they are like animals, They are not Human.*
> **Eli Ben-Dahan, Israeli Deputy Defence Minister, in a radio interview in 2013**

Can you imagine the wild wailing of a victimhood culture and the ostentatious outrage that would result if someone were to speak of Jews in that same manner? The Jewish State's utter contempt for Palestinians, and Judaism's intemperate and somewhat unfounded claim to the Holy Land in general and the Temple Mount in particular, is unfortunately — to the detriment of hopes for universal peace — also up against equally justified claims by two other Abrahamic religions. The Christian Church of the Holy Sepulchre — located within the walled Old City of Jerusalem — is venerated as the site of Calvary (Golgotha) where Jesus is said to have been crucified and subsequently buried. As it is also the alleged site of the resurrection, it has served as an important Christian pilgrimage destination since the fourth century.

Temple Mount is also the current site of three monumental Islamic structures consisting of the al-Aqsa Mosque, the Dome of the Rock, and the Dome of the Chain which have stood there since 705, 691, and 691 respectively. Despite that Islamic presence on Temple Mount for more than 1,300 years — far longer than any Judaic structures — the Temple Institute is nonetheless undeterred in its quest which does not appear to be a problem for its ultra-Orthodox/Zionist objective, even if it means either destroying or dismantling Islamic structures and moving them to an alternative site.

> *Now's the time to put one hundred kilos of explosives in the Mosque of Omar [the Dome of the Rock], and that's it, once and for all we'll be done with it."*
> **The army's chief rabbi, Shlomo Goren, later Israel's chief rabbi, immediately after Temple Mount was captured by Israeli paratroopers on June 7, 1967.**

During a panel discussion in February 2016 organised by the group Students For The Temple Mount, Deputy Speaker of the Knesset, Oren Hazan claimed "If the day comes and I have the opportunity to lead the country, not to mention become the prime minister, I will build the temple on the Temple Mount." When asked how he would demolish Al-Aqsa mosque and Dome of the Rock in order to make way for a temple, Hazan replied "It would not be responsible at this point in time to tell you how we would do it, but I will say it clear and loud: When I have the opportunity to do it, I will." Other likeminded god chosen people include members of the reestablished Sanhedrin — a Greek word for council or assembly — the highest court of justice and the supreme council in ancient Jerusalem.

> *The chief priests and the whole Sanhedrin were looking for evidence against Jesus so that they could put him to death, but they did not find any. Many testified falsely against him, but their statements did not agree.*
> **Mark 14:55-56**

The earliest known mention of a Sanhedrin is by Josephus — the Romano-Jewish scholar, historian and biographer (37- c. 100 CE) — who wrote of a political Sanhedrin convened by the Romans in 57 BCE. Hellenistic sources generally depict the Sanhedrin as a political and judicial council headed by the country's ruler. Tannaitic (rabbinic works written from about 10 - 220 CE) sources describe the Great Sanhedrin as a religious assembly of 71 sages who met in the Chamber of Hewn Stones in the Temple of Jerusalem. They are said to have constituted the supreme religious body in the Land of Israel during that time and had their own equivalent of a police force with powers to arrest people, as was the case with Jesus Christ.

Though the Sanhedrin heard both civil and criminal cases with authority to impose the death penalty, during the New Testament period that authority was restricted to the Romans, which was why Jesus was crucified — a Roman punishment — rather than being stoned in accordance with Mosaic law which was given specifically to the nation of Israel (Exodus 19; Leviticus 26:46; Romans 9:4). The law consisted of the Ten Commandments, the ordinances, and the worship system, which included the priesthood, the tabernacle, the offerings, and the festivals (Exodus 20 - 40; Leviticus 1 - 7; 23).

The Sanhedrin's last binding decision in ancient times appeared in 358 CE with the adoption of the Hebrew Calendar and their eventual dissolution was the consequence of continual persecution by the Roman Empire and the aspirations of Christendom. Efforts to reestablish the Sanhedrin, were initiated in 2004 in the form of a provisional body awaiting integration into the Israeli government as both a supreme court and upper house of the Knesset. Though the Israeli secular press regarded this new body as an illegitimate fundamentalist organisation of rabbis, it nonetheless claimed to enjoy recognition and support from the entire religious Jewish community in Israel, and has stirred debate in both religious and secularist circles. Since its reestablishment, the Sanhedrin has supported the Temple Institute whose "ultimate goal is to see Israel rebuild the Holy Temple on Mount Moriah in Jerusalem, in accord with the Biblical commandments."

Mount Moriah is in Judaism viewed as being identical with the Temple Mount of Jerusalem. In supporting the Temple Institute, the Sanhedrin has called upon all groups working in the area of Temple Mount and in Temple related activity/research to begin preparing detailed architectural plans for the construction of the Holy Temple with a view to its establishment in its proper place; had stated its intention to establish a forum of architects and engineers whose assignment would be to implement the Council's decision, so that detailed working plans could effectively be brought to an operational stage; had asked the Jewish people to contribute towards the acquisition of materials for the purpose of rebuilding the Holy Temple; had suggested that the gathering and preparation of prefabricated, disassembled portions of this building to be stored and ready for rapid assembly, in the manner of King David; and had ruled that such contributions would be considered as "chulin" — that is non-sacred — for the Temple's construction.

So how will the building of this Third Temple achieved on a site occupied by Islamic monuments for more than 1,300 years? Well, it will involve a long process that began by fooling the UN into believing the partitioning of Palestine was for the creation of independent Arab and jewish states; by then ignoring the agreed to demarcation lines for such states and instead launching a barbaric ethnic cleansing campaign against the indigenous Palestinians by murdering thousands and causing some 750,000 more of them to flee their homes in terror; by carrying out a policy of gradual illegal Jewish settlement building and in the event of anyone complaining remind them of the "Holocaust" and accuse them of being anti-Semitic; by controlling the US government so as to ensure it vetoes all UN resolutions condemning disregard for international law and crimes against humanity, while simultaneously conning the American people into believing that Israel is a staunch ally and bulwark against Islamic extremism and therefore deserving of billions of dollars in annual military aid; by illegally invading and occupying East Jerusalem while declaring that a united Jerusalem is the eternal capital of the Jewish people; by exploiting archaeology and concocted biblical narratives to deny Palestinian history and heritage so as to de-Arabise Palestine; by using spurious excuses and laws to expel Palestinians from areas around Temple Mount such as Silwan and replace them with Jewish families; by building a park adjoining Silwan and claiming it was where King David built a city even though there is no historical evidence of his or his city's existence; by making periodic controversial and confrontational visits to the Temple Mount that provoke riots and justify Israeli use of excessive violence; by allowing provocative visits to Temple Mount by Jewish settlers protected by police and the army while preventing Muslims accessing the holy sites; and by eventually orchestrating a violent confrontation where live ammunition and incendiary weapons are used so as to cause fires that will destroy the islamic monuments.

After that it will be relatively easy to start removing the debris from the destroyed buildings and start building the Temple. Furthermore, there will be no repercussions because not only have most western democracies been undermined by the control of their corrupt governments and pathetic mainstream media, but also because a god chosen and long suffering people are determined to ensure that ethnic cleansing/genocide shall "never again" occur on this planet, unless of course it means having to be rid of those "inhuman" Palestinians whose land was promised by god to his chosen people.

This raises the question of the Islamic world's reaction if that were to happen. If for example a seriously divided Muslim nations were to finally decide on standing up to Israel — having failed to do so for decades — then a nuclear holocaust would most certainly ensue with devastating consequences. This is not some unfounded and wild speculation, but a distinct possibility that previously arose during the 1973 Yom Kippur War.

Though at the time the Israeli intelligence system enjoyed an international reputation for efficiency, it nonetheless repeatedly — right up to the last minute — missed or ignored every possible indicator that Egypt was preparing for war. The coalition of Arab states led by Egypt and Syria had chosen to attack on October 6, 1973, which as the day of Yom Kippur (Day of Atonement) was the holiest and most solemn day of the year for Jewish people. Within forty-eight hours of the surprise Arab attack starting, Israel was reeling and in a desperate position with Syrian forces storming into the Golan Heights and their tanks taking positions on the hills overlooking the Sea of Galilee and pre-1967 Israel.

In the south, the Egyptians had sent five infantry and two armoured divisions across the entire length of the Suez Canal and penetrated Israeli front-line strongholds. Having initially estimated the possibility of up to 10,000 fatal casualties for the assault, the Egyptians lost only 200 men and the canal crossing has since been rated as one of the best-orchestrated obstacle crossings in history. By October 7, a defending Israeli regular division had 180 of its 270 tanks destroyed by Egyptian infantry antitank weapons. On 8 October 1973, the first two Israeli reserve armoured divisions finally arrived in the Sinai to launch a major counter-attack against Egyptian positions but one division was badly mauled and the other apparently indulged in aimless manoeuvres due to confused battle progress reports.

By the end of fighting on that fateful day the Israeli forces had suffered what the late Trevor Nevitt Dupuy (1916-1995) — a retired US Army Colonel, prolific author, and noted military historian — described as "the worst defeat in their history." On that same evening Israeli Defense Minister Moshe Dayan said to Prime Minister Golda Meir "the Third Temple [the state of Israel] is going under." It was probably at that moment that an Israeli decision was taken to use nuclear weapons as a last resort.

It is on record that on the following day Golda Meir was sufficiently concerned to propose travelling to Washington for a face-to-face meeting with US President Richard "I'm not a crook" Nixon but abandoned the idea after being assured that the US would replenish Israel's military hardware. On October 12, Meir stressed the urgency of the situation in a personal communication to Nixon that stated that Israel would be forced to use all "available means" to ensure national survival if the US military hardware was not immediately forthcoming. Meir's implicit threat to use nuclear weapons — a fact confirmed years later by Henry Kissinger to a trusted colleague — spurred the launching of US Operation Nickel Grass.

Nickel Grass involved — C-141 Starlifter and Lockheed C-5 Galaxy transport aircraft — which between October 14, and November 14 — transporting 22,325 tons of tanks, artillery, munitions, and supplies to the Israelis. This enabled the IDF — commanded by war criminal General Ariel Sharon — to turn the tide by initially disabling portions of the Egyptian air defences and crossing the Suez Canal to surround the Egyptian Third Army. On the Golan front, Israeli troops, at heavy cost, repulsed the Syrians and advanced to the edge of the Golan plateau on the road to Damascus. On October 22 the UN Security Council adopted resolution 338, which called for an immediate end to the fighting, but despite that, hostilities continued for several days thereafter before finally ceasing on October 26.

Bearing in mind the unconscionable ease with which Western leaders — led by an AIPAC-controlled US government — have unleashed illegal and still ongoing wars resulting in the death of millions in the Middle East, you can rest assured that Israel would have even less compunction in using nuclear weapons to do likewise. These racist humanity-hating fanatics — such as the criminal maniac Benjamin Netanyahu — would quite happily initiate a nuclear holocaust in order to retain Israel's grip on its ill-gotten gains.

> *In everything, we are destroyers — even in the instruments of destruction to which we turn for relief . . . We Jews, we, the destroyers, will remain the destroyers for ever. Nothing that you will do will meet our needs and demands. We will destroy because we want a world of our own.*
> **Maurice Samuel, You Gentiles**

22

Israel's Moral Degeneration

. . . Israel engages in the kinds of jaw-dropping lies that characterise despotic and totalitarian regimes. It does not deform the truth; it inverts it. It routinely paints a picture for the outside world that is diametrically opposed to reality. And all of us reporters who have covered the occupied territories have run into Israel's Alice-in-Wonderland narratives, which we dutifully insert into our stories — required under the rules of American journalism — although we know they are untrue.

Christopher Hitchens (1949-2011), English-born American journalist, author, and critic

If the downfall of Israel ever occurs, it will be due self-infliction rather than the result of some overwhelming attack by Arab armies or a pervasive pandemic with profound consequences. Zionist Israel's settler-colonial enterprise has been the most heinous in recent history: infinitely more inhumane than that experienced by black people in South Africa during Afrikanerdom\s era of Apartheid. The barbarity and violence by god's chosen people began with the market bombings of the 1930s; continued with the 1948 Naqba, or Palestinian exodus which unlike the biblical Israelite exodus from ancient Egypt was a reality and not a myth; followed by the massacres in Gaza, Lebanon, and Jordan; included thousands of illegal extrajudicial killings and deliberate targeting of civilian Palestinian men, women, and children; and featured the sick-minded bombing of apartment buildings, ambulances, hospitals, schools, and utility infrastructures with substantial losses of life. Israel's conduct was, and still is, inexcusable and an indication that not only has it disregarded the core essence of Judaism, but has also exploited the past suffering of Jews in general, and the Holocaust in particular as a means of avoiding accountability for its bestial behaviour.

Consequently, every year on January 27 — a Jewish lobby enforced International Holocaust Remembrance Day — people everywhere continue gorging themselves on a feast of guilt-inducing media reports that only mention the six million Jewish victims of the Holocaust while forgetting some 16 million others who also perished in World War Two. Western politicians, ecclesiastic notables, and other fawning hypocrites with suitably sombre expressions call to mind the number of Jews lost, while omitting any thought or mention of all the other Nazi victims including Romany gypsies and homosexuals. Meanwhile, the world continues to ignore other ethic groups under threat of genocide, crimes against humanity, war crimes, and ethnic cleansing.

While the heinous Nazi crimes of the Holocaust should always be remembered as an example of "man's inhumanity to man" which should "Never Again" happen, it is equally important not to forget that allowing such a fitting Memorial Day to be exploited to silence legitimate criticism of ethnic cleansing by Israel is reprehensible. Such memorial days should also include the hundreds of millions tragically lost in numerous other genocides. What about the hundreds of millions of innocent children that have died since World War Two as a result of hypocrisy, indifference, neglect, and wars waged by supposedly "civilised" nations as opposed to those countries that many "genius" Americans like former US President Donald Trump regard as being "shitholes"

Not being content with already having two-tier justice system — with one specifically for Palestinians that denies them due process — Zionism has also attacked the judiciary in an attempt to derail the legislative branch; to undermine individual rights by invoking emergency situations; and to warp Basic Laws under the guise of creating a unity government. Though the danger of such developments has been generally ignored by the media and most Israelis, some have nonetheless warned of the consequences with Supreme Court Chief Justice Esther Hayut in October 2019 condemning "unprecedented" efforts to politicise Israel's judicial system: "These days, unprecedented in our political history, require all of us to stand firm and to do our work without fear

. . . Politicisation of the judicial system is likely to completely undermine its foundations as an independent and objective system." Hayut also stressed that the courts are not immune from criticism and added that caution must be exercised to ensure that the fault-finding is not aimed at delegitimising public institutions and civil servants because "Without them all of us will have difficulty maintaining the rule of law."

Struggles on the political and legislative fronts, however, will not be enough to preserve Jewish State "democracy" and Judaic ethics, because it will also be necessary to radically overhaul an education system that has the textbooks used within the school system laced with a pro-Israel ideology that plays a part in priming Israeli children for military service by presenting images, maps, layouts and use of language that marginalises Palestinians, legitimises Israeli military action, and reinforces Jewish-Israeli territorial identity. The inculcation of such points of view produces a culture lacking the conscience, humanity, and values necessary for avoiding the nation's moral degeneration.

Unlike other democracies with a colonialist past who eventually recognised and accepted that the evils of colonialism facilitated morally unacceptable control and oppression, Israel has not allowed its conscience to be affected by a brutal occupation that while brutalising the Palestinians, has also desensitised Israelis to their own moral corruption, endemic use of violence, and diabolical disregard for democratic and humanitarian principles.

Actually — and this was where I began to feel seriously uncomfortable — some such divine claim underlay not just "the occupation" but the whole idea of a separate state for Jews in Palestine. Take away the divine warrant for the Holy Land and where were you, and what were you? Just another land-thief like the Turks or the British, except that in this case you wanted the land without the people. And the original Zionist slogan — "a land without a people for a people without a land" — disclosed its own negation when I saw the densely populated Arab towns dwelling sullenly under Jewish tutelage. You want irony? How about Jews becoming colonisers at just the moment when other Europeans had given up on the idea?

Christopher Hitchens, Hitch 22: A Memoir, 2010

The subterfuge employed by Zionism to fulfil its agenda, has also to some extent been helped by the coincidental rise of right-wing populism in the West which has engendered nationalist, racist, and ethnocentric sentiments that — along with the islamophobia stoked by Israel — have parallels with the Jewish State's way of thinking. The irrational and racist hatred of Islam by western right-wing movements has resulted in them having a shared interest with, and toleration of, the Jewish State's Fascist transgressions against Palestine's indigenous population.

While the extreme right-wing's philosophy on racism and violence is to some extent curbed in Western societies by the presence of humanitarian traditions and some degree of consensus regarding democratic principles, in Israel there are no such constraints whatsoever because the nation's collective conscience has been programmed by a brutally avaricious Zionist ideology — from kindergarten through to compulsory military service — with its incessant beat of war drums and chants of hatred. "KILL THEM ALL" is their mantra as with murderous intent they gather on hillsides and gloat gleefully as Israeli warplanes paid for by US taxpayer dollars bomb Gaza "back to the Middle Ages." The intensity of such hatred warps the mind and defiles the spirit. But not to worry and never mind because "This land is ours. All of it is ours and god himself has willed it."

Ultimately, however, invoking a concocted covenant with some mythical god does not excuse unlawful killings and war crimes with thousands of Palestinians being murdered; does not justify illegal settlement with the transfer of Israeli civilians to the occupied West Bank, including East Jerusalem, in violation of the Fourth Geneva Convention; does not license forced displacement with thousands of acres of Palestinian land being expropriated; and does not mitigate for either the blockade of Gaza, the unreasonable movement restrictions in West Bank, or the abusive detentions designed to dehumanise the Palestinian population.

Israeli authorities have incarcerated hundreds of thousands of Palestinians since 1967, the majority after trials in military courts, which have a near-100 percent conviction rate. In addition, on average, hundreds every year have been placed in administrative detention based on secret evidence without charge or trial. Some were detained or imprisoned for engaging in nonviolent activism. Israel also jails West Bank and Gaza Palestinian detainees inside Israel, creating onerous restrictions on family visits and violating international law requiring that they be held within the occupied territory. Many detainees, including children, face harsh conditions and mistreatment.

Human Rights Watch, Israel: 50 Years of Occupation Abuses, June 2017

Israel is in fact awash with dehumanising racial classifications — dehumanisation is an important weapon in Zionism's armoury for oppression of the Palestinian population — which include the Naqab Bedouin citizens of Israel. The Arab Bedouin minority of the Negev is one of the most discriminated against groups within the Arab population and within Israeli society as a whole. More than half of the estimated 160,000 Negev Bedouins reside in unrecognised villages, which the state refuses to provide with a planning structure and place under municipal jurisdiction. The government uses a variety of measures to pressure Bedouins into relocating to government-planned urban centres that disregard their lifestyle and needs. Whole communities have been issued demolition orders, while others are forced to continue living in unrecognised villages that are denied infrastructure and basic services such as electricity, running water, roads, and schools.

A report published in June of 2020 by the non-governmental agency Negev Coexistence Forum for Civil Equality (NCF) — whose mission is "to achieve full civil rights and equality for all those living in the Negev/Naqab, since the State of Israel fails to respect, protect and fulfil its human rights obligations, without discrimination, towards the Arab-Bedouin citizens in the Negev/Naqab" — stated that in 2017, 2018 and 2019, the State of Israel demolished over two thousand homes of Palestinian citizens of Israel per year in the Naqab region alone.

Intra-Jewish ethnic heterogeneities — between white European-Ashkenazy and black Arab-Mizrahi as well as Ethiopian Jews — also amount to racial classifications, but it is the racial segregation between Israeli Jews and Palestinian Arabs that ultimately enables Israel to ensure that Jewish settlers in the Occupied Palestinian Territories and also those Jewish Israelis in the State of Israel, are able live at the expense of the Palestinian "others." Michel Foucault —French philosopher, historian of ideas, social theorist, and literary critic — described it as establishing "a relationship between my life and the death of the other." Foucault's theories addressed the relationship between power and knowledge, and how they are used as a form of social control through societal institutions.

Such classifications assert Israel's control over Palestinian citizens and other occupied subjects by both the security services and the civil authorities that involve ongoing surveillance by Shin Bet; regular raids on Palestinian villages and homes; checkpoints, separation walls, and curfews; house and village demolitions, population transfers, widespread arrests, and administrative detentions; the detention and torture of Palestinian minors, an increasing number of extrajudicial executions, and forcing Palestinians to be subject to, and objects of an Apartheid Jewish State sovereignty.

In their endless fight to prevent criticism of Jewish State violations, pro-Israel lobby groups have managed to have draconian "anti-racist" laws imposed in many Western countries: laws that prohibit people who criticise Israel on social media, imprison pro-Palestinian activists, and condemn any expression of pro-Palestinian sentiment in the mainstream media. It was therefore business as usual when in early 2015, Israeli politicians requested that other nations across the world enact legislation that outlawed any criticism of Jews or Israel due to a global increase in "anti-semitism." Such efforts have been persistent and ongoing with the *Jewish Insider* reporting that Jewish groups were already lobbying President-elect Joe Biden — even before his inauguration — with a letter on the IHRA's working definition of anti-Semitism. The IHRA definition is a non-traditional definition promoted by Israel partisans in which many negative factual statements about Israel are considered "anti-Semitic." The definition is based on a formulation proposed by an Israeli official in 2004 that has been promoted world wide. The letter, sent to Biden by the Conference of Presidents of Major Jewish Organisations on January 12, 2021, called on "all federal departments and agencies" to use the definition.

It should be realised that Zionist Israel's attempts at suppression of the truth have nothing to do with concern over hate speech, anti-Semitism, or holocaust denial, but are instead about stifling critical comments about the Jewish State and its supporters. It is for example no secret that Israel with its advocates have a double standard on holocaust denial with iIsrael itself having denied of Armenian Genocide (1915-16) so as to reinforce the idea of Jews being the only victims. Further hypocrisy is evident from the fact that Zionist Israel is without doubt one of the most racist and anti-Semitic nations on earth.

Israel has also been frenziedly enacting anti-free speech laws, hiring internet trolls for the spreading of propaganda and disinformation, and even persuading the Jewish owners of social media websites Facebook, Google, Wikipedia, and Youtube to remove material which it did not like irrespective of veracity or merit. This Jewish State's "respect" for democracy has also included campaigns against political parties it did not approve of in Greece, Hungary, Ukraine, and as recently occurred, in Britain where the virtual destruction of the labour party — We "slaughtered" Jeremy Corbyn an Israel lobbyist boasted — was achieved. In Greece, the anti-Israel far-right Golden Dawn Party was disbanded and its leaders arrested. Apart from being illegal, such Jewish State activities also threaten human rights globally by disregarding the articles of UDHR.

Just as the destruction of others eventually results in one's own destruction, denying the right of free expression to others, will also in due course impact negatively on Israel. The result of that impact has over time created an Israeli society with a critical lack of public discourse which has been replaced by a dogmatic and explicit promotion of "Jewish values" where the pronouncements of intellectual thinkers have been silenced by the vacuous mumbo jumbo of pontificating rabbis whose rhetorical smokescreen — generously peppered with biblical quotations regarding the Jewish people's divine mission — overrides the reality of a nation consisting of people whose indoctrination and ethnocentrism has transformed them into brainwashed conformist Fscists lacking the basic civic considerations that are prevalent in western democracies. The modern Israeli therefore has a utilitarian view of the world that translates into the dehumanisation of the inferior "others" irrespective of whether they are Palestinians, Blacks, or white goyim.

It was reported on March 9, 2016, that a Palestinian man attacked a group of people in Jaffa, killing one American tourist before being chased off by security officials. Video footage subsequently emerged showing the assailant lying motionless on the ground after security officials had immobilised him. The baying of Jewish bystanders can be heard encouraging a police officer to shoot the subdued Palestinian: "Give it to him in the head, don't be afraid, give it to him in the head." Eventually, the officer heeded the demand of the bloodthirsty crowd and carried out an extrajudicial execution.

Later that same month, a video — there is no shortage of other such examples on YouTube — shot by Israeli human rights organisation B'Tselem that showed two Palestinian men lying motionless on the ground after reportedly stabbing Israeli soldiers in the centre of Hebron with a large group of Israeli soldiers and settlers busy establishing a crime scene. It is clearly evident that there is no further threat to anyone. A voice can be heard asking about one of the attackers in Hebrew: "Is the dog alive?" Then, a soldier carrying an M16 assault rifle, walks up, cocks his weapon, and shoots the wounded men in the head at point blank range. The soldier's compatriots and group surrounding the bodies barely register the execution that had just occurred before their very eyes.

The frequent occurrence of such extrajudicial killings — supported and cheered on by the general Israeli public — confirm the fact that the seeds of the nation's moral degeneration were sowed in kindergarten, nurtured during childhood and adolescence, and fully developed during compulsory military service at which time they become the means for the Jewish State's dehumanisation of the Palestinian people who are brutally denied their civil rights. Such contemptible conduct is then rationalised by narratives of victimhood and claims of Israel having "the most moral army in the world." There is also the mendacity promoting the myth that the conflict is being fought between two relatively equal sides vying for self-determination within secure and safe states, instead of how in reality the conflict is about an overwhelming military colonisation that denies Palestinians their heritage, history, human and civil rights, and of course their land.

Having such "informed" outlooks may explain why many Israelis have a preference for belligerent and bigoted leaders who favour the use of force over conciliatory dialogue — and are also amoral and corrupt to the core like Benjamin Netanyahu — instead of ones with some humanity and moral backbone. It is also evident that Israel's conveyer belt education system produces emotionally shallow technocrats who while being efficient in the use of applied knowledge, are totally deficient in their capacity for either critical thinking or moral judgment. For them decency, integrity, and adherence to veracity are but abject perceptions for those who are weak and in need of lofty ideals to compensate for their weakness.

Strong of "Zionist mind" Israelis, however, are not encumbered by the need for lofty ideals and have no compunction whatsoever about systematically poisoning one million Palestinian children (under 18s) who account for 50 percent of the two million population under threat of genocide in Gaza which has become "uninhabitable": not as a result of ecological disaster or poor Palestinian stewardship of the land, but because Israelis have chosen to destroy it by every available means including the poisoning of water supplies, starvation, disease, deliberate shootings, poverty, medical neglect, and invasions. They have even destroyed Palestinian COVID-19 Clinics.

Sara Roy of Harvard University's Centre for Middle Eastern studies, considered to be the leading scholar on Gaza's economy, wrote that "innocent human beings, most of them young, are slowly being poisoned in Gaza by the water they drink and likely by the soil in which they plant." According to the UN, 97 percent of Gaza's water is undrinkable with only the upper 10% of Gaza's population having access to clean water. Consequently, on the basis of conservative estimates, only 40 percent of Gaza's children are drinking water that is fit for human consumption with the result that parents in Gaza are faced with having to make the chilling decision of whether or not to allow their children to drink contaminated water as a means of survival. Apart from being efficient in their ethnic cleansing efforts, Israelis also excel in their own kosher brand of chutzpah hypocrisy and capacity for flat-out falsehoods. There is only one thing worse than lying to other people and that is the danger of hypocritically lying to oneself.

When I saw pictures of babies suffocating from a chemical attack in Syria, I was shocked and outraged.
Israeli Prime Minister Benjamin Netanyahu, a god chosen criminal — amongst other things — who is

never shocked or outraged by Israel's deliberate targeting and slaughter of Palestinian children.

Following the April 2017 chemical attack in Syria which Israel's stooge western leaders and mainstream media immediately blamed — without any significant evidence — on the government of President Bashar al-Assad, Zionist Israeli leaders jackbooted their way up to the moral high ground and loudly pontificated about the need for the world to act "against the chemical massacre in Syria" in which some 90 people were killed as opposed Israel's 2014 Operation Protective Edge when more than 2,000 Palestinians were killed — including more than 500 children — and more than 10,000 people injured. Such righteous Israeli condemnation, however, was to say the least, hypocritical considering the fact that during its past attacks on Gaza, Israel had no qualms about using prohibited white phosphorous munitions and flechette shells that spray out thousands of tiny and potentially lethal metal darts which Human Rights Watch described as indiscriminate and evidence of war crimes.

Some seriously burned patients were evacuated to Egypt for treatment, especially if they needed skin grafts, because Gazan hospitals could not offer proper care. "We have a lot of burns, actually chemical burns," a doctor in Cairo treating Gazans told Human Rights Watch. "Most are third degree burns, which look like chemical burns and not ordinary burns. There is no skin and sometimes even no muscle . . . "

All of the white phosphorus shells that Human Rights Watch found came from the same lot manufactured in the United States in 1989 by Thiokol Aerospace, which was running the Louisiana Army Ammunition Plant at the time. In addition, on January 4, 2009, Reuters photographed IDF artillery units handling projectiles whose markings indicate that they were produced in the United States at the Pine Bluff Arsenal in September 1991.

Human Rights Watch Report, Rain of Fire: Israel's Unlawful Use of White Phosphorus in Gaza, March 25, 2009

What is truly tragic about the situation in Palestine is that a Jewish people who suffered at the hands of the Nazis who denied them inalienable rights — the right to life, liberty, and the pursuit of happiness — should themselves degenerate into being the vicious perpetrators of evil against another ethnic group to whom they deny those same rights in order establish and expand a Jewish State for Jews only: Jews who vociferously accuse others of discrimination, anti-Semitism, and of being existential threats to Israel; Jews who misuse the UNHRC to scrutinise nations critical of Israel with a view to bringing them before the Human Rights Council to be reprimanded and punished; Jews who defy that very same UNHRC if it dares to consider examining Israel's crimes against humanity; and Jews who are relentless in their global silencing of any criticism of Israel irrespective of how true and justified it might be.

The plague is spreading. Under cover of the (just) war against anti-Semitism, Europe and the United States silence every voice daring to criticise Israel. Under cover of this war, they are undermining their freedom of speech. Incredibly, this new phenomenon is not triggering any protest, as one would expect. Laws labelling anti-Zionism as anti-Semitism and the anti-occupation movement as anti-Semitic, are passed with overwhelming majorities. Now they are playing into the hands of Israel and the Jewish establishment, but they are liable to ignite anti-Semitism when questions arise about the extent of their meddling.

Last week, the phenomenon hit France, cradle of the revolution. The French National Assembly passed by a sweeping majority a bill that adopts the definition of anti-Semitism issued by the International Holocaust Remembrance Alliance, which equates anti-Zionism with anti-Semitism.

Liberty? Equality? Fraternity? Not when it involves Israel. Here, these values are rendered mute.

Gideon Levy, Haaretz, December 8, 2019

There is no doubt in the face of overwhelming evidence that Israel's creation as a Jewish State was, at its core, a colonialist act of dispossession that deliberately established an Apartheid regime intent on systematic discrimination against, and subjugation of the indigenous population. The evidence is irrefutable.

At the Paris Peace conference in 1919, the Zionist Commission submitted a map of Palestine marked "grazing land," empty of all its towns and villages. That was certification of the Zionist myth of Palestine being "a land without people, for a people without a land." Britain and France — the colonial powers at the Paris conference — supported the outrageous lie of Palestine being empty, despite both of them having conducted extensive surveys in Palestine including the Survey of Palestine by the Palestine Exploration Fund, and published maps and volumes about 1,200 towns and villages, many of which were at least 2,000 years old.

People who call themselves supporters of Israel are actually supporters of its moral degeneration and ultimate destruction.
Noam Chomsky, Jewish American linguist, philosopher, cognitive scientist, and historian

Apartheid and racism are intrinsic components of a Zionist ideology which was pursued with the full knowledge that without the forcible expulsion of Palestinians, it would be impossible to establish an Israeli State. Consequently every single acre of Palestinian land acquired by Israel in 1948 was gained with brutal military force. It should be remembered that from the outset Zionism enjoyed little support from key Jewish figures including Albert Einstein. Zionism was regarded as an extreme form of Jewish nationalism that was criticised by western liberals along with most of the pre-eminent Orthodox and ultra-Orthodox rabbis in Russia and

Eastern Europe. Russian communists opposed Zionism and leading Marxist theorists saw it as complicit in the rise of antisemitism. Zionism was initially more vigorously criticised by Jews than by non-Jews, but that, sadly, was before Zionism instigated the degeneration of the Jewish conscience.

> *It became clear to me how hard it is to realise Zionism in a way compatible with the demands of universal ethics. I was quite depressed.*
> **Arthur Ruppin (1876-1943), Zionist thinker and leader, co-founder of Tel Aviv, director of Berlin's Bureau for Jewish Statistics and Demography from 1902 to 1907, and as of 1908 director of the Palestine Office of the Zionist Organisation in Jaffa for organising Zionist colonisation in Palestine.**

The Israeli group known by the name of its journal *Matzpen* (Hebrew for "Compass"), was a revolutionary socialist and anti-Zionist organisation founded in 1962 and active until the 1980s. It was opposed to all forms of human exploitation, oppression, and discrimination; viewed Zionism as a colonising project; strove for Arab-Jewish coexistence based on full equality; supported implementation of Palestinian human and national rights; and called for solving the region's national and social problems through revolutionary struggle.

> *The interesting point here is Ruppin's guilty conscience and, even more, the fact that Dayan had to bring up the question and confront it anew in 1968. In spite of all the ideological and ethical tranquil-*

lisers which the Israeli-Zionist establishment and its intellectual camp followers cram into Israeli youth, in spite of all the historical justifications and all the sermons about Jewish identity, in spite of all the work of the machinery which moulds national consciousness and national loyalty and which has, for many decades, been exerting immense pressure on Israeli minds at home, at school and in the media — in spite of all this, Zionism cannot rid itself of the demon that Ruppin calls the "demands of universal ethics."

Matzpen On Zionism and Universal Ethics, February 10, 1972

23

Future Prospects for the "Only Democracy in the Middle East"

. . . For almost a hundred years, Zionism fulfilled both roles, becoming not only Israel's state ideology but its citizens' secular religion, effectively supplanting Judaism as the primary source of self-identification and focus of allegiance. Yet the very success of Zionism resulted in disenchantment, because reality has fallen short of the founding fathers' utopian vision of a just, moral society — "a light unto the nations." The disillusionment, in turn, spawned a host of alternative ideological approaches, ultimately crystallising into a serious challenge to the very essence of Israel's national ethos.

Ilana Kass and Bard O'Neill, The Deadly Embrace: The Impact of Israeli and Palestinian Rejectionism on the Peace Process, 1996

Despite its complete and contemptuous disregard for "universal ethics," Israel has nonetheless managed to gradually erode the possibility of any united Arab opposition to its illegitimate and criminal existence: an existence facilitated by an ethnic cleansing financed by US taxpayer dollars, and favoured with timid toleration by a selfish and apathetic international community whose inexplicable inhumanity knows no limits.

When Egypt's President Anwar Sadat visited Israel in 1977, he did so not because of some altruistic motive, but out of an urgent necessity — he had already removed the Soviet military presence from Egypt during the summer of 1972 — to gain favour with the US as a means of getting economic aid and advanced weaponry. Sadat's realisation that getting US aid and support would not be possible without the Jewish lobby's influential approval in Washington, was the reason for his befriending Israel and the subsequent signing of the Egypt–Israel peace treaty on March 26, 1979, following the previous year's Camp David Accords. Though Sadat's 1977 address to the Knesset had reiterated the fact that a just solution for the Palestinian problem was still essential for peace in the Middle East, it turned out to be just a lot of hot desert air because even back then, Israel's perception of "peace" — despite the endless charade of "peace talks" — was, still is, and always will be, an emphatic denial of Palestinian human rights including the criteria for statehood as laid down in the 1933 Montevideo Convention which provided that a state must possess a permanent population, a defined territory, a government, and the capacity to conduct international relations.

First: I have not come here for a separate agreement between Egypt and Israel. This is not part of the policy of Egypt. The problem is not that of Egypt and Is-

rael. Any separate peace between Egypt and Israel, or between any Arab confrontation State and Israel, will not bring permanent peace based on justice in the entire region. Rather, even if peace between all the confrontation States and Israel were achieved, in the absence of a just solution to the Palestinian problem, never will there be that durable and just peace upon which the entire world insists today.

Second: I have not come to you to seek a partial peace, namely to terminate the state of belligerency at this stage, and put off the entire problem to a subsequent stage. This is not the radical solution that would steer us to permanent peace.

Equally, I have not come to you for a third disengagement agreement in Sinai, or in the Golan and the West Bank. For this would mean that we are merely delaying the ignition of the fuse; it would mean that we are lacking the courage to confront peace, that we are too weak to shoulder the burdens and responsibilities of a durable peace based on justice.

Anwar Sadat (1918-1981), address to the Knesset on November 20, 1977

With the signing of that peace agreement, Egypt not only became the first Arab State to officially recognise Israel, but it also set a precedent that if other nations desired getting US aid, arms, and political support, then they would first have to curry favour with Washington's pro-Israel lobby through diplomatic rapprochement with Israel. As a consequence of that precedence, other nations eventually began following suit starting in 1992 with India — until then a staunch backer of Palestinian rights — which changed its position on Israel with the hope that pro-Israel lobby influence would facilitate the release of much needed aid from the US, the International Monetary Fund, and the World Bank.

Though the Saudi Arabians — eminently guilty of war crimes against humanity in Yemen — have not officially normalised relations with Israel, they are nonetheless known to be working behind the scenes with Israel in opposing Iran: a ploy rewarded with protection from the pro-Israel lobby against accusations of genocide in Yemen, and the October 2018 murder at the Saudi Arabian consulate in Istanbul of Jamal Khashoggi, the Saudi dissident, author, and columnist for *The Washington Post*.

Other countries that sought to benefit from an Israeli connection have included the Democratic Republic of Congo which hired an Israeli company to lobby Washington in order to avoid sanctions for human rights violations; Tunisian efforts to normalise relations with Israel have included a 2019 presidential candidate paying $1 million to a Canadian company headed by a former Israeli intelligence agent in an attempt to get a meeting with Donald Trump; Qatar which in 2017 — desiring to be rid of its "pro-terrorist" label over previous support for the Palestinian cause — brownnosed the pro-Israel lobby by killing *Al Jazeera's* four-part documentary on the lobby's shenanigans in the US; United Arab Emirates signed a peace agreement with Israel on August 13, 2020, with the hope that broad benefits would follow including an easier path to buying the Lockheed Martin F-35 Lightning II stealth fighter, as well as other US-made military products; and all the other Arab Gulf states who are equally aware that improving relations with the US and the West requires rapprochement with Israel: which inevitably means abandoning support for the Palestinian cause.

Despite Israel's undoubted success in becoming an essential avenue for currying favour with the US and the West, it has, however, failed in most respects to become a "Jewish State" that Jews everywhere can be genuinely proud of; a state which the rest of the world can accept and recognise with unreserved respect rather than timid subservience and hypocrisy; and a state that has failed to fulfil the dream of the founding fathers who by signing the Declaration — considered the principle of equality as the bedrock of the society they were building — committed themselves, and the Jewish community, "to pursue peace and good relations with all neighbouring states and people".

Following Israel's June 1967 military victory against its Arab neighbours, euphoric Israelis and Jews in diaspora began believing that the dream of a democratic and secure Jewish State might actually become a reality. Three weeks later, during that period of national euphoria, David Ben-Gurion, at 81 years of age, stepped out from retirement to assert that Israel — which had conquered the Palestinian territories of

Gaza and the West Bank — must immediately withdraw and give up possession of the territories. Forcible occupation, he warned, would corrupt the Jewish State and possibly destroy it outright. His speech was mostly ignored by the Israeli press, and as is now apparent, also by the global Jewish community including Israelis.

> *Those of us who are today prepared to hazard our lives for the cause would regret having raised a finger if we were able to organise only a new social system, and not a more righteous one.*
> **Theodor Herzl**

That dream, with its promise of a democratic and secure state for the Jewish people, was always overshadowed by the stipulation that if the promise was in anyway broken, then Israel would be nothing more than an insignificant name on the world map. There is no doubt that Israel has failed to either adhere to the values of Judaism, or fulfil the vision of those who established its existence. According to the Israeli Voice Index for July 2020 and published on August 5, only slightly more than a third, 38 percent of Israelis were optimistic about the future of democratic governance in the country, as compared to a majority of 59 percent who were optimistic about the future of national security. Having a prime minister who is under indictment for bribery, fraud, and breach of trust — on February 5, 2021 he was ordered to appear for opening arguments in his trial — is hardly conducive to giving Israelis confidence in their government.

Your rulers are rogues and cronies of thieves, every one avid for presents and greedy for gifts; They do not judge the case of the orphan, And the widow's cause never reaches them.

Isaiah 1: 23

So why are the ultra-Orthodox Jews, right-wing nationalists, and others in Israel so firmly entrenched in Netanyahu's camp despite his being under investigation for bribery and various other unethical crimes? Have they not read the Torah and the prophetic readings from Isaiah, Jeremiah, Hosea, Micah, and others: readings full of calls for ethical behaviour from leaders and serious warnings regarding the negative effects on society when leaders are corrupt and abuse their power?

To be fair, Netanyahu is not alone and there have been others including President Moshe Katsav who was convicted for two counts of rape, obstruction of justice, and other offences; Prime Minister Ehud Olmert convicted and jailed; and eleven government ministers, sixteen members of the Knesset, two Chief Rabbis, six local government officials, and others who were also convicted of crimes including accepting bribes, bribery, breach of faith and trust, conspiracy to commit a crime, drug smuggling, electronic commerce fraud, forgery, fraud, illegal transfer of funds, harassment and sexual assault, larceny, moral turpitude, obstructing justice, perjury, physically assaulting a child, and theft of two million shekels.

You shall appoint magistrates and officials for your tribes, in all the settlements that the LORD your God is giving you, and they shall govern the people with due justice.

You shall not judge unfairly: you shall show no partiality; you shall not take bribes, for bribes blind the eyes of the discerning and upset the plea of the just.

Justice, justice shall you pursue, that you may thrive and occupy the land that the LORD your God is giving you.
Deuteronomy 16:18-20, Parshat Shoftim, Portion known as "Judges"

Zionist Israel's failure to fulfil the visions of its founders and to meet the moral principles of Judaism has created an internal turmoil which if not addressed will result in it becoming an undemocratic nation with an isolated existence behind an "Iron Wall" that runs counter to the ideals of its founders. While Israel has been primarily preoccupied with ensuring its physical security and empire building, it has gradually abandoned the democratic principles that were pledged on the day of its foundation: democratic principles that must be honoured if the Jewish State is to ultimately avoid self-destruction.

Look back over the past, with its changing empires that rose and fell, and you can foresee the future, too.
Marcus Aurelius (121-180), Roman Emperor, Philosopher

The possibility of that happening was addressed back in March 2015 in a Haaretz article, in which journalist Ravit Hecht, wrote that Netanyahu would make Israel the Middle East's next failed state with the country galloping toward an anti-democratic binational future saturated with hatred and racism. More recently in July 2020, Hecht wrote — in reference to the Black American killed by police while being restrained with a knee on his neck — "It's like George Floyd. We have our knee on the Palestinians' necks."

Democracy means freedom. Even a government of majority rule can negate freedom; and where there are no guarantees for freedom of the individual, there can be no democracy. These contradictions will have to be prevented. The Jewish State will have to be such, ensuring that the minority will not be rendered defenceless.

[Even] after the formation of a Jewish majority, a considerable Arab population will always remain in Palestine. If things fare badly for this group of inhabitants then things will fare badly for the entire country. The political, economic and cultural welfare of the Arabs will thus always remain one of the main conditions for the well-being of the Land of Israel.

Ze'ev Jabotinsky

Jabotinsky's commitment to equality was total and absolute. His attitude toward the Arab minority in the Land of Israel — and his vision for the Jewish State — stand in stark contrast to the thinking behind the recent introduction of illiberal legislation in the Knesset. Though Jabotinsky was the leader of the nationalist camp, which advanced the idea of the Jewish State with all its might, he nonetheless repeatedly emphasised that Arabs must be granted absolute equal rights within that state.

Fulfilment of Jabotinsky's vision, however, has recently been dealt another blow by Israel's most influential political group — the Right Block of mostly religious Zionists — whose primary objective is annexation of the entire West Bank and a declaration of Israeli sovereignty on all Jewish settlements. Annexation would not only increase the Right's political influence, but would also make it much easier to establish new settlements — which currently require approval from the Prime Minister — that would become the responsibility of local councils.

Israel's Jewish Underground — recognised as a terrorist organisation with some members being arrested on various charges in the 1980s including conspiring to blow up the Dome of the Rock shrine, attacking Palestinian students, and bombing Palestinian mayors before fading from view — has also been adding fuel to the fire since its recent resurgence with support from the settler movement, ultra-Orthodox Jews, and hardline Prime Minister Benjamin Netanyahu, who supports illegal settlements and annexation of the West Bank. Contrary to the general belief that it had completely disappeared in the late 1980s, it resurfaced with a different face and was probably responsible for the killing of Prime Minister Yitzhak Rabin after he signed the Oslo Peace Accords with the Palestinian leadership in 1995. This violent movement has been reenergised and is aiming to change the alleged secular nature of the state into a religious one.

Any further annexation would only exacerbate an already explosive situation in the Israeli-occupied territory which with its almost three million Palestinians is essential to hopes of a future independent Palestinian State. The viability of that State, however, has been undermined by the deliberate and illegal influx of Jewish immigrants of whom there were 12,000 in the 1980s but who now number some 500,000 living in settlements within an area of approximately 2,262 square miles. Dominated by ultra Orthodox groups, Underground members want to establish Jewish law as the official ideology of Israel and are a problem for Israel's political establishment because of their extensive influence over right-wing political parties. Netanyahu and other likeminded politicians have tacitly tolerated the jewish Underground's further growth because they regard its activities as serving their own political agenda

Israel's deceitful tactic of pretending to be interested in a peace agreement — while actually playing for time — has enabled it to continue pouring in more Jewish immigrants, thereby gradually negating any chance of either a peace deal or a Palestinian State. Under the "two-state solution" — the mirage that has for decades been supported by the US and the international community — the vast bulk of the West Bank would be returned to the Palestinians. The Israeli right, however, has been pushing Netanyahu's government to proceed with the unilateral annexation of significant areas of the West Bank which it wants to officially make a part of Israel proper, irrespective of what the Palestinians and international community may feel about it. Annexation of the West Bank would violate international law and would no doubt be "severely punished" with the customary ineffectual UN condemnations and mealy-mouthed objections from the West.

Jewish history has been tragic to the Jews and no less tragic to the neighbouring nations who have suffered them. Our major vice of old as of today is parasitism. We are a people of vultures living on the labor and good fortune of the rest of the world.
Samuel Roth (1893-1974), American publisher and writer, Jews Must Live: An Account of the Persecution of the World by Israel on All the Frontiers of Civilisation, 1934

Another political minefield that Israelis need to skirt around was the December 2019 announcement by the International Criminal Court (ICC) on the conclusion of the preliminary examination of the Situation in Palestine, that also sought a ruling on the scope of the Court's territorial jurisdiction. This does not necessarily mean that the ICC has abandoned its previous reluctance to investigate Israel's very obvious and barbaric crimes against humanity — due to the

Court and its members being relentlessly impugned by Israel and its US stooge — but it is at least a first step.

> *Today, I announce that following a thorough, independent and objective assessment of all reliable information available to my Office, the preliminary examination into the Situation in Palestine has concluded with the determination that all the statutory criteria under the Rome Statute for the opening of an investigation have been met . . .*
>
> **Fatou Bensouda, ICC Prosecutor**

As was to be expected the "incorruptible" Benjamin Netanyahu sent a letter to one of Israel's other reliable stooges — Canada's Prime Minister Justin Trudeau — nearly as smarmy as the UK's Tony Blair but not in the same league as a war criminal — asking him to condemn the possible ICC probe into alleged Israeli war crimes, and wasted no time in using Israel's ultimate weapon to launch an attack against the court with Judaism's holy Western Wall as a backdrop during a candle-lighting ceremony marking the start of the eight-day Hanukkah holiday:

> *"New edicts are being cast against the Jewish people — anti-Semitic edicts by the International Criminal Court telling us that we, the Jews standing here next to this wall . . . in this city, in this country, have no right to live here and that by doing so, we are committing a war crime . . . Pure anti-Semitism,"* he added, with a view to striking a chord with many

Israelis who believe that criticism, especially in Europe, of Israeli policies towards the Palestinians has its roots in anti-Jewish sentiment.

In an obligatory US followup to Netanyahu's disingenuous diatribes, US Secretary of State Mike Pompeo — who like his President is also an American paragon of unimpeachable political integrity and the four humanitarian principles of humanity, neutrality, impartiality, and independence — once again threatened the ICC by on this occasion stating that the Trump administration will "exact consequences" if the ICC "continues down its current course" of moving forward with an investigation of possible war crimes committed on Palestinian territory. With global concern for justice being in a shameful state, not one of the ICC's 123 member countries challenged Pompeo's toxic, vicious attack on the court.

Furthermore, on June 11, 2020, the ever-obliging US imposed unprecedented sanctions on the ICC, with President Donald Trump issuing an "executive order" authorising the freezing of assets and a travel ban against ICC officials and their families. The order also allowed for the punishing of other individuals or entities that assist the ICC in its investigation. The US decision to carry out punitive measures against the very Court — that was established for the sole purpose of holding war criminals accountable — is indicative of the extent of US depravity and hypocrisy because while claiming to be the ultimate defender of human rights, it is actually itself committing, cooperating with, and defending another major violator of those rights.

Another Israeli reaction came from Attorney General Avichai Mandelblit who suggested "The principled legal position of the State of Israel, which is not a party to the ICC, is that the Court lacks jurisdiction in relation to Israel and that any Palestinian actions with respect to the Court are legally invalid . . . Only sovereign states can delegate criminal jurisdiction to the court and the Palestinian Authority did not meet the criteria for statehood under international law and the Court's founding statute." Mandelblit's statement did not deny that Israel had committed war crimes, but simply focused on the issue of whether or not the ICC had the authority to prosecute the Israel.

Israel's campaign against the ICC was carried over into 2021 and in February Israeli Foreign Minister Gabi Ashkenazi spoke over the phone with US Secretary of State and fellow Jew Anthony Blinken who assured him that "we will continue to uphold President Biden's strong commitment to Israel and its security, including opposing actions that seek to target Israel unfairly,"; he then spoke with German Foreign Minister Heiko Maas stress that the ICC's decision damages the prospects for promoting peace, and strengthens extremists in the region; and on the following day continued with his harangue against the ICC with calls to other countries including Canada's foreign minister Marc Garneau.

Ashkenazi thanked Garneau for his Feb. 7 statement reiterating that Canada did not recognise the ICC's jurisdiction to proceed with this investigation against Israel: a statement that highlighted Canada's pathetic foreign policy on Palestinian statehood and human rights. While claiming to support the Palestinian right to self-determination, Canada nonetheless refuses to recognise any Palestinian state unless it has the stamp of approval from its occupier, Israel, in negotiations. In other words, Canada recognises the theoretical right to a state, but will in practice ensure that an independent Palestinian state will never become a reality.

The fact that a nation has not signed up to a particular international body or human rights law does not exempt it from being made accountable for any obvious violations. It should be noted that before the Universal Declaration of Human Rights document — establishing a set of principles for the rights of individuals — was accepted by the UN General Assembly on December 10,1948, there was no hesitation to establish Nuremberg trials — November 10, 1945, to October 1, 1946, — when of the 199 Nazi defendants who were tried, 161 were convicted, and 37 sentenced to death.

Israel's determined efforts to avoid facing accountability for its crimes have since remained persistent with Israeli President Reuven Rivlin asking France on March 19, 2021 to oppose the decision of the ICC to initiate a formal probe against "Israelis" for war crimes in the Occupied Palestinian Territories; with Israel on March 22 revoking Palestinian Authority Foreign Minister Riyad Al-Maliki's special travel permit after he returned from a meeting in the Hague with

British lawyer Karim Ahmad Khan, the ICC's new prosecutor; and with the IDF's Chief of Staff also condemning the court with the implication that it was unfamiliar with terror tactics and that that Israel would protect its service personnel from any prosecution.

In the opinion of international law experts, the ICC could lay charges against the heads of the IDF since 2014 — Generals Benny Gantz, Gadi Eizenkot and Aviv Kochavi — as well as senior officers and the current and past heads of the intelligence agencies, including Nadav Argaman and Yoran Cohen. Even PM Benjamin Netanyahu, former Defence Minister Avigdor Lieberman, and head of the Ministry of Defence Naftali Bennett could be indicted, as could the housing ministers responsible for construction in the settlements.

Any issuing of subpoenas or arrest warrants by the ICC would undoubtedly receive no cooperation from Israel which apart from not allowing its citizens to be questioned, would also take the precaution of preventing possible suspects from travelling abroad because all countries that are signatories to the Rome Statute, would be obliged to hand them over to The Hague. This forced Israel — according to an article in *Haaretz* on July 16, 2020, — to draft a Secret List of Hundreds of Officials Who May Stand Trial at the International Court.

Israel is drawing up a secret list of military and intelligence officials who might be subject to arrest abroad if the International Criminal Court in the Hague opens an investigation into alleged Israeli war crimes in the Palestinian territories.

Haaretz has learned that this list now includes between 200 and 300 officials, some of whom have not been informed. The great secrecy surrounding the issue stems from a fear that the mere disclosure of the list's existence could endanger the people on it. The assessment is that the court is likely to view a list of names as an official Israeli admission of these officials' involvement in the incidents under investigation.

Based on the international community's failure to date to unconditionally condemn Israel and make it accountable for the psychopathic and barbaric tendencies of its leaders and citizens, it seems improbable that the ICC will achieve any significant success in its endeavour to get some justice for the Palestinian people. This, however, will not mean that Israel will survive unscathed because the very nature of its malicious mentality and insidious behaviour will ultimately result in self-inflicted punishment. These are a people who are either unable to comprehend, or are deliberately choosing to ignore the fact that the ethnic cleansing of an indigenous population in illegally occupied territories, is definitely not "self-defence."

The soul of Judaism is currently in a deep peril that does not bode well for the future. Saving that soul requires that it be wrenched from the clutches of Zionism, and for Israeli Jews to seriously examine their collective conscience while listening to these amongst them who are wiser including Yehoshafat Harkabi — Chief of Israeli Military Intelligence (1955-9) and subsequently a professor of International Relations and Middle East Studies at the Hebrew University of Jerusalem — who in his 1989 book, *Israel's Fateful Hour*, called for Israel's withdrawal from the occupied territories and warned that:

> *We Israelis must be careful lest we become not a source of pride for Jews but a distressing burden. Israel is the criterion according to which all Jews will tend to be judged. Israel as a Jewish state is an example of the Jewish character, which finds free and concentrated expression within it. Anti-Semitism has deep and historical roots. Nevertheless, any flaw in Israeli conduct, which initially is cited as anti-Israelism, is likely to be transformed into empirical proof of the validity of anti-Semitism. It would be a tragic irony if the Jewish state, which was intended to solve the problem of anti-Semitism, was to become a factor in the rise of anti-Semitism. Israelis must be aware that the price of their misconduct is paid not only by them but also Jews throughout the world. In the struggle against anti-Semitism, the frontline begins in Israel.*

Conclusion

Justice in the life and conduct of the State is possible only
as first it resides in the hearts and souls of the citizens.
Plato, Ancient Greek philosopher (428/427-348/347 BCE)

On January 6, 2021, with an unhinged Donald Trump still insisting he had won the election, the US Capitol was temporarily but violently taken over by a rioting mob of disgruntled and bigoted white "citizens" — with some brandishing Israeli flags in recognition of white Jewish supremacy being the guiding principle in that country — who after incitement by Trump tried to prevent the Congress from exercising its constitutional duty to confirm Joe Biden as the next president. The relative ease with which the takeover was achieved prompted criticism of the somewhat restrained, if not at times accommodating police response. It was even suggested that had this illegal insurrection been carried out by coloured people, then many of them would have been killed by the police who in the US are renowned for being notoriously racist and trigger-happy whenever dealing with African Americans. Police in the US killed 1,000 Americans in 2020.

That assault on what little remained of American democracy resulted in predictable, unreserved, and ostentatious expressions of selective outrage by world leaders and cascades of critical condemnation by corrupt and compliant corporate media journalists and ended with Trump becoming the only US President in US history to be impeached twice. These champions of democracy, human rights, justice, and truth have, however — just like most of their predecessors since 1948 — inexplicably never felt comparable outrage over the far more brutal violence that Israel has with arrogant impunity perpetrated, is perpetrating, and will continue to perpetrate against the Palestinian people while the rest of so-called humanity watches with complicit silence.

> *Throughout history and in contemporary times, belligerent armies, colonial authorities and occupying powers have commonly employed a spectrum of collective punishment methods against civilian populations hostile to their alien rule. The methods used have included civilian executions, sustained curfews and closures of towns, food confiscation and starvation, punitive property destruction, the capture of hostages, economic closures on civilian populations, cutting off of power and water supplies, withholding medical supplies, collective fines and mass detentions. These punishments are, in the words of the International Committee of the Red Cross ("ICRC"), "in defiance of the most elementary principles of humanity."*
>
> **Human Rights Council, Forty-fourth session, 15 June - 3 July 2020, Report of the Special Rapporteur on the situation of human rights in the Palestinian territories occupied since 1967.**

Such egregious disregard for the most elementary principles of humanity has for more than seventy years plagued the Palestinian people who are subject to a brutal siege of occupation, constant intimidation, and disenfranchisement. They have been denied world-endorsed nationhood, thwarted in the preservation of their culture, barred from free movement and travel, abandoned, betrayed, and mistreated by Arab regimes, and spurned by a heartless international community. On January 12, 2021, B'Tselem — Israel's most prominent and respected human rights group broke ranks to declare what has been obvious for many decades — that Israel had created the permanent reality of "a regime of Jewish supremacy" that unequivocally qualified as Apartheid.

> *. . . A regime that uses laws, practices and organised violence to cement the supremacy of one group over another is an apartheid regime. Israeli apartheid, which promotes the supremacy of Jews over Palestinians, was not born in one day or of a single speech. It is a process that has gradually grown more institutionalised and explicit, with mechanisms introduced over time in law and practice to promote Jewish supremacy. These accumulated measures, their pervasiveness in legislation and political practice, and the public and judicial support they receive — all form the basis for our conclusion that the bar for labelling the Israeli regime as apartheid has been met . . .*

B'Tselem

Needless to say, The New York Times and The Washington Post led most of the so-called US news media in avoiding to report B'Tselem's finding that Israel is without question an abhorrent "apartheid regime" guilty of crimes against humanity. The failure by the mainstream media to report such news, only serves to help drag the US and other western "democracies" into the same amoral gutter where the body of Israeli society is already putrefying.

Opinion | Judaism Dies in Darkness – and When Netanyahu Wins

In the quarter century that passed since he first took office, Netanyahu has transformed Judaism in destructive ways. In the end, that will be his main legacy.

When I was small, not so many years after the Holocaust, I remember wondering if I would live to see a day when Judaism was over.

We had a teacher in Hebrew school, a survivor of concentration camps and of subsequent wars in Israel, who seemed to be haunted by the idea.

"Halev nikra," he told us once. The heart is torn. "Your generation," he went on, to our uncomprehending ears, "May it not be the last." No Judaism left to practice. The teachings lost. The wisdom gone. The traditions and subcultures all but forgotten, disfigured out of existence, turned inside out, unrecognisable, dead.

Over time, I understood him to mean that that the State of Israel was then still terrifyingly vulnerable, that assimilation was growing among Diaspora communities. Age-old centres of Jewish life in Europe and in the Muslim world were already extinct.

The fears were real. But there was one threat to Judaism our teacher hadn't seen coming:

Benjamin Netanyahu.

Maybe our teacher would have seen it now, had he lived. You can't miss it now.

In the quarter-century since he first took office, Benjamin Netanyahu has transformed Judaism more dramatically and more destructively than any other single figure of his time.

This, in the end, is his legacy. Post-Judaism.
Bradley Burston, Haaretz, March 18, 2021

The recent result of the fourth Israeli election in two years — held on March 23, 2021 and contested by 39 parties with only 13 actually winning seats — was a continuation of the divisive Israeli politics that resulted in deadlock with neither the Netanyahu-led Likud and its allies or the opposition parties being able to secure a majority capable of forming a government with a scintilla of credibility or honour. So irrespective of which coalition finally prevails and who becomes prime minister, Zionism will still have the stranglehold that is choking the life out of Judaism.

When the victims of Zionism finally have their day in court, the world will see just how cruel and racist the early Zionists really were. The world will see that Israel, today's Zionist state, is a perfect reflection of what the early Zionists were: racist, violent, and hateful.

Miko Peled, March 19, 2021

Bibliography

Colonisation and Christianity: A Popular History of the Treatment of the Natives by the Europeans in All Their Colonies, William Howitt, 1838,

The Secret Societies of all Ages and Countries (two volumes), C. W. Heckethorn, 1875

The Book of the Dead, E. A. Wallis Budge, 1895

Egyptian Religion: Egyptian Ideas of the Future Life, E. A. Wallis Budge, 1900

The Outline of History, H.G. Wells, 1922

You Gentiles, Maurice Samuel, 1924

Aegyptiaca, J. D. S. Pendlebury, 1930

Jews Must Live: An Account of the Persecution of the World by Israel on All the Frontiers of Civilisation, Samuel Roth, 1934

Axis Rule in Occupied Europe, Raphael Lemkin, 1944

The Arrogance of Power, Senator J. William Fulbright, 1967

The Origins of Totalitarianism, Hannah Arendt, 1968

The Chronicles of the Crusades, Jean de Joinville, 1970

Zionism in the Age of the Dictators, Lenni Brenner, 1983

Zionist Revisionism from Jabotinsky to Shamir, Lenni Brenner, 1984

They Dare to Speak Out, Paul Findley, 1985

My Friend, the Enemy, Uri Avnery, 1986

South Africa Inc.: Oppenheimer Empire, Pallister, Stewart, and Lepper, 1987

Balaam's Curse: How Israel Lost Its Way, and How It Can Find It Again, Moshe Leshem, 1989

Israel's Fateful Hour, Yehoshafat Harkabi, 1989

The Hidden History of Zionism, Ralph Schoenman, 1989

The Passionate Attachment: America's Involvement with Israel, 1947 to the Present, George W. Ball, 1992

American Holocaust: The Conquest of the New World, David E. Stannard, 1992

Asimov Laughs Again: More Than 700 Jokes, Limericks and Anecdotes, Isaac Asimov, 1993

America and the founding of Israel: An investigation of the morality of America's role, John W. Mulhall, 1995

Torture: Human Rights, Medical Ethics and the Case of Israel, Neve Gordon, 1995

Below the Temple Mount in Jerusalem: A sourcebook on the cisterns subterranean chambers and conduits of Haram al-Sharif, Shimon Gibson and David M. Jacobson, 1996

Who Is Esau-Edom? Charles A. Weisman, 1996

The Deadly Embrace: The Impact of Israeli and Palestinian Rejectionism on the Peace Process, Ilana Kass and Bard O'Neill, 1996

The Invention of Ancient Israel: The Silencing of Palestinian History, K.W. Whitelam, 1996

THE BROKEN PROMISE OF A PROMISED LAND

From Freedom To Slavery: The Rebirth of Tyranny in America, Gerry Spence, 1996

Colonialism: A Theoretical Overview, Jurgen Osterhammel, 1997

The World's Banker. The History of the House of Rothschild, Niall Ferguson, 1998

The House of Rothschild: Money's Prophets 1798-1848, Niall Ferguson, 1999

The Golden Ass, Apuleius (Author), E. J. Kenney (Translator), 1999

The Albigensian Crusade, Jonathan Sumption, 1999

The Bible in History: How Writers Create a Past, Thomas L. Thompson, 1999

Science and Creationism: A View from the National Academy of Sciences, Second Edition, 1999

Deconstructing the walls of Jericho, Ze'ev Herzog, 1999

The Mythic Past: Biblical Archaeology And The Myth Of Israel, Thomas L. Thompson, 2000

The Politics of Genocide: Holocaust in Hungary, Randolph L. Braham, 2000

Righteous Victims: A History of the Zionist-Arab Conflict, 1881-1999, Ben Morris, 2000

The Glory of Kings, Kebra Nagast, 2001

Separate and Unequal: The Inside Story of Israeli Rule in East Jerusalem, Amir S. Cheshin, 2001

Seeds of Fire: China and the Story Behind the Attack on America, Gordon Thomas, 2001

51 Documents: Zionist Collaboration with the Nazis, Lenni Brenner, 2002

They Dare to Speak Out: People and Institutions Confront Israel's Lobby, Paul Findley, 2003

Final Judgment: The Missing link in the JFK Assassination Conspiracy, Michael Collins Piper, 2004

Bad News: The Decline of Reporting, the Business of News, and the Danger to Us All, Tom Fenton, 2005

The Case Against Israel, Michael Neumann, 2005

The Heirs Of The Prophet Muhammad: And the Roots of the Sunni-Shia Schism, Barnaby Rogerson, 2006

The Power of Israel in the United States, James Petras, 2006

Creating Judaism: History, Tradition, Practice, Michael L. Satlow, 2006

Cultural Insurrections: Essays on Western Civilisation, Jewish Influence, and Anti-Semitism, Kevin B. MacDonald, 2007

The Bible and Zionism: Invented Traditions, Archaeology and Post-Colonialism in Palestine-Israel, Nur Masalha, 2007

The Secret History of the World, Jonathan Black, 2007

The Neoconservative Revolution: Jewish Intellectuals and the Shaping of Public Policy, Murray Friedman, 2007

Man in the Shadows: Inside the Middle East Crisis with a Man who Led the Mossad, Efraim Halevy, 2007

Emotional Blackmail: When the People in Your Life Use Fear, Obligation, and Guilt to Manipulate You, Susan Forward, 2007

God Is Not Great: How Religion Poisons Everything, Christopher Hitchens, 2007

1948: A Soldier's Tale - The Bloody Road to Jerusalem, Uri Avnery, 2008

Israel's Vicious Circle: Ten Years of Writings on Israel and Palestine, Uri Avnery, 2008

The Age of the Warrior: Selected Writings, Robert Fisk, 2008

The Templars: History and Myth: From Solomon's Temple to the Freemasons, Michael Hagg, 2008

Hitch 22: A Memoir, Christopher Hitchens, 2010

Jerusalem: The Biography, Simon Sebag Montefiore, 2011

The Middle East: 2000 Years Of History From The Rise Of Christianity to the Present Day, Bernard Lewis, 2011

Legacy: A Genetic History of the Jewish People, Harry Ostrer, 2012

Mossad: The Greatest Missions of the Israeli Secret Service, Michael Bar-Zohar, 2012

The General's Son: Journey of an Israeli in Palestine, Miko Peled, 2012

Palestine in Israeli School Books: Ideology and Propaganda in Education, Nurit Peled-Elhanan, 2012

Solving 9-11: The Deception That Changed the World, Christopher Lee Bollyn, 2014

Gideon's Spies: The Secret History of the Mossad, Gordon Thomas, 2015

100 Years of Deception: A Blueprint for the Destruction of a Nation, Alan R. Adaschik, 2015

A Theory of Imperialism, Utsa Patnaik, Prabhat Patnaik, 2016

Moses Restored: The Oldest Religious Secret Never Told, Jonathon A Perrin, 2017

The Origins of the Druze People and Religion, Philip K. Hitti, 2017

The Earth is Weeping: The Epic Story of the Indian Wars for the American West, Peter Cozzens, 2018

America's Forgotten Middle East Initiative: The King-Crane Commission of 1919, Andrew Patrick, 2018

Rise and Kill First: The Secret History of Israel's Targeted Assassinations, Ronen Bergman, 2019

About the Author

William Hanna is a London-based freelance writer on democracy and human rights and author of several books including *The Grim Reaper*.

Further information about book reviews, articles, sample chapters, videos, and contact details at:

https://www.williamhannaauthor.com

CPSIA information can be obtained
at www.ICGtesting.com
Printed in the USA
BVHW081712220721
612646BV00006B/84